Archie & Edith, Mike & Gloria

Archie & Edith, Mike & Gloria

THE TUMULTUOUS HISTORY OF ALL IN THE FAMILY

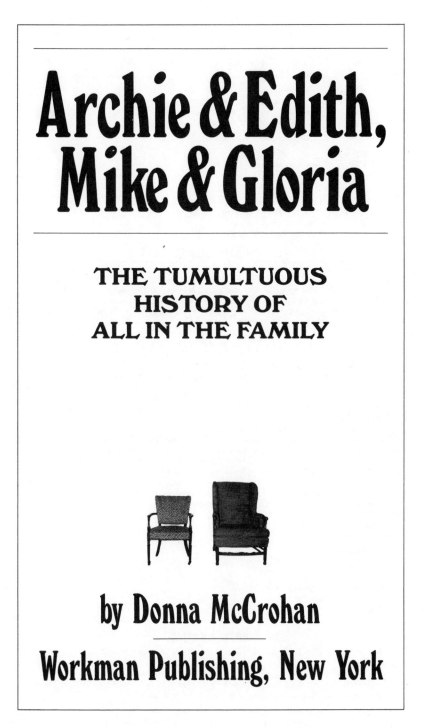

by Donna McCrohan

Workman Publishing, New York

Library of Congress Cataloging-in-Publication Data

McCrohan, Donna.
  Archie & Edith, Mike & Gloria revisited.

  Includes index.
  1. All in the family (Television program)
I. Title   II. Title: Archie and Edith, Mike and Gloria revisited.
PN1992.77.A483M34 1987   791.43'72   87-43743
ISBN 0-89480-527-4 (pbk.)

Photo Credits

p. 2, UPI/Bettmann Newsphotos; *p. 3*, Copyright © 1972 by Triangle Publications, Inc., Radnor, Pennsylvania. Reprinted with permission from TV GUIDE® Magazine; *pp. 4–5*, Copyright © 1971 by New Tandem Music Co., courtesy of Columbia Pictures Publications; *p. 32*, Copyright © 1971 by Triangle Publications, Inc., Radnor, Pennsylvania. Reprinted with permission from TV GUIDE® Magazine: *p. 39*, AP/Wide World Photos; *p. 48*, Copyright © Yoram Kahana; *p. 56*, Copyright © Yoram Kahana; *p. 59*, AP/Wide World Photos; *p. 62*, AP/Wide World Photos; *p. 70*, AP/Wide World Photos; *p. 81*, courtesy of Smithsonian Institution; *p. 85*, AP/Wide World Photos; *p. 88*, The Bettmann Archive; *p. 91*, The Bettmann Archive; *p. 97*, AP/Wide World Photos; *p. 104*, AP/Wide World Photos; *p. 108*, AP/Wide World Photos; *p. 115*, The Bettmann Archive; *p. 118*, AP/Wide World Photos; *p. 131*, AP/Wide World Photos; *p. 139*, courtesy of the Movieland Wax Museum; *p. 140*, "All in the Family Game" reproduced by permission of Milton Bradley Company, a subsidiary of Hasbro, Inc.; *p. 143*, AP/Wide World Photos; *p. 146*, AP/Wide World Photos; *p. 156*, AP/Wide World Photos; *p. 160*, AP/Wide World Photos; *p. 162*, AP/Wide World Photos; *p. 165*, AP/Wide World Photos; *p. 168*, AP/Wide World Photos; *p. 198*, Copyright © 1972 Spencer Gifts, courtesy of Spencer Gifts, Inc.; *p. 264*, courtesy of Central Synagogue, New York City; *p. 265*, courtesy of the Pearl S. Buck Foundation, Inc., photographer Deng Jeng Lee; *p. 266*, (Rob Reiner) Copyright © Yoram Kahana; (Sally Struthers) courtesy of the Christian Children's Fund, Inc.; *p. 267*, AP/Wide World Photos; *pp. 268–269*, Copyright © 1971 by New Tandem Music, Co., courtesy of Columbia Pictures Publications.

Front cover: Color photograph Ken Whitmore. Black-and-white photographs (top left and right) Gene Trindl; (bottom left) Ken Whitmore. Map courtesy Metropolitan Transit Authority
Back cover: Color photograph Gene Trindl
Cover design: Kathy Herlihy Paoli
Book design: Judith Doud Design

Workman Publishing
1 West 39 Street
New York, New York 10018

Manufactured in the United States of America
First printing November 1987
10 9 8 7 6 5 4 3 2 1

Acknowledgments

Very special thanks to all those—both on the record and off—who contributed their insights, remembrances and assistance toward the completion of this book; to the private and public collectors who shared their extensive documentation, above and beyond the call of duty; and to those who, while they did not participate in the preparation of this book, enriched our lives with work that became an American institution known as *All in the Family*.

Special thanks, too, to my editor Sally Kovalchick, and Bob Gilbert, her assistant, whose patience and iron constitutions belong in the Smithsonian alongside the Bunker chairs.

To Mom:
Vera said you have all of Edith's virtues,
but none of Edith's faults.

CONTENTS

Introduction

**"The secret of success is to offend
the greatest number of people."
—George Bernard Shaw**

When a TV series engenders hyperbole from its fans, that's no great rarity as television goes. Best show. Funniest show. Greatest show. As Archie Bunker would say, "Whatever."

But only one show in TV's entire history has seemed to *demand* sweeping hyperbole, then force even its critics to concede that statistics support every apparent exaggeration: most widely seen show; most controversial; most influential. As Archie might say, sadistics don't lie.

Most widely seen show in the history of television? According to *The Wall Street Journal*, "in its heyday, [*All in the Family*] was watched regularly by nearly one-third of all Americans." As a series, it remained secure among the top ten shows for eight seasons and was the top-rated show for five consecutive seasons. Before its final season, on a per-episode basis, *All in the Family* had delivered six of the top 50 highest-rated programs of all time.

Most controversial series? For 13 seasons (nine on *All in the Family* and four on *Archie Bunker's Place*), Archie spun an elaborate web of bigotry that very few escaped. No other TV character, before or since, spent more time expressing inflam-

All in the family—including Edith (Jean Stapleton), Archie (Carroll O'Connor), Gloria (Sally Struthers), Mike (Rob Reiner), chairs, beer can, television, and elephant.

matory opinions on race, religion, politics, and sex. Within the context of each episode, an opposite voice—Mike's, Gloria's, Lionel's, Henry's, Irene's, even Edith's—answered Archie's every charge. Within the context of our lives, their exchanges became focal points among educators, psychologists, politicians, the clergy, and the worldwide press. Did *All in the Family* expose bigotry or encourage it? Was Archie too much the bigot or not bigot enough to give his beliefs a bad name? Were decent beliefs made ridiculous by association with the Bunkers? Did ridiculous beliefs become decent before undiscerning eyes? For the million who argued "yes" on each burning issue, another million asserted the contrary view. It is unlikely that any other show has been as thoroughly dissected in every medium, or will be again.

Most influential series ever on television? *All in the Family*, first merely unique and then uniquely successful, broke ground not only for imitators but in fact for the whole of comedy. As Carl Reiner remarked, and few would deny, it "reshaped the face of television." For years, every new sitcom on the air was either liberated by or reacting to it. Within a few years of its debut in 1971, *All in the Family*, together with its spin-offs and godchildren—*The Jeffersons*, *Maude*, *Good Times*, and *Sanford and Son*—reached 120 million Americans, more than half the nation's population. *Playboy* calculated in 1976 that their combined ratings and mixture of humor plus social comment "have earned for their creator [Norman Lear] a power and influence perhaps never attained by anyone in the history of entertainment."

All in the Family reflected, then went on to contribute to, both our history and our culture. Its finest shows frequently earned the accolade of "national theater," and its best scripts fall not an iota short of national literature, while Archie has joined the pantheon of American folk heroes.

For his portrayal of Archie Bunker, Carroll O'Connor earned more awards than any other actor ever received for a single TV characterization. When *The Guinness Book of World Records* recognized *All in the Family* as commanding TV's highest advertising rates, the series became known as the Super Bowl of sitcoms, and Archie as "the most expensive racist on TV." No mean distinction.

Although, as Archie would surely observe, "It ain't got nothing to do with being mean."

TV Guide **records the media high points of 1971.**

T.V. Theme from "ALL IN THE FAMILY"

THOSE WERE THE DAYS

Words by LEE ADAMS
(Medium Ragtime)

Music by CHARLES STROUSE

Those Were the Days

"Norman, you're the laziest white
man I ever saw."
—Herman Lear

Norman Milton Lear, son of Herman and Jeanette Lear, was born July 27, 1922, in New Haven, Connecticut. His father, a second-generation Russian Jew, was a salesman by trade and the head of his household by nature. Not knowing how famous his words were destined to become when spewed from the mouth of Archie Bunker, Herman Lear had the habit of silencing his wife with "stifle yourself" and labeling his son Norman "the laziest white man I ever saw."

The Lears moved to Hartford, moved to Boston, moved to New York. The family lived, by Norman Lear's description, "at the top of its lungs and the end of its nerves." As a result of the Depression, "all we ever talked about at the dinner table was who could afford this and who could afford that, because we couldn't afford anything."

His Uncle Jack represented the opposite extreme. A

theatrical press agent rumored to pull in over $100 a week, he had the wherewithal to flip Norman a quarter whenever he came to visit—several times a year. From this, Lear formed a goal—to grow up to be the sort of uncle who could flip quarters to his nephew. Since press agents had this capacity, the route to prosperity seemed patently clear.

Lear graduated from Weaver High School in Hartford, Connecticut, in 1940; attended Emerson College in Boston for a year; enlisted in the U.S. Army Air Force in 1942, flying 57 missions as a radioman. Returning to civilian life and investigating the possibility of entering Uncle Jack's field, he turned up a $40-a-week job writing bon mots for gossip columnists. This led to ghosting whole pieces for top columnists of the day.

With his star on the ascendant and his professional credentials falling into place, Lear segued not quite predictably into manufacturing aluminum hot plates with his father. When the venture failed, he took off for Los Angeles to resume his former role. Finding a job that paid no salary, he moonlighted by selling baby pictures. When not doing either, he spent time with his cousin's husband Ed.

Ed Simmons had gone west to write comedy. Norman Lear, so far as either of them knew, had not. But one night, just to be doing something, Simmons and Lear wrote a parody. Once they had it, they drove around until they sold it. It earned them a fast $25—better money than Lear made selling baby pictures. Thereafter, the two collaborated on a nightly basis, generally selling material as soon as it was written. The decade that had begun for them on an infinitely leaner note drew to a fairly lucrative close.

At this point, Lear thought up a routine ideally suited to Danny Thomas, at the time one of the biggest names in nightclub entertainment. Wanting to pitch it directly, he phoned Thomas' agency posing as a *New York Times* writer. He said he needed to ask a few quick questions to finish an interview he'd just done with the man. The agency gave him Danny Thomas' private number. Lear called Thomas, confessed his subterfuge, elicited a laugh, and explained that he had a comedy routine for him. To the question "How long is it?," Lear replied, "How long do you want it to be?" To the answer "About seven minutes," Lear responded, "That's how long it is." Thomas wanted to see it right away. Lear countered with another subterfuge—that he wouldn't be free for a few hours—because the routine had yet to be written.

Once finished, the piece scored a hit with Danny Thomas, and with the public when Thomas did it at Ciro's in Hollywood for a benefit. There followed a call from New York agent David Susskind, and an invitation for Norman Lear and Ed Simmons to write for NBC's *Ford Star Revue*. Borrowing money, they flew back east and instantly found themselves creating sketches for a full-fledged network comedy/variety show at the whopping sum of $350 a week *each*. Seeing their work, Jerry Lewis wooed them over to NBC-TV's *Colgate Comedy Hour*, on which he and partner Dean Martin were hot going on hotter.

Lear doubled as a writer for the Martin and Lewis radio show, as well as for some of their motion pictures. As the team added triumph to triumph, Norman Lear had quarters to flip and to spare. To Bud Yorkin, who made Lear's acquaintance on *The Colgate Comedy Hour*, "Norman was big-time. He lived at the Waldorf and moved in a different world than my own."

Bud Yorkin, born February 22, 1926, in the coal-mining town of Washington, Pennsylvania, served as one of four stage managers on *The Colgate Comedy Hour*. A former TV repairman with an electrical engineering degree from Carnegie Tech, he first went to NBC as a cameraman, then stepped up to stage manager, then to the control booth. At Lear's suggestion, Martin and Lewis promoted him to director.

Lear and Simmons left *Colgate* to write for *The Martha Raye Show*, which Lear also directed. A new team of comedy writers worked under them—the brothers Danny and Neil Simon. The program was short-lived, its early end often attributed in part to a curtain call during which Martha Raye and Tallulah Bankhead embraced Gloria Lockerman, a young black child who had won a bankroll on *The $64,000 Question*. Appalled letters of protest ensued, as did the show's demise.

Lear and Simmons next received an offer from Bud Yorkin, who had gone to Tennessee Ernie Ford's *The Ford Show* (named for the sponsor, not the star). But the call wasn't for head writers, nor was the salary anything like what they'd been getting. Simmons preferred to look elsewhere. Lear felt he'd rather be employed. He took the job, and then one as writer and director for *The George Gobel Show.* After two years with Gobel, he fell in with Bud Yorkin again.

Particularly in 1958, Bud Yorkin was a magical man to know—big-time, as Lear had seemed to him to be a few years earlier. The breathtaking, never-to-be-forgotten *An Evening with Fred Astaire* had captivated the nation. It would win nine Emmys, including Best Special Musical or Variety Program (one hour or longer), Best Single Performance by an Actor (for Fred Astaire), Best Writing of a Single Musical or Variety Program (Bud Yorkin and Herbert Baker), and Best Direction of a Single Musical or Variety Program (for Bud Yorkin).

Yorkin approached Lear to form a company, which they did in 1959 with the hope, Lear has said, "that one and one would make three." Yorkin's primary bailiwick would be directing. Lear would essentially write. Inspired by the image of two men pedaling a bicycle uphill, they dubbed their effort Tandem Productions.

Tandem contracted with Paramount to provide six TV pilots. Early in the deal, Neil Simon—at this point writing comedy for the stage instead of television—sent Lear a play, which Lear and Yorkin promptly interested Paramount in making as a movie. The play, about a swinging bachelor who teaches his brother the ropes, rocked Broadway as *Come Blow Your Horn.* Yorkin and Lear didn't doubt for a minute that Frank Sinatra should realize the role on screen. When Sinatra failed to share this enthusiasm, they hired a plane to skywrite their phone number over his house. They set up a cozy reading nook on the corner of his lawn. They kept after him for eight months, until he agreed. *Come Blow Your Horn* came through in 1963 in no uncertain terms, giving Lear and Yorkin their first cinematic hit.

The team followed up in 1965 with a film version of the

Broadway comedy *Never Too Late* (Lear produced, Yorkin directed), and in 1967 with *Divorce American Style* (produced and written by Lear, directed by Yorkin). *Never Too Late* made sport of a middle-aged couple on the brink of unplanned parenthood. Some critics gasped in horror that such things could be treated in fun, while the majority delighted in the handling and portrayal of the theme. *Divorce American Style* offered laughs, insights, and surprises in another delicate area, and earned Lear an Oscar nomination. While neither subject was, strictly speaking, taboo, each ventured close enough to the cutting edge to give Tandem a taste of its destiny.

Yorkin and Lear were represented by two more films in 1968. Yorkin directed Alan Arkin in the title role of *Inspector Clouseau*; and Lear, in collaboration with Arnold Schulman and Sidney Michaels, wrote the script for *The Night They Raided Minsky's* (produced by Lear, directed by William Friedkin, with Bud Yorkin as executive producer). The story centered on an Amish girl who unintentionally invents the striptease at Minsky's Burlesque. A brief topless scene at the climax occasioned predictable controversy. Reviews were generally enthusiastic. Box office receipts soared.

As popular as the movie turned out to be, two behind-the-scenes moments conjure as many memories as the picture itself. One, sadly, is the death of Bert Lahr during filming, making his appearance in *Minsky's* all too short—and the editing process unusually complex. It was during this troubled period that a second behind-the-scenes story unfolded. Norman Lear happened upon a few words in *Variety* about a superbly rendered BBC-TV series which had England on its ears. According to the piece he read, *Till Death Us Do Part* threw Alf, a Cockney father, up against his son-in-law. They lived under the same roof in the heart of London's East End docks area, arguing constantly about politics and social issues. Thought Lear, "If that could happen on American television! I grew up on that. My father and I fought those battles." He readily envisioned the father, the mother, the daughter, and the son-in-law, and set about acquiring American adaptation rights before he ever saw a program.

Till Death Us Do Part, written by Johnny Speight, had originally appeared as a single episode of a BBC anthology offering. As a short-run series—short runs being a common series form on British television—it began in June 1966. (A movie version in 1968 would become a major box office smash. Scenes included a wartime flashback wherein during rationing, Alf steals milk for his tea from a baby's bottle; springs to patriotic attention while naked in the bathtub; and scolds people for singing about the prostitute "Lili Marlene.") Series episodes centered around working-class ultra bigot Alf Garnett (Warren Mitchell), his wife Else (Dandy Nichols), his daughter Rita (Una Stubbs), and Rita's husband Mike (Anthony Booth). Alf Garnett is bald, with glasses and a fat mustache. Else is a joyless, tough old bird, with a tongue sharp enough to slice concrete.

> ALF: I'm not a bloody mouse.

> ELSE: I wish you were . . . I'd set a trap for you.

When initially conceived by Johnny Speight, Alf would confine himself to racism, confuse his facts, and once in a while get something right. As the characters and their roles expanded, Speight found himself investing Alf with opinions on everything from the royal family to the nature of God.

As reported in *Variety*'s synopsis of January 11, 1967:

TILL DEATH US DO PART
With Warren Mitchell, Dandy Nichols, Anthony Booth,
    Una Stubbs
Producer: Dennis Main Wilson
Writer: Johnny Speight
30 Min., Mon., 7 p.m.
BBC-1, from London.

This click comedy situationer, already discussed in terms reserved for the revered "Steptoe" skein, returned to the schedules in superb form, and shapes as a Top-10 ranker and certainly as the most inventive and yockful newcomer to its class in 1966. Johnny Speight, who contrived it, was the scribe behind the late, much-lamented Arthur Haynes, and he has an explosive gift for working-man truculence and opinionated absurdity.

Here it's concentrated on Alf Garnett, a Cockney paterfamilias who booms and blusters at wife, daughter, and son-in-law. Riddled with prejudice and political non sequiturs—Speight has made him a bigoted Tory in outlook, thus giving a rebellious contrast to his aitch-dropping personality—he's never happier than when arguing, and this segment had him inveighing against Harold Wilson, Socialism, the welfare state, and explaining with sublime idiocy the relationships between God and Lucifer and the background to the Queen's annual Christmas message. The series has previously aroused protests about its language—Garnett is not sparing of his "bloodys"—and its general irreverence. But perhaps its saltiest ingredient is its vein of invective against sacred cows, and it doesn't offend because its train of thought is so bizarre.

Lynch-pin of the show is Warren Mitchell's over-whelming performance as Garnett, and it has elevated this able actor into stardom. Mitchell bristles and splut-ters from all pores, and the only danger in the format, apparent here, is that the half-hour should turn into an hilarious monolog, hinting at monotony. But he is splen-didly supported by Dandy Nichols, as his long-suffering, word-weary spouse, by Anthony Booth, as his Socialist son-in-law always ready with the needle, and by Una Stubbs, as his giggly daughter.*

As *All in the Family* would shortly do on this side of the Atlantic, *Till Death* represented a breakthrough on British television, becoming the first story-line comedy to hone in on prejudice and political controversy. As would be the case with *All in the Family*, the gibes did not go unnoticed. One broadcast described Conservative Party leader (later Prime Minister) Edward Heath as a "grammar school twit," provoking the Conservative Central Office to obtain the script from the

*Reprinted by permission of *Variety*.

BBC, though it ultimately declined to protest.

In the United States in 1968, Lear assembled the pieces of his pilot. He considered naming it *Justice for All*, and his bigot, Archie Justice. An early thought for the lead was Mickey Rooney, who appreciated the offer but had misgivings about the character. By the time ABC financed the pilot, its title was *Those Were the Days,* and Carroll O'Connor played its blue-collar bigot. Lear inclined to O'Connor for the "combination of bombast and sweetness" the actor exuded as a general in the 1966 film *What Did You Do in the War, Daddy?*, which Lear had seen during an airplane screening.

To answer the question of what he did in the war: Carroll O'Connor had served with the merchant marine in World War II, then taught school and pursued an advanced degree,

A pre-*All in the Family* Carroll O'Connor—Raymond Chandler's *Marlowe* (1969), with James Garner (left) and Kenneth Tobey (right).

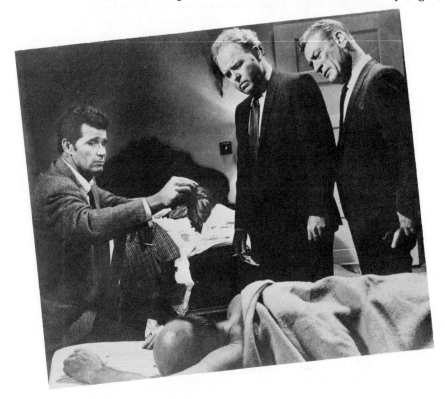

living in Montana and in a Queens, New York neighborhood not far from the Bunkers's TV home. His studies in English and interest in the theater persuaded him to try acting, at which he distinguished himself—in classical drama at the Gate Theatre in Dublin, Ireland, in BBC teleplays, on Broadway, and on Off-Broadway. Of his performance in Clifford Odets's *The Big Knife,* directed by Peter Bogdanovich, Judith Crist wrote, "Carroll O'Connor is indeed a powerful caricature as the self-made man, sharply cruel and unctuously powerful—a fine villain."

On TV, he appeared in over 100 roles, for *The U.S. Steel Hour, Kraft Television Theatre, Armstrong Circle Theatre, The Untouchables, The Defenders, Naked City, East Side/West Side, Gunsmoke, Bonanza, Adventures in Paradise, The Man from U.N.C.L.E.,* and *The Outer Limits,* to name a few. In the movies, he established himself as one of the industry's most versatile character actors, in parts ranging from a trucker in *Lonely Are the Brave* (1962) to the assassin Casca who stabs Caesar in *Cleopatra* (1963).

One role he had not gotten: the role of the Skipper in *Gilligan's Island.* Recalls that show's producer, Sherwood Schwartz:

> That was the most difficult part to cast on *Gilligan's Island* because I needed someone who was going to be physically bigger than poor little Bob Denver's Gilligan, and who would berate him and bawl him out for this and that, and just be annoyed with him all the time. I really needed a sort of Hardy who would suffer the tortures Laurel put him through and yet this kinship between them would surmount it. Someone who, through all of that, could remain sympathetic, and that was very, very difficult. I'd written a particularly vicious two pages for the test. They weren't even in the script. I figured if someone could live through those lines and remain sympathetic, that would be the Skipper. Everyone flunked that test.
>
> We tested everyone here in town whom we could think of, and when they didn't work out, CBS sent for

four or five actors from New York who were primarily stage actors at that point. Carroll O'Connor was among them. Obviously, it has nothing to do with talent that he didn't fit the part. Some people have even pointed out similarities between the Skipper's role and Archie Bunker, although the big difference is that Archie was up against Mike, who was more than his equal. You were sometimes sorry for Archie that he was so clearly beyond his depths with Mike. Mike was definitely not poor, hapless Gilligan.

Anyway, it's the luckiest thing that could have happened to Carroll O'Connor when he didn't get the part. If he'd become identified with the Skipper, no way would he have been chosen for Archie Bunker.

When Norman Lear approached O'Connor to play Archie Justice, O'Connor believed in the character but not in its chances on television. Residing in Rome at the time, he opted to keep paying rent on his apartment in case he might need to go back. He felt sure, as he told *Playboy* in 1972, "that the American public would explode in indignation about this show and force [the network] to take it off the air. In my contract, I insisted on round-trip air transportation from Rome for myself and my family. I just didn't think the American people could stand to listen to a character who talked about coons and Hebes and spicks, even though the public knows damn well that most people talk this way in their homes."

From the first ABC pilot, Jean Stapleton (no relation to actress Maureen Stapleton) portrayed Edith, Archie's wife. A popular character actress, her past performances ran the gamut from *Naked City, The Defenders, Philco Television Playhouse, True Story,* and *Dr. Kildare* to *Laugh-In,* and *Car 54, Where Are You?* on the home screen, *Up the Down Staircase* (1967) in the cinema, and on stage in *Damn Yankees, Funny Girl* ("as an Irish yenta"), and *Bells Are Ringing* (its star, Judy Holliday, "taught me a lot about the need for honesty in comedy").

Norman Lear invited Jean Stapleton to read for the Edith role. She couldn't get over the script: "This on TV? I was

reminded of my own parents, terribly amused by it, by its
reality and honesty and humor and by the fact that the subject
would be *treated* on TV." Lear gave her a key to Edith's
character—that Edith no longer hears what Archie is saying,
having tuned out years ago.

Rob Reiner and Sally Struthers hadn't yet assumed the
roles of Mike and Gloria. The pilot went before ABC network
executives. ABC laughed, but it didn't get on the air. When
ABC's option was about to lapse, they requested another
pilot, attributing their earlier refusal to "the kids." Lear shot a
second pilot in 1969, with Chip Oliver and Candice Azzara as
Mike and Gloria. Mike wasn't named Mike nor was he Polish
in it, and he had the look of an all-American jock. The set
didn't quite look like the now familiar one—for instance, the
kitchen opened onto the living room rather than being a
separate room—but the pilot was essentially the one the
world later saw. It struck ABC executive funny bones but also
whacked a nerve. They withdrew from the project, leaving
Lear free to try elsewhere.

The possible elsewheres included CBS, where network
president Robert D. Wood, entering his second year in office,
had instituted sweeping programming changes. Though CBS
held the lead in ratings, Wood feared that the demographics
—the age range and geographical distribution of viewers—
needed a boost to better attract advertisers' dollars. In a
startling move bound to leave the industry reeling, he
planned to jettison many longtime favorite programs, among
them Jackie Gleason's, Red Skelton's, and Ed Sullivan's. Over-
board with them would go the rural sitcoms *The Beverly
Hillbillies, Green Acres,* and *Petticoat Junction.* In their place
came fare which Wood considered to have "contemporary
relevance." The intended result—to attract a young urban
audience—was achieved.

In 1970, Tandem's pilot went to CBS with the same
Archie and Edith but a new pair of "kids"—Rob Reiner and
Sally Struthers. Rob or Bob Reiner—the name appeared
interchangeably then—had grown up surrounded by his father's comedy genius friends, men like Mel Brooks, Sid Cae-

sar, and Dick Van Dyke. Says Rob/Bob, "That was my kinder-
garten and they were my teachers." Lear, a friend of Rob's
father, Carl, had known Rob for over a decade. There had
even been one day, when Lear stopped by Reiner's house, that
Rob made him laugh with a routine about cheating at jacks.
Noted Lear to Carl Reiner, "You've got a funny kid there."
Answered poppa Carl, "Get out of here. He's not a funny kid."
Years after, Carl Reiner expanded on the exchange. "Oh, I
knew the kid was funny. A funny kid can't help being funny.
What I didn't know until a long time later was that he had
talent."

Talent he had, and he found himself writing, performing, and engaged in summer stock by the age of 17. He
majored in theater arts at UCLA, leaving the program after
two and a half years because "In school they can teach you
about acting, but they can't teach you how to act." While
attending UCLA, he formed the improvisational comedy
group "The Session," then formed a comedy twosome with
Joey Bishop's son Larry, and from there went on to join the
renowned inprovisational genii, "The Committee." He became half of the gifted writing team of Rob Reiner and Phil
Mishkin, and the youngest writer on *The Summer Brothers
Smothers Show* (summer replacement for *The Smothers Brothers
Comedy Hour,* for which he next wrote). By 1970, his acting
credits included the portrayal of a chunky nerd in the movie
version of his father's autobiographical novel *Enter Laughing*
(1967), and the TV shows *Hey Landlord!, The Partridge Family* (as
a hippie), and *Gomer Pyle, U.S.M.C.* (as a hippie).

Sally Struthers, meanwhile—who originally dreamed of
being a doctor, then an artist—captained the cheerleading
squad in her Portland, Oregon high school and founded its
girls' track team. After graduation, she attended the famed
Pasadena Playhouse College of Theatre Arts, winning a schol-
arship as its most promising new student. She went on to
commercials, played a musical pogo stick with the Spike
Jones, Jr. Band, danced on the *Herb Alpert and The Tijuana
Brass Special,* and appeared as a regular on *The Summer Brothers
Smothers Show, The Smothers Brothers Comedy Hour,* and *The Tim*

Before the CBS Pilot

- Archie's name was Archie Justice.
- Mike was Irish, not Polish; his name was Dickie.
- Different performers played Gloria, Mike and Lionel.
- Edith didn't play the piano as well.

Conway Comedy Hour (on which she provided occasional highlights as, among other things, the entire chorus in musical production numbers). Before ever meeting Reiner through *All in the Family*, she dated him briefly, though both went on in real life to marry others. Reiner married an actress Struthers beat out for the Gloria role—Penny Marshall—whom he'd met during his days with "The Committee." Undaunted, she went on to star in *Laverne & Shirley*.

Struthers particularly caught Norman Lear's eye with her film work as Jack Nicholson's bowling-alley pickup in *Five Easy Pieces* (1970); and she reportedly cinched *All in the Family*—over a reputed 200 other candidates—by having severe laryngitis when she read for the Gloria role. Her attempts to bellow an argument with a hoarse, fading voice came across as endearingly funny.

With the age factor against them, neither Rob Reiner nor Sally Struthers could have gone very far in the original (ABC) pilots. But by 1970, they were perfect. As Norman Lear has frequently remarked, "I think we were blessed...five years before, neither one of them could have played it."

The pilot offered Archie and Edith returning prematurely from church to find Mike cajoling Gloria to make love. Archie is scandalized. It's still daylight "of a Sunday morning." He proceeds to tell them how wrong they are, as well as what's wrong with longhairs and hippies, welfare chiselers, Jews, blacks, campus subversives, and the sermon he heard that morning.

When CBS's Mike Dann (senior vice-president of programs) and Fred Silverman (vice-president of program planning and development) saw it, Silverman reportedly exclaimed, "Don't let that tape leave the building!" After a screening for Robert D. Wood, 13 episodes were ordered.

But despite in-house support for *All in the Family,* the research department had reservations, recommending that Archie be a family man, subdued in manner and far more supportive of his brood. CBS chairman William Paley likewise expressed doubt as to its taste and suitability, feeling it might be vulgar and insulting. If a new sort of sitcom had to be launched, he had no objection to another network assuming the honor. Yet he recognized the value of assent, having since written, in his autobiography *As It Happened,* "We came out and said, in effect, we'll do it the way it is and not be afraid of the complaints we expected. Some would say that white people do not have black people coming into their houses, and if you, Mr. CBS, think they do, you're mistaken and we're not going to listen to your network any more. That would have been, I think, the kind of reaction we would have received ten years earlier. But we felt the time had come to catch up with some of the developments that had taken place in the United States."

Robert Wood argued that CBS, from its top-ranked position in the ratings, could afford to take risks. The risk ultimately wangled by Wood was no devil-may-care, full-fledged season opener, but rather, a mid-season replacement. Noted one CBS veteran, "If he hadn't needed a replacement that winter, *All in the Family* might never have gotten on." Wood held a special screening for affiliate owners, calling their attention to the show's innovative qualities and its "spirit of the Broadway theater."

After numerous meetings with Paley, Wood managed to slot the half-hour show for 9:30 P.M. on Tuesday nights, between an hour of *Hee Haw* (8:30–9:30) and an hour of CBS news (10:00–11:00). It replaced John Forsythe's *To Rome with*

Love, which moved to Wednesday night, bumping *The Governor & J.J.* (Dan Dailey and Julie Sommars) into oblivion except for reruns. Within a few months, *To Rome with Love* got axed entirely. Both comedies dared less in the way of Wood's "contemporary relevance." The question was: Did *All in the Family* dare too much?

The answer—the acid test—loomed large. What would the public think? As Bud Yorkin once observed, "When we first did *All in the Family,* we had to explain to them what an Archie Bunker is and how he would relate and how he isn't a guy who would go out and burn a cross but he is a bigot. But *now* when Archie Bunker walks out on the set, the audience is ahead of you. There's nothing more delicious in comedy than expectation...."

As January 1971 drew closer for CBS and for Tandem, expectant tension was not merely in the air, but the order of each new day.

All Wet at Once

> "Humor has a liberating element
> ...Humor is not resigned. It is
> rebellious."
> —Sigmund Freud

Along with having its roots in *Till Death Us Do Part,*
All in the Family drew sustenance from everything
television had been, everything comedy had been,
and everything comedic rebellion had promised to be.

Looking back in 1986, Norman Lear told *The New York
Times:*

> I didn't know this when I started with *All in the
> Family,* but that show was the first to make social issues
> integral to evening-television sitcom. All the way through
> *All in the Family* and *Maude* and *Mary Hartman,* I was asked
> what made me think I was right to insert a point of view
> in shows. That was never my intention. It was to enter-
> tain. If it wasn't funny, it wouldn't work.
>
> We followed a whole bunch of shows like *Father*

Knows Best, Leave It to Beaver, Green Acres, and other shows of the '60s. They were all fine shows, but you would think by watching them that America had no blacks, no racial tension, that there was no Vietnam. As people asked me about the points of view, I thought, "My God, by omission, look at the points of view of the earlier shows: wall-to-wall television comedy that would let you think there were no problems in the 1960s."

Before *All in the Family,* situation comedies could be counted on not to raise too many difficult questions—*I Love Lucy, Father Knows Best, The Adventures of Ozzie and Harriet* (Adventures? Name one.) Lucy Ricardo pestered Ricky for permission to sing at his club. Bud Anderson broke curfew or maneuvered to buy bongo drums. Ozzie Nelson wondered where he dropped his sweater. Sitcoms entertained. They reinforced homespun values. If they touched on controversial issues at all, they minimized the controversy, presenting instead either straight-out satire or a morality play.

Get Smart (NBC 1965–1969; CBS 1969–1970) spoofed government cutbacks, policies, and the previously sacrosanct federal espionage network. Strictly speaking, it revolved around incompetence in high places, thereby fingering a leading sacred cow. For that matter, so had Phil Silvers' Sergeant Bilko on *The Phil Silvers Show: You'll Never Get Rich* (1955–1959). But neither was *about* issues per se.

Several notable episodes of CBS's *Dick Van Dyke Show* (1961–1966; created by Carl Reiner) challenged racial barriers. In one, Rob Petrie (Van Dyke) is convinced that his wife got the wrong baby at the hospital. He phones the father who he thinks has his real baby, insisting they make a swap. The father protests: It's impossible. Rob won't budge. When the two couples meet, it's obvious Rob made the error. The other couple is black. The four, becoming friendly, enjoy a good joke at Rob's expense.

In another episode, Rob accidentally darkens his hands in a pot of dye before speaking to a black community organization. As the dye won't wash off, he wears gloves like Mickey

Mouse to avoid seeming insensitive to the group. But that evening, addressing the club members, he decides he's been silly. He confesses what's happened, expressing his conviction that they can all share the humor of the situation. They do. And, again, enjoy a good joke at Rob's expense.

Due credit must be given. These episodes, though tame by the standards of the 1980s, at least took notice of racial tension in an effort to dispel it. They were brave and effective in their day, but also gentle, with every character a model of racial accord. Moreover, *The Dick Van Dyke Show* didn't revolve around burning issues, even when occasional episodes considered them.

Along the same lines, NBC's *Julia* (1968–1971) starred Diahann Carroll as the widow of a Vietnam helicopter pilot. She independently raised her son on the income derived from her career as a nurse. The first black female performer with her own comedy series not about maids or servants, Carroll blazed a trail of sorts, as in the series opener when she phones to apply for a job:

JULIA: Did they tell you I'm colored?

DOCTOR: Hmmm. What color are you?

JULIA: Why, I'm Negro.

DOCTOR: Oh, have you always been a Negro, or are you just trying to be fashionable?

The series, completely integrated—and with such episode titles as "Am I, Pardon the Expression, Blacklisted?"—presented an ideal that sidestepped really thorny issues. Observed Harry Belafonte of it and other black vehicles then around, "For the shuffling, simpleminded Amos-and-Andy type of Negro, TV has substituted a new, one-dimensional Negro without reality."

In terms of taboo-shattering and issue-lambasting, *All in the Family*'s TV comic predecessors included virtually no sitcoms and precious few other programs—and before them comedically, controversial nightclub satirists on the order of

Lenny Bruce, Mort Sahl, Dick Gregory, Godfrey Cambridge, and the Second City-spawned team of Jack Burns and Avery Schreiber:

> CONVENTIONEER (Burns): I hate those people who make derogatory remarks about someone's ancestry. You've heard it, you've heard it! You know who says that the most?
>
> CABBIE (Schreiber): Who's that?
>
> CONVENTIONEER: Your Hunkies. A'right, we're having fun here, we're having fun here. All the guys brought their wives. I was gonna bring my wife but we've been separated twelve years.
>
> CABBIE: Good idea not to bring her.
>
> CONVENTIONEER: Oh, yeh. You kidding me? She was a saint! She was too good for me. I was a bum, she's a saint. She's a saint. Here I got a picture of her right here. That's a saint. That's a saint!
>
> CABBIE: Yeah, I never saw one before.
>
> CONVENTIONEER: Of course not, you're Jewish. You don't have saints.
>
> CABBIE: We got prophets...

What ground was broken on television gave way primarily under the jackhammer blows of NBC's news-and-revue format *That Was the Week That Was* (1964–1965), which satirized each week's headlines; CBS's topical variety *The Smothers Brothers Comedy Hour* (1967–1969, subsequently on the other networks in varying formats), which went through sacred cows like an irreverent barbecue; and NBC's rapid-fire grab bag *Rowan & Martin's Laugh-In* (1968–1973), which socked it to everything for over five years—until, inside sources said, "there was simply nothing left to make fun of."

Paving the road for the latter two, *That Was the Week That Was* ("TW3" to the short-winded) went for the jugular, demolishing political and social targets with devastating panache.

One news flash had UN paratroopers dropping from Guatemalan planes to rescue civil rights activists in Mississippi. Another, set to music, nailed National Brotherhood Week as the seven days set aside to patronize people barred from your schools or your neighborhood the other 51 weeks of the year. And "The Vatican Rag" summed up Catholic church reform to a snappy ragtime beat, with genuflection reduced to a dance step. "TW3"—strong stuff by any standard—demanded intelligence and a high reference level from its audience. For all the brilliance legitimately attributed to it, this diet of unrelenting mockery ran little more than a year.

On *The Smothers Brothers Comedy Hour*, Pat Paulsen, one of its regulars, campaigned for the U.S. presidency on a string of ridiculous platforms.* Pete Seeger, once blacklisted on television, guested several times on the *Comedy Hour*. Yet when the Smothers Brothers asked him to sing his antiwar protest "Big Muddy," censors rejected the song. For a sketch about sex education, with Barbara Eden as the instructor, censors deleted the words *sex* and *sex education*. Tommy Smothers and Elaine May had a sketch about TV censors. It never got on the air.

In 1968, guesting on *The Smothers Brothers Comedy Hour*, David Steinberg delivered a "sermonette" that some viewers denounced as blasphemous. As *Time* magazine has since quipped, "the vein in which Steinberg took the Lord's name was comic." But the vein was opened, and CBS saw red. The network demanded greater scrutiny each week. In short order, they permitted folksinger Joan Baez to tell viewers of her husband's imprisonment; then they cut the reason (resisting selective service), thereby leaving the uninformed to guess at the nature of his crime.

Tommy Smothers responded by lobbying for greater freedom, talking to senators Edward Kennedy and Alan Cran-

---

*Back at it in 1985, Pat Paulsen (Emmy-winner turned award-winning vintner) announced plans to run again in 1988, as a Democrat, having previously assaulted the Republican ticket. "I like to mix it up. In 1992 I may run as a Royalist." Asked to detail allocation of supporter dollars, he promised they could anticipate "Two dollars for an amaretto at the Chicago airport, that sort of thing. Certainly nothing will be spent on politics."

ston, F.C.C. commissioners Kenneth Cox and Nicholas John-son, and interested parties attending the National Association of Broadcasters Convention in Washington, D.C. CBS, embarrassed but able to stand the heat, had its fill only when the brothers failed to deliver a program in time for the prescreening mandated by CBS. Robert D. Wood, with barely a month under his belt as CBS-TV president, felt compelled to cancel the show mid-season. Replacing it, ironically, came *Hee Haw*, which in another two years and in another time slot, would become the lead-in for *All in the Family* and which, more ironically still, would shortly after fall victim to Wood's purge of rural comedies in favor of "contemporary relevance."

A less rapacious gadfly than either "TW3" or *Comedy Hour, Laugh-In* tossed its issues at the audience like confetti. A calculated average of 200 pages of jokes, 25 hours of taping time, and 4.4 miles of unedited tape went into a single *Laugh-In* edition. Plenty of viewers questioned its tastefulness, but plenty more embraced its iconoclasm, putting it number one in the ratings for two straight seasons. (*Marcus Welby, M.D.* would outpull it in the 1970–1971 season, to be unseated in 1971–1972 by *All in the Family*.) Just weeks before *All in the Family*'s debut, *Laugh-In* devoted an hour to outrageous ethnic jokes. (Reported *Advertising Age*, "No group escaped the 'Laugh-In' poniard and, so far as is known, nobody batted an eye.")

A decidedly liberal program, *Laugh-In* nonetheless happily enlisted guest appearances by conservative figures such as Billy Graham, Richard Nixon, and John Wayne, who joined in the general spirit of fun. Even when perceived as naughty or deadly or dangerous, *Laugh–In* went about its business like a salesman with his foot in the door. As long as Dan Rowan and Dick Martin kept the door open, America couldn't avoid hearing what they had to say.

Getting a foot in the door is one thing. Keeping your toes is another. When his turn came, Norman Lear managed both. Quite a coup in light of the degree to which he favored openness—saying it, showing it, facing it. As he told *Los Angeles Times* editor Digby Diehl early in the life of the show,

"If you're looking for where *All in the Family* began in American life, though, it began with Lenny Bruce. He really was a prophet." Lear went on to credit Bruce as a "strong influence" on his thinking, "particularly in these television series."

When he and Yorkin sold *Those Were the Days* to CBS in 1970, they were proposing, in effect, the marriage of Lucy Ricardo and Lenny Bruce. They knew they were dealing with a network that only a year earlier had canceled the Smothers Brothers but now—no doubt mindful of *Laugh-In*'s success on a rival network—sought "contemporary relevance." At the same time, outspokenness in theory is far less nerve-racking than outspokenness in actual practice. As air date approached, temerity retreated. CBS pushed for changes.

Tandem held its ground, having other irons in the fire. The team's earlier TV successes with such fare as *The Many Sides of Don Rickles, An Evening with Carol Channing, Another Evening with Fred Astaire,* and the original *Andy Williams Show* proved their versatility. Nor had either man twiddled so much as one thumb in the wake of ABC's rejections. Bud Yorkin, directing Donald Sutherland, Gene Wilder, and a cast of wildmen in *Start the Revolution Without Me* (1970), had created

Bud Yorkin directed *Start the Revolution Without Me* (1970), starring Donald Sutherland (left) and Gene Wilder (right).

Norman Lear's *Cold Turkey* (1971), with Vincent Gardenia (seated) and Dick Van Dyke (standing).

a comic gem that today commands its own cult following. Norman Lear had written, directed, and produced *Cold Turkey* (1971), a trenchant satire about a town that gives up smoking. A multi-picture deal from United Artists presented the ready alternative to caving in for CBS.

In 1972, Lear recalled the chain of events in a hearing before a Senate subcommittee reviewing freedom of the press:*

> I was editing the film I had written and directed in the intervening two years when the call came that CBS was interested in *All in the Family* and wished to meet with me to discuss it. In the ensuing months, I spent literally dozens of hours in conversation with various mem-

---

*Hearing before the Subcommittee on Constitutional Rights of the Committee on the Judiciary of the United States Senate, 92nd Congress.

bers of the department of program practices, especially its head, Mr. William Tankersley, a vice president of the network....

In reflecting upon that first meeting, I realize that Mr. Tankersley and I had really not reached a meeting of the minds. We had enjoyed a lively discussion and had reached a degree of mutual respect which allowed each of us to think that the other fellow was so reasonable we could ultimately change his mind. For example, in that first meeting Mr. Tankersley stated objections to certain areas of the pilot script, which he termed explicit sex....

All of my early talks with the department of program practices at CBS were on this rather esoteric, nonspecific plane, until a week before the show was scheduled to premiere. By that time we were in production and had already filmed four episodes....

In the week prior to the premiere of *All in the Family*, Mr. Tankersley first asked me if I would agree to plan the second show as the premiere episode. He felt the second show was a lot more tame than the first and would therefore offend fewer viewers and affiliates.

I neglected to mention that one of the network's prime concerns was the affiliate stations around the country and their owner-managers. They did not want to air a show which might cause these men to drop the series after one episode.

I explained to Mr. Tankersley that I had designed the first show to introduce Archie Bunker as fully as I knew how so that there was no doubt as to what he was. In my opinion, CBS, and *All in the Family* had to jump in the water together and get fully wet the first time out. I felt if we didn't do that with the very first episode, the series would never get further than wading.

And so, in the hours of discussion on the subject, I held firm to my position that the first show—the pilot show—must air first.

Two days before the scheduled premiere, program practices agreed to air the first show first. With two or three suggestions and trims, however, said trims of deletions were all in the area of what program practices called, explicit sex.

I refused to allow the trims and in literally hours and hours of cross-country conversation with Mr. Tankersley I held to my theory that the American public was ready to accept the degree of reality that *All in the Family* represented.

And I preferred not to go on the air at all if it meant tampering with the reality one iota. I suppose again it was in the last hours of these discussions that Mr. Tankersley and I learned that neither of us was as reasonable as we had believed at the beginning. In any event, it wasn't until 7:05 P.M., California time, the day before *All in the Family* was to premiere that I could call my wife, Frances, and tell her the show was going on the air.

The network was committed to making, or at least paying for 13 episodes, but until that moment when Mr. Tankersley agreed to air the first show with no deletions, I had absolutely no reason to be certain that *All in the Family* would make it to the air at all.

Lear added, some time after the hearing but discussing the same heady dissent, "When the network saw there wasn't a

close up	ALL IN THE FAMILY © 9:30 ❷
A LIGHTHEARTED LOOK AT PREJUDICE	**Debut:** Situation comedy takes a giant step with this adult social satire. This series will explore American prejudices by looking at those of one middle-class family—if viewers can take the heat. There's plenty of abrasive language and subject matter to keep the cards and letters pouring in. The show is based on the BBC's highly controversial—and successful—"Till Death Us Do Part," which didn't pull any punches either. Anyway, it's "All in the Family," made up of . . . bigoted Archie Bunker (Carroll O'Connor); his spiritless wife Edith (Jean Stapleton); their naively idealistic daughter Gloria (Sally Struthers); and Gloria's husband Mike (Bob Reiner), an argumentative liberal who sorely tries Archie's soul. Mike Evans plays Lionel, a young black friend of the younger couple. True to the series' controversial nature, the subject matter for tonight's episode was undecided at press time—CBS executives might even change the program's title. Produced by Norman Lear and Bud Yorkin.

As *TV Guide* introduced *All in the Family.*

single state that seceded, we were able to talk constructively with them."

In an article appearing on the day the show debuted, critic Clarence Petersen opined, "Unless there is a third world war, a double axe murder in a convent or one heck of a storm in the next 24 hours, there seems little doubt about what the chief topic of conversation will be tomorrow morning: the new CBS-TV comedy *All in the Family* which debuts tonight."

It premiered January 12, 1971. Opposite it on ABC was the Movie of the Week, *Assault of the Wayne* starring Joseph Cotten and Leonard Nimoy, and on NBC, Elizabeth Taylor and Mia Farrow in *Secret Ceremony.* Promotion for *All in the Family* had been slight because, as one CBS official conceded, "we weren't exactly sure how to promote it."

When *Hee Haw* went off the air that evening, a voice announced, "The program you are about to see is *All in the Family*. It seeks to throw a humorous spotlight on our frailties, prejudices, and concerns. By making them a source of laughter, we hope to show—in a mature fashion—just how absurd they are." It opened with the now-familiar theme song by Archie and Edith, belting away an ode to the good old days. Many a viewer sat not in shock but annoyance: "This is new? A dowdy middle-aged couple singing claptrap at the piano? Terrific. She'll burn the roast. He'll probably lose his sweater. Be still my quaking heart."

Then Archie let loose with his epithets, using words TV never heard before, Mike answered from the opposite mindset, his vocabulary sharp and his notions fit to wake a large segment of the dead. Race. Politics. Religion. Sex. Irretrievably out in the open.

Anticipating the worst, CBS had extra operators stationed at major switchboards across the country for the deluge of calls that would certainly pour in. The flood amounted to a modest 1000 phone-ins,* over 60 percent

---

*Fewer, for instance, than the number generated by Vice-President Spiro Agnew's 1969 attack on the media.

favorable (a rarity, considering folks generally dial in to complain). According to the New York Nielsen ratings, the show had attracted only a 15 percent audience share, trailing *Assault on the Wayne* (38 percent share) and *Secret Ceremony* (30 percent share).

Critics who did not reserve their judgment for a few weeks or months registered mixed reactions. Fred Ferretti of *The New York Times* said he liked it much better when it was *Till Death Us Do Part* or the pilot *Those Were the Days. Variety* hailed it as "the best TV comedy since the original *The Honeymooners*" and "the best casting since Sgt. Bilko's squad ...A broad, sharp double-edged sword [that] sliced right and left," while the *Daily Variety* found it "nothing less than an insult to any unbigoted televiewer...something for every prejudice...too bad this bundle from Britain wasn't turned back at the shoreline."

In *The Washington Post,* William C. Woods termed it "a welcome breath of stale air in a show that was all shock and no story...every racial epithet and prejudiced social stance available in the long catalogue of the ways we find to be cruel to each other." The piece recorded a comment called into the local station by someone who might as well have sprung from one of Lear's scripts: "I wouldn't let my kids watch it. I don't want them to hear words like that. They pick up enough of that crap on the street."

In the weeks following *All in the Family*'s debut, CBS initiated and financed an opinion poll. The majority of people questioned, including minority group members, indicated that they hadn't been offended. On the street, depending on whom you talked to, the show registered as great or brilliant, hideous or stupid, or "I haven't seen it yet."

The furor, such as it was, perked along through February, March, April, May. People saw and enjoyed the show, or saw it in disbelief, or with contempt. People who saw it discussed it. People who hadn't, discussed it anyhow. "Bunker gives conservatives a bad name." "Stivic gives liberals a bad name." "At last someone is speaking the truth"—an opinion expressed from widely disparate positions of the political spectrum.

Accolades began to roll in. "At least the brightest new thing on commercial TV since the early *Laugh-In,*" said Clifford A. Ridley in *National Observer.* "The best show on commercial television," wrote Cleveland Amory in *TV Guide.*

Concurrently, other critics doggedly dumped it. From Richard Burgheim in *Time*: "This show proves that bigotry can be as boring and predictable as the upthink fluff of *The Brady Bunch.*" From *Life,* "Something fresh must be acutely missing if CBS' recent *All in the Family,* a minstrel show that's big with bigotry and revives half-forgotten hate words, is hailed as a breakthrough." John Leonard, in another *Life* article, denounced it as a "wretched program. Why review a wretched program? Well, why vacuum the living room or fix the septic tank? Every once in a while the reviewer must assume the role of a bottle of Johnson's No-Roach with the spray applicator: let's clean up this culture!"

To *Advertising Age,* "in the tradition of tv sitcom, there'd be no show without the kids, in this case daughter Gloria (Sally Struthers) and son-in-law Michael (Rob Reiner), whom Archie calls 'Meatball.'" Meatball? There's always somebody, somewhere, who hasn't quite been listening.

Ratings registered low for the first weeks, causing reports, as in *Saturday Review* (March 27, 1971) that "mail response has been 75 to 80 percent favorable. Nevertheless, as this is written, CBS has still not decided to renew the series for the fall." An inspired Merv Griffin saluted it on his own CBS program, an event he recalls in his autobiography, *Merv*: "It wasn't doing much in the ratings yet, but it was innovative and lively, and the stars were good talkers. Carroll O'Connor, Jean Stapleton, Rob Reiner and Sally Struthers were my guests. Next day the call came. 'Why are you putting *them* on? The show probably won't last the season. It was a CBS show, and *still* we drew fire from the network."

Yet by May, enough sets had tuned in—out of curiosity, or on the strength of reviews, or because formerly preferred shows were in reruns—to make *All in the Family* a viable item. Remarked Rob Reiner, "It really shakes me up that it's still around and is a hit. When we went on the air four months ago, you couldn't get a bet down we'd last through spring. Even the cast wouldn't book the bet. We did the show because we believed it was good and healthy for television to do it, but deep down I don't think any of us believed it would last more than a few token weeks."

It took one Emmy as Outstanding Comedy Series, and Jean Stapleton walked away with a second as Best Actress in that category. Fred Silverman insisted on running the show during the summer, drawing a still larger audience. By September, it climbed to number one in the Nielsen ratings, in the top-ten company of *The Flip Wilson Show* (NBC), *Marcus Welby, M.D.* (ABC), *Here's Lucy* (CBS), *Gunsmoke* (CBS), and other heavy-hitters of predominantly CBS stock.

Before the close of 1971, Bud Yorkin asserted a mind-boggling statistic. "Recently we had a 70 share in New York City. Unbelievable. That means 70 percent of the sets were turned to us, and the other stations had to split up the rest. There aren't many specials that get a rating like that."

By the beginning of 1972, an estimated 50 million plus watched *All in the Family* on a weekly basis—an unprecedented viewership for a regulary scheduled series.

In May of 1972, *All in the Family* swept the Emmy Awards: Carroll O'Connor for Outstanding Continued Performance by an Actor in a Leading Role in a Comedy Series; Jean Stapleton, Outstanding Continued Performance by an Actress (etc.); *All in the Family*, Best Comedy Series; Sally Struthers, Outstanding Performance by an Actress in a Supporting Role in Comedy;* John Rich, Outstanding Directorial Achievement in Comedy (Series) for the episode "Sammy's Visit"; and Burt Styler, Outstanding Writing Achievement in Comedy (Series) for "Edith's Problem."

Johnny Carson, dubbing the ceremonies "an evening with Norman Lear," joked, "I understand Norman has just sold his acceptance speech as a new series."

Not bad for a show that wasn't expected to last the winter.

---

*In a tie with Valerie Harper of *The Mary Tyler Moore Show.*

Archie

"I don't think you should strip people of their prejudice—that's all they have, some of them. We should just leave them alone until they mature."
—Butterfly McQueen

To describe *All in the Family* as a series about a bigot is as comprehensive a statement as saying *Gone with the Wind* is about a much-married woman of Irish ancestry during the Civil War, or that *Casablanca* is about a man who runs a nightclub in Africa.

As Norman Lear has told interviewers, *Till Death Us Do Part* "did stick figures. The characters simply fought, and the shows were about nothing more than the argument," whereas Archie on *All in the Family* might be watching television and toss off a remark a bigot might make, thereby setting off a quibble with Mike. "But the show in which that challenge occurs might be about losing his job and being worried all night about losing his job. The show that treated that, for example, had a great deal to say about the fabric of our American economic system, and the little thing about bigotry was about two lines."

To declare Archie a bigot is easy—so was Scarlett

O'Hara. Were this the only issue, their stories would be the same. And if Archie's sum total is being the antihero, then his bar might as well be in Casablanca, and Rick's could be in Queens. Said Carroll O'Connor, "This is a monumental character in American literature, not just a stick figure on television."

Far from being a stick figure, Archie is his whole history. His parents and childhood. Growing up in the Depression, and his father who never got over the Depression. Having to quit school in order to work and support his family. Fighting the war. Getting the best blue-collar job available, given his skills and education. He's the world he lives in, with its problems. He's his armchair. His white shirt that never launders really white.* The woman he married. The daughter they had. The pacifist with no job she married. The boy who, precisely the opposite of Archie, permits a family to support him while he stays in school so that he can, he hopes, get a terrific job, and go on from it to solve the world's problems.

Physically, Archie—like the actor behind him—is five feet eleven, blue-eyed, about 200 pounds, with thinning gray hair. Geographically, he's a new Yorker. Wrote O'Connor, "When Norman and I first began talking about a pilot show ...we considered all regional possibilities, but we decided to follow the lead of the hit British comedy *Till Death Us Do Part,* which Norman had transferred to America. That is to say, the counterpart of London is New York, so we fixed on New York; and that being our locale, it remained for us to construct a character-counterpart of the Cockney Alf Garnett."

Archie in all things is the product of his genesis, underscored by his name. Another Archie, "the typical New York mug" in the words of his creator Ed Gardner, kept bar on radio's *Duffy Tavern.* The archy of Don Marquis's *archy & mehitabel* was a cockroach with the soul of a poet. Archie Leach, to avoid sounding too ordinary, changed his name to Cary Grant. "*Arch,*" notes Thomas Berger in *The TV-Guided*

---

*Perhaps the only thing about Archie that isn't really white. But for technical reasons, it can't be. White would photograph blindingly.

American, "is defined in the dictionary as 'extreme, most fully embodying the qualities of his or its kind,'" then adds, "*bunker,* 'full of bunk, nonsense....' He is a pipsqueak with petty hatreds and ignorant prejudices. He is the American common man." On one level, perhaps Archie is, inescapably. Therein lies the true bunker. He builds defenses around himself to keep things from getting worse, which can only be accomplished by sealing himself in, shutting out in the process most chances that things might get better.

Dug into his bunker, he's not out to get anybody. Commented arch conservative Al Capp—first comic-strip cartoon-

Archie Bunker strikes a characteristic pose.

ist to engage in overt political satire—"Archie Bunker's purpose in life is to do his job and be left alone." Threaten Archie's job, he'll panic. Threaten his self-respect, he'll set you straight. He has to. Except for twenty or thirty pounds, he has nothing left that he can afford to lose.

Archie is a white, Anglo-Saxon, Protestant American—qualities he pulls into the bunker with him. In these, he takes absolute pride. They're his only link with the likes of the Rockefellers. He works on a loading dock (an early thought was to make him a virtually outmoded elevator operator), and drives a taxi. He's a working stiff and he knows it. He looks to the link for self-dignity. Besides, the Rockefellers aren't after his job the way unskilled minority citizenry seems to be.

Archie has been compared to Ralph Kramden (Jackie Gleason) of *The Honeymooners*. O'Connor, in fact, once wrote to Gleason, "I know I am doing some of the things you did." Gleason replied, "I wish I had done some of the things you're doing." Indeed, both Kramden and Bunker are blue-collar, bellicose, prone to oversimplification, and hard on their wives. Both are trapped in the basement. But Ralph schemes with dreams of the penthouse. Archie complains he's locked in and some idiot lost the key. Ralph goes on TV to sell useless kitchen utensils, makes a fool of himself and knows it, and blows his investment. Archie goes on TV to knock gun control, makes a fool of himself without knowing it, and is robbed by thieves at gunpoint while watching the show in a bar. Ralph strives, though clumsily, to be a millionaire overnight. Archie figures he's lucky to keep the wolf from the door. The American Dream spurs Ralph Kramden. Archie Bunker has nightmares, not dreams.

Archie, sure his best days are behind him, shapes a lifestyle of waxing politically and socially nostalgic, a theme reflected in *All in the Family*'s opening and closing tunes ("Those Were the Days" and "Remembering You"). Compared to his present and future, the past looks rosy. Not because wars and depressions make for happy times, but only because he didn't know then what he knows now: that his moments of material progress will fall few and far between.

His current pleasures derive essentially from grumbling over big disappointments to wear them down to size, and reveling in such diminutive joys as getting his bagged lunch all the way to work without the oil from the tuna fish leaking onto his Twinkie.

"Ralph Kramden..." wrote Tom Shales in *The Washington Post*, "was a victim of the system before people talked about victims of the system, but he didn't blame the system." Ralph Kramden, survivor of the war and the Depression, is assured by his very survival that things can only improve. Archie Bunker, from a similar background, remembers the system before it betrayed him. Not these, but "those were the days."

To Archie, all his allies in the struggle—his values, his ideals, the sweat of his brow—have just set him up for a great cosmic joke. At last he's gotten ahead, a little, only to see the rewards withheld for the ones who were left behind. David Hapgood gave this a name, in his book *The Screwing of the Average Man*:

> As we emerged from the dream of endless progress and a bigger share for everyone, it became obvious that today's screwing of the average man was far different from the straightforward exploitation of the past. It has, in fact, become hard to tell the difference between victim and hustler, to identify ourselves with either the average man or his oppressors. We find, instead, that most people are on both sides—taking some, giving some—and are themselves not sure whether they are ahead of the game or behind. This problem, which never bothered the average man in the past, we shall call *net screwing*.

If Archie Bunker is Average Man, Common Man, Everyman, it's certainly not by choice. No thanks. When you're Adlai Stevenson or Jimmy Carter campaigning for the presidency, there's a strategy to telling folks you're the average Joe. When you're an aging foreman on a loading dock, you want someone believing, somewhere, that you're better than average somehow. To Archie, "average" smacks of mediocrity. That's why "silent majority" rings of strength. Afraid he might be a meaningless speck on the planet, Archie shores up his bunker, convincing himself that at least he's not a meaningless spic (or Hebe, or coon, or wop, or Polack).

Yet in Archie's eyes, Archie's no bigot. A bigot spouts mindless prejudice, whereas Archie believes that he's thought things through—that he's simply aware of the rules ordained by nature to make some people sluggish and other people cheats. Besides, to Archie, a racist would only use negative labels—while he's the first to declare that the sharpest lawyers are Jews.

Wrote *Saturday Review* critic Robert Lewis Shapiro, "The constraints of *All in the Family* formula dictate that Archie shall never become aware that he is a bigot." Carroll O'Connor felt much the same way: "Archie's dilemma is coping with a world that is changing in front of him. He isn't a totally evil man. He wouldn't burn a cross. He's shrewd. But he won't get to the problem, because the root of the problem is himself, and he doesn't know it." Archie knows what he sees, and when what he sees doesn't fit with what he thinks he knows, he reconnoiters around it until the obvious conforms to his prejudgment (a.k.a. prejudice) of what it ought to be.

Along these lines, one of Archie's finest moments comes in the episode "Mike's Move." Archie, not wanting to live so far from daughter Gloria and grandson Joey, has resisted son-in-law Mike's plans to take a better teaching job in Minnesota. Ironically Mike, the peace-marching liberal, might lose the position to a black man in a case of reverse discrimination. Archie, for purely selfish motives, decries Mike's wanting to steal work from a minority member. He ludicrously proclaims that here stands living proof: All along not he but Mike had it in for those people. Virtually transforming himself into the Statue of Liberty, Archie ringingly paraphrases its promises of justice and equality: "send me your poor, your deadbeats, your filthy" to come and live in their own separate neighborhoods where they'll brain you if you enter.

Not the bias, but its strained application to Archie's daily struggle, provides the axle on which *All in the Family* revolves. Said Carroll O'Connor, back in *All in the Family*'s infancy, "We try to follow a plan of confrontation situations with which Archie can't cope, due to his ingrained prejudices." Archie must choose between laying off a Puerto Rican, a black man, and a white man who's the least qualified of the lot; a realtor offers Archie a bundle to sell his house, but the realtor is black; Archie's most macho friend at Kelcy's bar admits to being gay.

Archie is often stymied in trying to act on a given prejudice, but seldom has trouble declaring what it is. His face-to-face greeting to the realtor, whom he invited over sight unseen by phone: "You're colored!" His description of Mike, authority on everything: "A regular Marco Polish." Carlos from Kelcy's: "the spic kid."

Conceivably, Archie would do things differently were he less gullible, or more bright. But he's such a patsy in some ways, so often his own worst enemy in undermining his cause. Lionel Jefferson constantly bests him by agreeing with everything he says, then embellishing ad ridiculum. When Archie inquires what Lionel will be after graduating college, Lionel grins, "a 'lectical ingineer." Another time, describing the transplant of a "black heart" into a "white body" in South Africa, Lionel adds that the man wouldn't know what public restroom to visit. Archie admits that he never quite saw this aspect of the surgery before. When trying to help Mike over sexual difficulties with Gloria, Archie asks Lionel's uncle Henry what blacks do to attain the prowess for which they're justifiably famous. Henry comes on straight, playing Archie for a sap. Archie presses for the secret—which he heard had something to do with soul food. Reluctantly, Henry admits— well, okay, it's hog jowls. Archie, no longer 100 percent sold, keeps listening. Only when Henry enumerates side effects— from the urge to shine shoes to a terminal tap-dancing syndrome—does Archie realize he's been had.

Significantly, Archie, for all his brights, sways a small but appreciative audience outside his home. Catalyst and occasional activist among those of similar bent, he wields a powerful signature, as when George Jefferson circulates a petition that no one in the neighborhood will sign until

Archie does first. Not only Archie's life, but also his cronies, reinforce his philosophy.

Outside his home. But in the family, it's a no-man's-land for bigots. There, no longer expecting to win the war, he relishes victory in the forays. Archie knows for a fact that Mike and Gloria will hoot down each justification, "which indeed they do," wrote Norman Lear in *The New York Times,* "so he tries forever to sneak them by."

For each sincere conviction, Archie marshals a thousand candid reasons in support: nature, human; biology, about which not to be too vocal in his presence; the Constitution, interpreted selectively and with a limited knowledge of history (being unable to believe, for instance, that the United States ever mistreated the Indians or committed acts of imperialist aggression); the Bible, which he quotes incorrectly (as when he notes that Abel was killed by his brother with a cane) and "misconscrews" (as when he holds that Jesus is proved to be God's son because, were he not, you couldn't shut business down all over the world on his birthday).

He *has* thought things through, his way. When things get *in* his way, that's where he draws the line. "Ministers are selling a kind of morality that he doesn't accept," Carroll O'Connor has explained. "They're telling him what he should do for his fellow man, and his concept is that he should do *nothing* for his fellow man, because there's no man that's doing anything for him. If he's getting along under his own steam, then everybody else should do the same."

Though Archie is in fact presented as a bigot, he emerges fully formed as much more. Had Archie the money and social station of, for example, Philip Drummond (Conrad Bain) on *Diff'rent Strokes,* there would be no story, and no point. Archie's background and history, while hardly excusing his bigotry, nonetheless effectively explain it. Since few social problems can be solved by understanding but a single side of the issue, *All in the Family,* by offering up the oppressions on both sides of the picture, dramatically explores the reality in which all oppression exists.

Archie, oppressed, oppresses. That's real. Archie, oppressing, is lovable. He tells a good story and drinks beer with his friends. Such is the nature of ultimate reality. Bigots are people, not symbols; not stick figures, but people who perceive themselves as stuck with the wrong end of the stick. In everyone, Norman Lear identifies "what the Jews call *tam*, the quality of being embraceable and human even at our worst." Of his father, a model for Bunker, Lear has said, "I could never forgive him for being a bigot—but I found there were other things to love him for."

And as John J. O'Connor cautioned in *The New York Times*, "As truly enlightened observers, we don't want to become too bigoted about bigots, do we?"

Mike

"In England there are only two
things to be, basically: You are
either for the labour movement or
for the capitalist movement. You
either become a right-wing Archie
Bunker if you were in the class I
am, or you become an instinctive
socialist, which I was."
—John Lennon

Chicago-born Mike Casimir Stivic married Archie's daughter, doesn't hold a job, is of Polish descent, sports long hair in a parted Prince Valiant cut, and a mustache (which Rob Reiner grew, at 24, to look old enough to get the part of Mike, 24). Such deeds in themselves could unhinge a man like Archie. But Archie is marked for worse, because Mike is a sociology major of heavily liberal persuasion.

Other than that Mike is balding from the forehead and has the round-shouldered slouch of a tall man used to talking eye-to-eye with a short wife, he has the best of all possible worlds: a fine and loving spouse; a nurturing mother-in-law; a father-in-law who provides his food and the roof over his head; a healthy body and a sharp mind, along with the opportunity to decide when he will apply which, and how. This final good fortune he sometimes takes for granted, forgetting that Archie never had many options nor Mike's exposure to what Mike knows. At the same time, Mike routinely neglects to consider that Archie has lived, firsthand, a life Mike only reads about in sociology books.

Archie, of course, is as bad. Convinced that Mike has no experience at anything, nor an idea worth hearing, he prepares himself in advance to refute whatever Mike has to say.

Mike would think like Mike, and Archie like Archie, whether or not the two had ever met. But if they weren't both so stubborn, they could actually learn from each other once in a while. This confrontation is the essence of *All in the Family*—a stark reminder of the dove/hawk polarization that characterized America in the Seventies. As Norman Lear said of himself and his father, "We never agreed about anything; we fought about everything. I'd tell him he was a bigot, he'd call me a goddamn bleedin'-heart liberal, and we were both right—but also wrong." Lear's father also referred to Norman

Meathead vs. Archie.

as "dead from the neck up," an expletive which Lear has Archie hurling at Mike as early as the first episode, and subsequently too, by way of definition. "You're a meathead, dead from the neck up...."

Mike, in Mike's eyes, is patriotic, motivated, socially adjusted, and intellectually mature. Mike, to Archie, is a commie pinko, lazy "prevert atheist," "ivory shower" meathead.

Mike's patriotism urges sweeping reforms. He envisions a better United States, free of inequities in the system, and free for all. Archie, certain Mike's line of attack will *incite* a free-for-all, suggests that Mike love America or leave it. Mike argues that if the protestors left, it wouldn't solve the problems. War, racial strife, poverty, and pollution would remain. Responds Archie, "If you're gonna nitpick." Besides, to Archie's way of thinking, what's wrong with the system isn't the system—it's the breaks.

Mike reads up on the issues, supports candidates, votes even in local elections. Archie doesn't vote locally, rationalizing that it dilutes the majesty of his vote. When Archie does decide to oppose Mike's neighborhood candidate at the polls, he can't anyhow. It's been so long since he voted, his registration has lapsed.

In one episode, Mike mails off a letter protesting government policies. A disgusted Archie feels compelled to send one too, to offset Mike's. Falling asleep, Archie pictures President Nixon reading the letter aloud on TV. Imagining Nixon's gratitude, he swells to a fervor approaching worship. The act of writing the president is, for Archie, high drama. Largely because he reveres the nation, he extends this reverence to its top office holder. Mike can't believe the fuss. Sure, stating his views was important enough to Mike that he troubled to write. But he didn't go bananas. President Nixon is neither Mike's idol nor his ideal.

Archie's Nixon is the Nixon who, in the wake of the bloody riots that beset the 1968 Democratic national convention, addressed its Republican counterpart with a message of peace and hope: "I think my principles are consistent. I believe very deeply in the American system. I believe very deeply in what is needed to defend that system at home and abroad."

Mike's Nixon is the Nixon he sees, only four years later, mortified by Watergate.

To Archie, patriotism means defending the country, not criticizing it. Defending, to Archie—who fought World War II (Fifteenth Army Air Force Unit, same as Norman Lear)— demands both your mouth and your gun. On the subject of guns, Archie would like to end hijacking by arming every plane passenger. Mike, a pacifist, rejects violence as an answer, to the point of having a personal crisis after he slugs a creep on the subway to defend a woman being strangled. Where Mike admires Ché Guevara, Archie esteems John Wayne.

Mike, enrolled in college full-time, studies diligently, committed to this process as the means to achieve his praiseworthy goals. He therefore isn't free to hold a job, a circumstance Archie equates with *free* ride. Even Andy Warhol went on record as loving "*Sanford and Son* and *That's My Mama* and most of all *All in the Family* because it's great to see working people and people working." What Archie would love to see most of all is *Mike* working. Adding insult to injury, Mike inherits money, which he decides to donate to McGovern's campaign instead of toward repaying Archie. Archie can't get over the feeling of being beleaguered by a son-in-law whose lifestyle he subsidizes, who reads books Archie will never read, and who then pontificates that Archie doesn't do enough for his fellow man. And into the bargain, since Archie doesn't personally choose to give more of his money away, Mike advocates a system that will call him nasty names and give it away on his behalf.

Ironically but not surprisingly, several years later when Mike, with a wife and son to support, loses a job to a black friend because of reverse discrimination, he's closer to standing in Archie's shoes than ever before. In this case, he doesn't feel his family should lose out to a minority family to atone for centuries of prejudice. To his credit, he thinks again, sincerely congratulates his friend, and invites the man to celebrate over dinner.

Mike also advocates a permissiveness Archie can't abide. Mike is openly affectionate with Gloria, believes in sex before marriage, and allows a friend to paint Gloria in the nude (although this ultimately bothers him more than he's willing to let on). Archie, who has nothing against humankind but totally distrusts people, fears such behavior as the beginning of the end—which he intends to avoid by ending it at the beginning. Accordingly, he flies off the handle at the use of the word *breast* in mixed company, even when it refers to swimming strokes or chicken. He prefers not to touch his wife anywhere but upstairs. He wouldn't support a clinic that gave free shots for VD: When he was a lad, they weren't free unless you joined the armed forces.

Mike is an atheist, for which Archie has visions of God striking Mike down with lightning. Where Mike rejects, Archie confuses. Mike renounced his own Catholic baptism long ago. Archie believes so much in baptism that he kidnaps Mike's son to have him baptized, yet in the selfsame hour he can speak of how Edith goes to church every Sunday and even prays during the week when God isn't listening. Archie's God made man in His image—white, as "that dago artist" Michelangelo depicted Him. Theologists, atheists, and agnostics may never be able to prove whether Mike is or isn't right, but all would agree that Archie is wrong. Archie's God, in truth, is made in Archie's image—whereas Mike's deepest convictions are those widely considered by people who uphold God's existence to be in synch with God. *All in the Family* neither proves nor disproves God's existence. What it shows is how much damage to public relations a loudmouth perverting His message can do. As Edith tells Archie, who glibly expounds on the thoughts of God sitting in Judgment, "But He's God. You ain't."

In a given political, economic, biological, or religious debate with Archie, Mike regards himself as the voice of educated reason, while to Archie, Mike is just one more nattering voice. Where Mike cites figures and statistics, Archie spiels convolutions enriched by dazzling malaprops: "The sexual act was never constipated," "Goodbye and good

ribbons," "Groinocologist." Malaprops, though neither in-
vented nor perfected by Archie, fit his tongue like a glove.

Mike is not above belittling Archie's brain power, as
when Archie inquires why Mike doesn't ask him an intelligent
question, and Mike ripostes, "I don't want to confuse you."

Mike freely ridicules Archie, but is deeply wounded
when accused of insensitivity in himself. During a *Scruples*-
type game, friends mention that Mike can be preachy, biased,
and ungrateful. Lionel, for instance, wishes Mike would treat
him less as a spokesman for black people everywhere, and
more like the guy next door. Mike explodes that they're
ganging up, and storms off to his room.

Archie spars with Mike, insult for insult, but he'd swear
it stems from legitimate contempt. He's the wildebeest drag-
ging himself to the waterhole, while Mike zips by in a Land
Rover, snapping photos for a survey on the extinction of
African wildebeests. In the long run, the survey may do more
good than the wildebeest, but wildebeests don't read surveys,
so Archie doesn't care. Even had Archie no bias against
intellectuals before, he'd readily develop one after living with
Mike. He resents knowing that someone can eat the food
from his table (or in Mike's case, inhale it—when he's hungry,
he wants to know if he has time to make a sandwich before
lunch) yet dismiss him as a buffoon—whether a son-in-law or
a welfare recipient.

Critics have argued that *All in the Family* presents Archie
as always wrong, and Mike as always right. But in fact, each is
both right and wrong. Comments Rob Reiner, "They don't
understand that Mike Stivic may be right in many things but
the way he's wrong is more subtle than the way Archie Bunker
is full of nonsense."

Though steeped in behavioral sciences, Mike can't discern what Edith eventually tells him—that Archie envies
Mike's potential. Mike embodies more promise than Archie
ever dared dream, while Archie will always be just the
schlump he is now. Sociologist Mike conceivably should pick
up on this without coaching, but he can't see the forest for the
trees. Too bad. If he'd learn how to get through to Archie,

instead of being an armchair activist, he could indeed begin to change the world.

In due course, Mike graduates and foots his own bills; moves with Gloria to the house next door; and lands a teaching post in California, taking Gloria and son Joey three thousand miles away. In the March 19, 1978 episode, Mike and Archie say goodbye.

Archie warns that they'll be murdered in California. It's different than in New York, he adds, where the police can explain why it happened. In California, you get snuffed because a rich kid is bored with playing the guitar.

Mike, in turn, hugs Archie with the passion he usually saves for minority groups. He thanks him, says he loves him, declares Archie has been like a father to him. Responds Archie, "You're like a son to me. You never did do anything I told you."

Gloria

**"A man in general is better pleased
when he has a good dinner upon
his table, than when his wife
talks Greek."
—Samuel Johnson**

Gloria Bunker Stivic is much to be admired once you manage to detect her. Overshadowed in the war of Mike versus Archie, upstaged by her mother in the realm of emotional pyrotechnics, she struggles to be her own woman when the easier course would be simply not to make waves.

Consider Gloria's predicament. She combines Archie's obstinance (slapping Archie's head and shooting him raspberries) with Edith's compassion (happily bustling after her man); is torn between Archie and Mike, the two men in her life; works her husband's way through school, forgoing her own education; loves Edith dearly but disdains her complacent servility; has the face of a child and the body of a full-figured woman; and has sometimes been labeled a "dizzy blonde."

"A sexy and slightly addled minigirl in miniskirts" is how critic Clarence Petersen described Gloria when the show debuted in 1971. But like Sally Struthers, the actress who plays her, she proved herself to be wonderfully complex. Said

Struthers in 1973, "Every time I have a television role, I'm a sweet, young, apple-pie-all-American girl, but every time I do a movie I'm sort of a loose woman, a bit more voluptuous, sexy, earthy."

It took time, but Gloria spread her wings. In the same year, she wished the writers would "develop Gloria more. She's not as much of a nitwit as she is a nonentity. After all, she did at least graduate from high school and she is married. But she's a parrot for her husband. Much of the time it's mostly 'Oh, Daddy, stop it,' 'Michael!' and 'Where are you going?'"

Within the structure of antecedent sitcoms, two traditional formats prevailed: parent/children family and couple/couple friendship. *All in the Family*, in a sense, offers both. In this regard, Gloria serves as a daughter, daddy's princess—in the vein of Betty Anderson on *Father Knows Best*; and as chum—à la Ethel Mertz of *I Love Lucy* or Trixie Norton of *The Honeymooners*—to Edith. Yet, in suiting these necessary purposes, the role could evolve into little more than the purposes it fulfilled—a concept to hang ideas from, furniture that talked.

A flashback to Gloria's wedding day. Edith tells Gloria the facts of life—but Gloria does all the talking.

Observed *All in the Family*'s director, John Rich, "It's been easy to underwrite her, to let her serve as a feeder of lines.... We received letters from a women's lib group asking 'What does she do? What's her job, her education? Is she just around all the time?' Norman Lear showed me a letter signed by about 50 women in bold signatures, and said, 'What do you think?' I said, 'I have to agree. We have somewhat ignored Gloria. I think we should write stories that give her another function than being another ear on the set.'"

She's daddy's little girl, and doubtless one thing Archie holds against Mike is that Mike's mere annexation to the family means Gloria has grown up. She's momma's little girl too; but as often happens with mothers in contrast with fathers, Edith relishes the knowledge that her daughter is a smart, insightful adult: her little girl in some ways, but in many more, almost her sister.

Gloria persuades Archie—who would just as soon drop it—to comfort Edith when Edith barely escapes being raped, and urges Edith to report the incident to the police. And, in "The Battle of the Month," she and Edith quarrel. This episode sparked tremendous post-episode reaction, because it dealt with Gloria's menstrual period. Revealed writer Michael Ross to *The New York Times*, "We needed Gloria irritated to the point where she would blow up at Edith. In fact, we got the idea from Sally herself. When she has her menstrual period, forget it...."

Each time mom and daughter argue, they learn from each other. They listen, unlike Archie and Mike, who run their mouths but close their ears. Gloria encourages Edith to become a liberated woman. Edith reaffirms for Gloria the beauty of selfless love.

Providing one of *All in the Family*'s most realistic ironies, Gloria learns from not Mike but Edith, while at the same time, she teaches Mike. The Stivics share similar views on a great many issues, which is admirable. But Mike tends to respect his wife for sharing his ideas more than for having her own. Mike is capable of telling Gloria not to worry about it, since no one expects her to be as smart as he is. He has school friends over, and remarks that it's fun to have bright company for a change. His friends frequently seem to appreciate Gloria more than he does. Indeed, in many ways, he treats Gloria just as Archie treats Edith, with the difference that maybe he'll kiss her in the living room.

But Gloria stands her ground, and generally gets through to Mike. She dons a black wig as a gag. Mike is so turned on, he wants her to wear it in bed. She sets him straight. He sees the light. Mike announces that he's going to have a vasectomy. Gloria brings him to realize it's not his unilateral decision to make. To Mike's credit, he softens because he finally lets her words penetrate. To Gloria's credit, she—like her mother—has a gift for knowing what to say.

Sometimes, because Mike can be so stubborn, Gloria convinces him only after the fact. For the early years of their marriage, their entire income is the money Gloria earns. When Mike needs an appendectomy, she pleads with him to use a female surgeon who comes highly recommended. Not only is the woman a minority member and hence deserving of Mike's support, but her fees fall within the range of what Gloria can afford. Professed convictions aside, Mike hammers away at going with the more expensive Dr. McKenzie whose name was mentioned to him, because when it comes to surgery on his personal person, he'd feel safer in the hands of a male surgeon. Mike prevails. Dr. McKenzie cuts. Only after the operation does Mike see the Dr. McKenzie about whom he's heard so much. The one thing he didn't hear: She's a woman.

Frequently Mike and Gloria unite to wage battle against a common enemy who is not always Archie. When Kressler's department store fires Gloria over her pregnancy in the belief that she no longer presents an alluring image to the public, Mike marches her up to confront her boss. Mike takes over the vocal battle, but when it fails, the two together plot the rest of the war. Mike plans a protest against the store. Gloria hits on the idea of calling her doctor for the names of other pregnant women, who eagerly form a picket line. TV coverage ensues. Gloria gets her job back.

Pregnant twice (the first ended in miscarriage), she announces her second bun in the oven at the close of the 1974 season, between commercials for Geritol and Preparation H. Joseph Michael (Joey) Stivic—played alternately by twins Jason and Justin Draeger—is born on December 22, 1975, suspiciously close to Christmas day. (The event is rated one of the 16 most-awaited TV shows and episodes of all time in Gabe Essoe's *The Book of TV Lists*.)

In a twinkling, the ideal Toy Corporation released Joey Stivic in plastic, "the first physically correct male doll." Strictly speaking, Petit Frère (Little Brother) copped those honors several years earlier. A French doll introduced to the United States in 1967 and promptly apprehended by U. S.

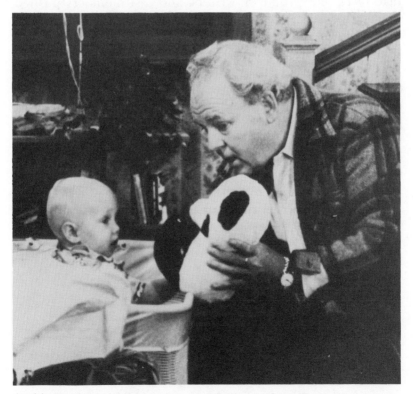

Archie Bunker with his "controversial" grandson, Joey.

Customs, Little Brother convinced authorities of his good intentions and was soon released. Joey's first, therefore, consisted in being the first U.S.-made p.c.m.d., as well as our first Polish-American doll.

Reported the *New York Daily News,* "Jeffrey Breslow, one of the general partners of Marvin Glass [Chicago-based creators of the toy], thinks the public is ready to accept the Joey doll. 'We're not making a special deal of the doll's anatomy, and we're certainly not going to take a zoom lens and focus on the penis.'"

But this is precisely what censors feared. They'd have preferred the Stivic child to be a girl. Someone's going to diaper it, right? On camera? An infant prevert, flashing and mooning the nation! Oh, baby! CBS suggested the scene not take place, but producer, writers, and cast members pushed that Archie be allowed to diaper his grandson's bottom. CBS backed down. Archie performed his task. Joey flashed accordingly.

With Joey, the Stivics and Bunkers had new reasons to clash: Who will be the godparents? Will he be baptized in the church? Archie responds to the latter debate by snatching Joey against his folks' wishes and doing the deed himself.

Motherhood permits Gloria many a rare moment to explore how the child of parents like Archie and Edith would raise a youngster of her own. Edith's compassion. Archie's assertiveness. Bonded together by Gloria's own smarts.

The combination held such promise that it spun off a sitcom, *Gloria,* in 1982.

Edith

"You'll stoop to anything to be good."
—Archie Bunker

I n *The Complete Book of Nerds*, Bob Stine lists her name as Dingbat, her nickname as Edith Bunker, and her hobby as taking abuse. A frump in a washed-out double-knit dress that frequently matches the wallpaper, she makes do with her budget and with her life. Easily placated, difficult to insult, Edith Baines Bunker scurries to do the bidding of a husband who orders "Stifle yourself, dingbat!"—the equivalent in *Till Death Us Do Part* being "silly moo"—and seemingly thrives on it.

The scurry is revealing—the illusion of speed to get nowhere; the frustration of being goal-oriented with infinitesimal goals. Shirley Booth used the motion sublimely on stage and in the movies in *Come Back Little Sheba*. Stapleton perfects the move and its nuances as Edith, Mrs. Mouse in a maze. How hard does Edith have to run to emerge from the kitchen with a beer? But her point is not the minute mile. Her message is: I aim to please.

Archie comes home in a mood. Edith greets him cheerily: "You're home!" Archie does a sarcastic routine on how clever she must be to have guessed this—upon seeing him enter, doff his hat and coat, and stash his bowling ball.

Undeterred, Edith persists in her bliss: "Plus, there's the sound of your voice."

On the surface, Edith isn't too bright. (Scratch deeper, and you still won't get Einstein.) She sends money to the OTB (Off-Track Betting) to help in their fight against lung disease. She wishes the poor people in England could have, instead of the Common Market, a really good one. She quotes Hallmark cards as though they were Shakespearean sonnets, and tells interminable stories with infinite detours, every detail having equal weight. Archie no longer can bear to listen. Adopting a pained expression, he pantomimes a gun blowing off the top of his head.

But Edith unfolds her stories the same way she does everything else—with total impartiality. She wouldn't dream of slighting a cousin who was somehow around for a tale, even if his place in it is totally immaterial. If he wore his favorite socks that day, she's going to tell you that, too.

Archie laments the loss of his easy chair.

Edith, being totally impartial, is naturally free of prejudice. Attending a high school reunion, she instantly recog-
nizes a man who, in his Adonis days, used to set her swooning.
Now he's changed for the worse—fat, receding hairline—
thrilling Archie, who feared the competition. But to Edith, he
looks as he always did. He's still the same man, with the same
warmth in his eyes. When a convict on work furlough does
chores around her house, Edith panics momentarily, only to
form an empathetic bond with him when she sees that they
both can quote the homespun poetry of Edgar A. Guest.

When Cousin Liz dies a spinster, Edith laments that Liz
died without having known love. Then Edith learns that she
did love—another woman. Though Edith only slowly compre-
hends the relationship, she immediately intuits the depth of
the other woman's grief—the despair of a widow surrounded
by people who don't acknowledge her loss. Edith isn't school-
smart, but her insights merit a Ph.D.

Soaking up experience like a sponge, Edith learns from
everything, valuing her lessons however gravely they are come
by. Her father taught her two things about survival: never
order hamburgers in a drugstore, and how to knee a man
when he attacks you. Once, as a teenager, she was forced to
apply the second lesson, then felt so ashamed she never
reported the incident. Years later when Gloria is molested,
Edith draws on her own failure to follow through, urging
Gloria to take her assailant to court—if not for herself, at
least to protect others from being his future victims. As well
as she learns, Edith teaches even better—sometimes with
words; often, just by example.

Without flying off the handle as Mike would, Edith can
take in whole lectures from Archie, nod hesitantly, then go do
what she planned to do all along—reach out to a friend in
need. When Louise Jefferson moves in next door, Edith
welcomes her happily. The Jeffersons, as blacks coming into a
white neighborhood, face societal pressures of which Edith is
doubtless aware. But she's at least as anxious that Louise
should know which grocery stores have the best produce
sections. From the first, Edith relates to Louise not in a token

gesture of positive race relations, but as one housewife to another. From before their first meeting, she looks forward to Louise's company, and to the fun she hopes they'll share.

Edith is like this with everyone, from senior citizens to transvestites: open, enthusiastic, with no preconceived notions about anyone, except to consider everybody a potential friend.

Instinctively drawn to the good in people, judging their intentions more than their actions—it's this attitude that enables Edith to adore Archie, which she does emphatically. Were she more critical, she'd have no use for him, which for Edith would be a tragedy. Archie is the center of her universe, warts and all. Edith serenades Archie in shrill, shrieking devotion when he'll let her, and smothers him with kisses. Warned by her mother before she was married that sex would be no pleasure, she's never quite stopped feeling guilty that she likes it with Archie so much. They don't talk about affection as she'd wish to, because Archie is a prude:

> ARCHIE: This ain't somethin' a man usually tells a woman
> ...I—I love you, Edith!
>
> EDITH: I know that, Archie.
>
> ARCHIE: You mean I didn't have to say it?

But they do it. "In spite of Edith's seeming innocence," observed Sander Vanocur in *The Washington Post,* "a strong sexuality cements their relationship. It is a sexuality based on the deepest kind of love." Carroll O'Connor fully concurs, and complained when series writers implied a sexual inertia inconsistent with a relationship obviously there.

Clearly, Archie loves and takes pride in Edith, though he'd rather she not hold a job, or express an opinion either privately or in public. Partly, he'd as soon not be shown up or embarrassed; but also, he thinks he's protecting Edith from getting in over her head. At such times, Archie's brain is no match for Edith's heart. Edith prevails, Archie gripes, and in the end, these very instances leave him respecting her more.

Only when Edith begins helping out at the Sunshine

Home does Archie stray, in the three-part story "Archie's Brief Encounter." He goes only so far as kissing the other woman, then confesses to Edith, who's guessed anyway. Edith walks out, deserting him for the Sunshine Home full-time. Archie, first stubborn, then bereft, wins Edith's heart all over again. Confessing he's missed her, Archie assumes she's been lonely too. Edith answers that, actually, she only missed him when she gave it thought, which wasn't very often. Before the separation, she'd concentrated her full energies on Archie, the only one she could count on. But now, beams Edith, she's learned she can count on herself too.

Edith counts on Archie more or less by definition. He puts food on the table, but so could most men, and Edith doesn't adore most men, just Archie. His fondness for her, however real, is generally unspoken, and his declarations of support and affection are hard won. What she can count on are his demands and expectations running true to form—get the beer, dinner at six, stifle. Yet she wouldn't have it any other way. Fish swim, birds fly, Edith needs Archie.

As totally as Edith anchors her life in Archie, he counts on her to an equal if not greater degree. When Edith needs Archie, he's often not there; or if there physically, then frequently not there in spirit, not caring enough. But when Archie needs Edith, she's there in all things and all ways, surrounding him with a toasty blanket of omnipresent love. Whoever or whatever might belittle him in the course of a day, he knows Edith will build him up again.

Besides, she's really the strong one of their twosome. When Archie disappoints Edith, she's strong enough to draw on inner resources until he makes things right; because he needs her so much, he always does. When Edith withdraws her strength from Archie, he has all the resilience of soggy bread. And when, for instance, Bernard Bernstein passes from life to death on their sofa, Archie senses what has happened but is powerless to do anything other than call Edith in from the kitchen. Edith takes his pulse, confirming Archie's fears. Archie, wishing not to face it, says the doctor will come and cure Mr. Bernstein. Of the two, only Edith is strong enough to accept the reality of the old man's demise, and her strength carries Archie through the ordeal.

Along with her strength, Archie both depends on and is at the mercy of Edith's goodness. She's so fair-minded, she can't get a joke that hinges on playing on words. To her, if a word can have two meanings, you have to explain which one you intend. Otherwise, you're cruel, not funny. When Archie tells her about the spaceman who mistakes a pinball machine for a female of his species, Edith can't see the joke. She can only hope the pinball machine will respond to his advances.

When menopause (a condition Archie terms "mental pause") makes Edith grouchy, he's nearly driven insane. Yet when she dents a car with a can of cling peaches and leaves a note for the unknowing victim, Archie is fit to be tied. She was kind to a stranger at his expense! Goodness as goodness is all well and good, but Archie will never fathom Edith's extremes.

Discovering that Edith has let him win at cards throughout their marriage, Archie rails that she's too good. Never swearing, nor angering anyone, she doesn't even cheat to win; Edith cheats to lose. Archie defies her to do something human, which he clarifies: "Do something rotten." The words break her heart but not her will. Transcendent humanity like Edith's can't be compromised.

Edith, with her radiant soul (and those blue-green eyes of Jean Stapleton's) has inspired countless sermons. Without pom-poms or a stadium, she's a cheerleader for the Lord. If you never saw her in action, you could read the Sermon on the Mount and know the woman anyway: "Blessed are the meek...Blessed are they which do hunger and thirst after righteousness...Blessed are the merciful...Blessed are the pure in heart...Blessed are the peacemakers." One can even imagine how she would have behaved had she been there when Jesus fed the multitudes. Some scoffed, some marveled at the miracle of loaves and fishes. Edith, though spriritually awestruck, would not have neglected asking Jesus to whip up a batch of leftovers for her to take to the poor the next day.

While Edith Bunker in some regards changed during her

TV tenure, she never abandoned this goodness. In fact, over time (and Archie's objections), she vastly expanded its scope —along with her own horizons. Said scriptwriter Bernie West in 1974, alluding to the gradual transformation, "We try very hard not to make her too dumb, too much of a Gracie Allen character. Edith is growing. She is not going to be a doormat."

In the same year, Jean Stapleton observed, "I couldn't be more thrilled with the effects of women's lib—all that con-sciousness-raising. But we can't hide the kind of woman who is restricted by her domestic life. She exists. And I think that by showing Edith as she really is, we are doing more good than an instant out-of-character liberationist would accom-plish. There's a slow development going on with Edith and that's the way it's really going to happen in this country."

Three years later, Norman Lear spoke of Edith's savvy at a seminar for the American Film Institute: "The women's movement caught our awareness, our consciousness, and so caught Edith's. After all, we are providing her with her thoughts and her words and her reactions and her attitudes ...so as we grow as people and artists, and as times change, I think the characters reflect it."

In October of 1977, as a member of the International Women's Year Commission, Jean Stapleton updated the thought: "The image of Edith Bunker is good for the women's movement because Edith is a homemaker." and the women's movement is at least as much about the women running households as it is about female nuclear physicists. Stapleton went on to elaborate that the role reflected sensibilities of the women's movement in terms of the need to dignify home-makers and evaluate their contributions to the nation's well-being and economy. She even indicated that the ever more knowledgeable Mrs. Bunker might support the ERA: "Edith Bunker is the soul of justice, and of course to me the ERA is a matter of simple justice...I think she'd vote for it, if she understood it."

Upon receiving a doctor of humane letters degree at Emerson College, Boston, in 1978, Jean Stapleton was able to add, "Thanks to the influence of her enlightened daughter and neighbor, Edith is growing...to know herself as a whole person with rights and power."

In the course of all this growing, Edith persuaded at least one critic, Arthur Unger of *The Christian Science Monitor*, that "Archie Bunker has outgrown the series just as the series has outgrown him. He is a vestigial central figure—still superbly conceived and acted, but now a sad, gloriously inglorious marginal figure. Instead, the central figure has become Edith Bunker."

Archie would not have agreed, though her scorecard showed significant gains over Archie. In the last analysis, Edith has everything she ever wanted—from life, from the world, from her mate. When Archie rants, Edith shuffles, by choice. But when she holds her ground against him, Archie, for all his sound and fury, can't win.

The Perfect Victim

**"The value of a sentiment is the amount of sacrifice you are prepared to make for it."
—John Galsworthy**

N o wonder Edith moves the way she does. Her gears are permanently out of whack from a lifetime of turning the other cheek. Her self-abasement is self-imposed. The abundant joys she finds in life, she seeks in the hearts of others.

Edith accedes to Archie's commands not from obligation, but desire. The cans of beer, the dinners promptly at six, sitting in her chair when his is more comfortable, doing him the extreme favor of hearing in his bluster the endearments he rarely has courtesy enough to speak—these are Edith's love offerings to Archie. She never fails to stand up to Archie, which is to say, she doesn't *fail* to do it; she simply chooses not to most of the time. When she does, it's not for herself, but only because Archie intends to hurt others—or, when for herself, only because she wants to help others.

The immovable force and the irresistible object.

When Edith holds a big-money lottery ticket belonging to Louise Jefferson ("Edith's Winning Ticket"), Archie connives to keep the booty. Edith turns a deaf ear. When Cousin Liz dies leaving Edith as her next of kin, Archie tingles over the price her silver set will fetch ("Cousin Liz"). Then Edith learns that Liz had been a lesbian, and over Archie's outraged objections, presents the pricey heirloom to Liz's longtime lover.

When a plumber's assistant turns out to be a convict on daytime work furlough from Sing Sing Penitentiary ("Prisoner in the House"), Archie grabs for the phone, determined to be rid of the man. Edith pleads with him to put the receiver down, but Archie persists. When Edith sees her entreaties getting nowhere, she orders Archie to hang up the phone, *damn it*. The audience, as in all such cases when Edith utters strong language in disobedience to her mate, goes wild. Yet Edith, far from wanting to play Pin the Tail on Archie, holds firm only to make a point. The audience, not Edith, derives jollies from her scoring one. Even in "Edith's Night Out," when Archie declines to go out with her and she sashays off to Kelcy's alone (instantly making scads of friends), she never speaks up to put Archie down. What she puts is her heart on the line.

Nor is it just Archie she challenges. In "Edith Has Jury Duty"—playing a role similar to one she had on *Naked City* some 20 years before—she holds out single-handedly against the rest of the jurors, ultimately saving an innocent man from a murder conviction.

When Edith dents a car with a can of cling peaches ("Edith's Accident"), she leaves a note for the driver. Archie resents her actions. The Goody Two Shoes dingbat strikes again when she could have run off scott free. Now Archie is stuck with the liability. But Edith, who chooses the times that she'll square off with Archie, can see no aspect of choice in this. Since she did the damage, she'd be afraid not to confess; afraid not of the law and the wrath of God, but of hurting another human being. When Edith learns that the driver is a Catholic priest, she welcomes him into her home as an honest man and a servant of mankind. Yet when Archie discerns the fellow's line of work, his suspicions have a field day. It wouldn't occur to him to fear God in this—because Archie, a professed believer, is invulnerable to facts. He assumes the Bible will bear out whatever he's thinking, and legitimatize whatever hurt he "has to" inflict.

However inaccurately, Archie prides himself on his knack for quoting the Bible. But Edith, who clearly knows the text—at least well enough to correct Archie when he allows as how "Honor your parents" must be the third or fourth Commandment, and she quietly identifies it as the fifth ("The Dinner Guest")—refrains from quotations for the same reason she doesn't cite pulmonary mechanics before drawing breath. Some things come too naturally to justify. Edith doesn't thump the Bible, she lives it.

While Edith doesn't quote the Bible, she waxes rhapsodic over the simplest sentiments, finding sanctity in a Hallmark card, and a postscript to the Scriptures in the *Reader's Digest*. Far from betraying a shallowness, her jubilant pleasure in such modest lines confirms the true belief of a woman who sees as much of her faith in a neighbor's smile as she does in a holy writ.

She's Edith the Good, in Archie's derisive words, and as the highest accolade in Presbyterian clergyman Spencer Marsh's book of the same name. She is good both in a theological and in a humanistic sense, with a depth of caring that makes sense even to Mike the atheist, who in the episode "Edith's Crisis of Faith," contends on the side of the angels to restore her religious convictions when a friend is brutally murdered. Because she is Edith, this moment of spiritual crisis stirs even those viewers with no strong convictions of their own.

Because she is Edith, viewers know that her patient compassion soars above reproach, beyond question. In "Edith Gets Fired," a lonely old woman at the Sunshine Home asks pitiably and eloquently to be allowed the dignity of death. When the time comes, Edith respects her wishes. Instead of alerting the doctors, she lets the woman slip away. Charged with fatal negligence, Edith is out of a job. But the Sunshine Home has it easy compared to the lot of the viewers, who must suddenly deal with the issue of euthanasia in their living rooms, in the context of a so-called comedy show.

Leave It to Beaver wouldn't have tried it ("Golly, Wally, should we let her croak?" "Naw, Beave. Dad'll yell and Mom'll cry into the mashed potatoes."). But *All in the Family* could, and did. A controversial issue deemed anything but the foundation of comedy works on *this* show because Edith is Edith, her motives so purely unimpeachable that the usual clichés don't apply.

Moreover, because Edith recoils at the thought of harming anyone, viewers ache when anyone or anything injures her. When Edith cries out for help, we listen. From a crusading scriptwriter's perspective, the victimization of Edith can focus tremendous sympathetic attention on sensitive issues drawn from life.

When the dread of breast cancer haunts Edith in "Edith's Christmas Story," viewers respond as if to a cherished friend. Neighbor Irene Lorenzo reassures her—speaking from the personal experience of a mastectomy—giving courage to Edith and viewers as well. Edith's fears are, mercifully, unfounded, but the audience suffers with her until the outcome is known. The profound effect of this episode was confirmed when, having seen it, large numbers of women made appointments for mammograms, and community service societies requested tapes of the program.

In "Edith's 50th Birthday" (parts one and two, as a one-hour special), a rapist traps Edith alone in her home. Viewers watch in horror, some realizing perhaps for the first time that rape victims don't have to "ask for it." Anyone can be victimized.

As the story begins, Archie, Mike, and Gloria are at the Stivics' preparing for Edith's birthday party. Edith, alone at 704 Hauser, answers her door. A handsome, well-dressed man identifies himself as a detective investigating rape in the area. Edith, unsuspecting, lets him in. Then he makes his intentions known. Edith's terror is real enough, but like many people in hideous situations, she can't quite connect with it happening to her. He begins to undo her clothes. Completely in character (and in a state of shock), she offers him coffee. He says he doesn't drink coffee. Desperately, she suggests Sanka, trying to wrest control in the only way she knows how. When at last Edith sees that he can't be dissuaded, she pleads that he leave his clothes on. Saintlike, she divorces flesh from spirit. If it must be, then let it be as impersonal as possible. She resigns her body to violation, only imploring that he not force a kiss.

Edith is saved by a cake burning in the oven. She rushes to rescue it. Her attacker follows. She hurls the cake into his face, runs next door, and cries her heart out to her family.

Archie wants her to forget the incident, since "nothing happened." Gloria urges her to take it to the police. Because
Edith is Edith, the idea of reporting such indignities sickens
her. But also because Edith is Edith, she consents to go, rather
than leave her assailant free to endanger others.

Some critics complained that much of Edith's reaction

**A molester (David Dukes) assaults Edith just before her fiftieth
birthday party (October 16, 1977).**

merely strained the bounds of comedy: offering coffee to a rapist, worrying about kissing, and crying over a ruined cake. But Edith Bunker runs true to form, even in the worst of straits. She's not Farrah Fawcett in *Extremities;* she's Archie Bunker's wife. Her arsenal of a lifetime consists of self-abnegation and plying people with food. Critic Cecil Smith of the *Los Angeles Times* defended Edith's actions in his column: "The attack was not treated lightly; the humor was hysterical and in keeping with the Edith character...A number of letters I have received in this vein seem to be from people who did not see the program."

Other critics voiced different objections. Wrote the *New York Post*'s Harriet Van Horne of the special, "This historic episode demonstrates anew what a fine actress Jean Stapleton is, and how far down Norman Lear and CBS will reach to push up the Sunday ratings a point or two." Said Val Adams of New York's *Daily News,* "There are some who think that Lear, TV comedy producer, is a genius. A more moderate view is that he's a good showman." The facts are that Lear consulted with experts, among them the director of the rape treatment center at Santa Barbara hospital; arranged multi-city private screenings for legal authorities and social workers; and devoted over a year to writing, rewriting, and producing the piece.

Recalls David Dukes, who portrayed the rapist, "I was sitting in a bar in Hawaii after a day of skindiving. The TV was on, and I heard the news program discussing this episode. This job I did for five days of my life was suddenly on the national news. I was astounded how people reacted to it. Another time, I was at a cocktail party, and a guy came up to me and said, "I know you. You're the guy who raped Edith Bunker." I answered, 'Uh, attempted rape.' He went on, 'Yeah, you're right, attempted. I saw the show in my class.' It turned out he was a detective with the NYPD, and this along with other films is used to convey the woman's side of rape. Actually, a lot of crisis centers have used this episode since it first aired."

The care in development of the episode paid handsome

dividends. Edith as victim makes its point. Said Jean Stapleton in 1974, "I love Edith—maybe because she's so well loved
by the fans. So many people approach me with special
affection that I know they are doing it because of Edith."
Edith's pain awakens compassion in viewers who, in sharing
her crises, better understand real-life others who share each
plight.

In terms of issues, Edith's character perfectly balances
Archie's. Through Archie, writers debunk the lies of bigotry.
Through Edith, writers belie the myth that selflessness is
bunk.

Archie's Thrones

> "A man may build himself a throne
> of bayonets, but he cannot sit
> on it."
> —Dean Inge

Traditional sitcoms open simply with shots of upper-middle-class dwellings—the Andersons' on *Father Knows Best*, the Cleavers' on *Leave It to Beaver*, the Nelsons' on *The Adventures of Ozzie and Harriet*. But *All in the Family* pulls back from Archie and Edith to bird's-eye, for a helicopter view of Manhattan...then Queens, just outside Manhattan...then the Bunkers' block, a row of two-family houses...then the Bunkers' home. As quickly as we know from *Leave It to Beaver*'s opening that the Cleavers are well-heeled, we realize from *All in the Family*'s footage that the Bunkers are strictly working-class.

We zoom inside—a close-up—for Edith and Archie at the piano. When an episode proper begins, we are usually once more inside. Facing the living room dead center, we see a staircase leading to the bedrooms and bathroom upstairs; to

Queens

One of the five boroughs of New York City, the one that's attached to both Brooklyn and Long Island and in which the Bunkers live. Other famous people born in Queens include Roone Arledge (Forest Hills), Tony Bennett (Astoria), Eddie Bracken (Astoria), Jimmy Breslin (Jamaica), Morton Gould (Richmond Hill), Michael Landon (Forest Hills), Patrick McGoohan (Astoria), Ethel Merman (Astoria), Lewis Mumford (Flushing), and Edward Villella (Bayside).

our left, a dining area; to its left, a door, with the kitchen on the other side. The kitchen door opens in such a way that whatever side Archie stands on, someone is bound to slam it into him. Another door in the kitchen opens on the outside alley. The front door, in the living room, extreme right, opens on the porch. From the porch, you can look through a window into the living room.

Though a two-family house, ostensibly, from the opening footage, reference is never made to a family living on the opposite side of a central wall. On the surface, this subtle detail reeks of suburban insight: Families in two-family houses frequently pretend their mirror-image counterparts don't exist. But presumably, Edith would acknowledge such neighbors, and Archie would express some opinion about them, since he has opinions on everything else. Perhaps 704 Hauser is not quite the house of the bird's-eye view credits—particularly since, unlike the Bunkers', it doesn't have a porch. Perhaps, but this is purely irrelevant. Spiritually, the two houses are one.

An early thought for *All in the Family* was to shoot it in

black and white. Though CBS preferred color, the set remained as near monochrome as color would allow. The faded
carpet—in fact painted on the floor of the set—if not hand-
me-down, ought to be. The impression emerges of drabness
trying for cheery. Enhancing it are keepsakes, inspirational
plaques, and cheap pictures, no doubt selected or received as
gifts by Edith's loving hand. Because her house cannot be a
showplace, she fills it with show-and-tell. A ceramic elephant
of no distinction is Edith's cherished objet d'art. (As a prop, it
was knocked down and repaired so often that only the
Bunkers could have wanted it.)

These pieces—like the candy dish and ice box on *The
Honeymooners*—assume special significance. Few remember
accoutrements of the Andersons and Cleavers, whose impec-
cable homes reflect their owners through the eyes of interior
decorators. Margaret Anderson and June Cleaver can regularly reupholster. The furniture that the Kramdens and Bunkers have, they'll have for the rest of their lives.

Both Jim Anderson on *Father Knows Best* and Ward
Cleaver on *Leave It to Beaver* possess impressive home li-
braries, echoing Judge Hardy's room in Andy Hardy movies.
A wall of books as a backdrop dignifies fatherly advice. A wall
of books behind Archie would be incongruous and absurd;
actually *buying* a stock of books would reduce him to quiver-
ing jelly.

Whole books have been written which Archie would
devour if Archie read books, but he doesn't. Except for the
telephone directory, books in his lair intrude. When Edith
reads so much as a *Reader's Digest,* he promptly senses danger,
since it puts new ideas in her head. When Edith reads books
about bettering sex in marriage, Archie is so embarrassed,
he'd almost rather she couldn't read. When Mike reads anything, Archie definitely suspects. Mike and Mike's books
spout pinko subversion. No, Archie's style isn't books—
neither reading them nor owning them. His style inclines to
that fifth member of his family, the television set.

No sitcom prior to *All in the Family* placed such an
emphasis on TV, but by 1971 when the show debuted, the

mesmerizing box as a family presence could no longer realistically be ignored. Wrote Michael Arlen in 1975 in *The New Yorker*, "The basis of the Lear programs is not so much the family and its problems as it is the commonality that seems to have been created largely by television itself."

Along with its presence comes its authority, a popular and increasingly pronounced criticism of the medium being that TV reduces and slants what it then presents as unadorned fact. An issue is "covered" in five minutes on the news, or addressed at length on soap operas, making viewers instant experts at aping others' views.

On the same theme, Kenneth M. Pierce noted, in "The Bunkers, the Critics, and the News": "The children in this family are tuned in; their views, which they offer at the slightest provocation, seem formed by the news media. Mike and Gloria know about (and favor) such developments as daytime release of prison convicts, election of women to public office, and natural childbirth. Still, they don't know very much." They are, as Pierce contends that we all are, "in this age of television and other forms of instant communication, forced to talk—if we wish to talk at all—of things about which we know very little."

Maude Findlay on *Maude*—another Lear creation—said it differently, but more succinctly: "As *Mary Tyler Moore* goes, so goes the nation." Wherever TV was going in 1971 and the years that followed, it was taking us along. *All in the Family*, by acknowledging as much, confirmed its own reality, involved us in its story, and influenced us in a way no sitcom ever had before.

Facing the TV set—which often sparks *All in the Family*'s discourse—rests Archie's armchair bastion. Edith's living room seat is a chair, nothing more, with spindly legs and support not even for her shoulders. Archie's, though hardly a modern recliner, is a statement, a stronghold, a throne. The original pair of Bunker chairs, now on display at the Smithsonian in Washington, came from a Goodwill thrift store in Los Angeles. Preceding them, the idea for the chairs began in Norman Lear's childhood home: "My father had a red leather

The Bunker chairs with Archie's beer can on display at the National Museum of American History, Smithsonian Institution, "A Nation of Nations" exhibit, Washington, D.C.

chair which was his territorial imperative. We would all gather around and listen to Eddie Cantor on Sunday nights, and my father would sit in that red leather chair and control the radio dial. So on the first episode of *All in the Family*, we had Archie sit on his chair and control the television dial, and it stayed in the show from then on."

Of his father's chair, Lear has also observed, "Now, I don't remember my father thinking that way about his chair. But I remember how I felt about his chair," and also, "I think something about home and family was locked in, some understanding of home and family and its importance."

Commanding people out of his chair is Archie's idea of a power play. From it, he controls discussions and watches old movies. In it, particularly with a beer in his hand, he feels he's the king of his castle. As Cervantes fancies in the preface to *Don Quixote*, "You are a King by your own Fireside, as much as any Monarch in his Throne."

Archie's second throne flushes, and can be heard

downstairs—maybe even down the block. Archie extols its location as the only room in the house affording peace and quiet. This throne he can retreat to when the first fails to confirm his kingship, which it fails to do most of the time.

The truth is that Archie as monarch of his fireside is a legend in his own mind. Mike, Gloria, everyone else, and sometimes Edith, contribute fuel to the fire. But the thrones look most like thrones to Archie. To many another less credulous eye, they are merely where he parks his brains.

Letting the Outside In

"If it is abuse—why one is always
sure to hear of it from one damned
good-natured friend or other!"
—Richard Brinsley Sheridan

A rchie's bunker so much defines Archie that many an episode revolves solely around his home (and pivots around his armchair), with only the four principals (Archie, Edith, Mike, Gloria) in evidence on the screen. But because the world outside drove Archie into his bunker, the world outside also defines him insofar as eliciting his reactions to it. Sometimes these uninvited forces enter the Bunker domain through the modern miracle of television, or through the time-honored plot device of one of the principals commenting on something that happened in the course of the day. On other occasions, however, these unwelcome intruders knock on Archie's door and walk through it—or knock into Archie in the world outside, and walk all over him.

Each of these figures, however fully rounded, embodies a trait or combination of traits designed to bring out the worst in Archie and, not unintentionally, the best in Edith. To Edith, who delights in making new acquaintances, everyone on the planet is potentially a friend with something positive to offer, perhaps even one of the *Reader's Digest*'s "Most Unforgettable Characters." To her, every person who walks through the door may provide an unimagined avenue of discovery or self-discovery. But to Archie, each incursion and excursion brings with it the definite likelihood of assault with still more bad news: What he will discover of himself through them is that a relative wants his money, his insurance ran out, he broke the law, his body is going to science, and the government thinks he's dead.

Maude, Edith's cousin, is Archie's living embodiment of bad news when she visits to nurse the Bunker brood through a flu crisis in "Cousin Maude's Visit" (December 1971; story by Rob Reiner's writing partner Philip Mishkin). Maude is played by Beatrice Arthur, considered by Norman Lear to be one of the funniest comediennes in the world. Arthur had worked with Lear on *The George Gobel Show,* and in addition had comic and serious credits ranging from *Lysistrata, No Exit, Taming of the Shrew, Three Penny Opera,* and *Ulysses in Nighttown* to *Fiddler on the Roof, Mame* (which won her a Tony for best supporting actress in a musical), and a nightclub act.

Pitted against Archie, Maude brings to bear her thirty-plus years of experience as an FDR Democrat and a long history of bad blood with Archie. She treats him to infinite contempt, served up on a platter of withering sarcasm. He reacts to her presence as he would to choking up lunch. CBS saw great possibilities for a spin-off in this. Another episode, "Maude" (March 1972), lays out the framework for a series—presented on what will become the *Maude* set, with some members of the ultimate cast, though with Marcia Rodd rather than Adrienne Barbeau as her daughter whose wedding to a Jew, Archie sabotages.

Maude premiered in September 1972. The politically active, ultrafeminist, outspoken heroine is rumored to draw certain traits from Lear's then-wife, Frances (the Lord & Taylor sportswear buyer had been twice divorced when she

Maude (Beatrice Arthur) and Walter (Bill Macy) consider her bid for the State Senate, on *Maude*.

met Lear, and was so liberated, she asked him out on a date). Exulted CBS-TV head Robert Wood, "Maude breaks every rule of television from the start."

With the arrival of the Jeffersons, Archie has to deal with blacks as neighbors, a novelty for which life simply never prepared him. He's worked with blacks, ridden beside them on the subway, and held forth about their proclivities at length. But as neighbors, they confront him with a woman (Louise Jefferson) who becomes his wife's best friend, two men (Henry and George Jefferson) as anti-Archie as Archie is anti-them, and a young man (Lionel) who patronizes Archie as skillfully as Archie clumsily condescends to him.

Louise Jefferson (portrayed by Isabel Sanford, whose jobs included keypunch operator for the New York City welfare department before her first showbiz breaks in the American Negro Theatre and such movies as *The Last Angry Man* and as the cook in *Guess Who's Coming to Dinner*) has little

Sherman Hemsley before *All in the Family*.

patience with Archie. Yet because her husband is the same sort of irritant, Louise takes Archie in her stride. On the other hand, she is no Edith Bunker in the sense of playing kowtow to her husband's whimsies. In standing up to husband George, Louise provides a model for Edith, whose relationship with Archie benefits from the example.

George Jefferson (Sherman Hemsley, with prior stage experience in Vinnette Carroll's Urban Art Corps, *Purlie* on Broadway, *Don't Bother Me I Can't Cope* and *The Odd Couple* on tour) is a tough little dude with colossal moxie. When Hemsley first appeared at rehearsals, he seemed shy, sheepish, and destined to disappear in his role, but he proved the doubters wrong. In Clarence Major's *Black Slang: Dictionary of Afro-American Talk*, George is defined as "any Negro pullman porter (picked up from white usage)." Hemsley's George Jefferson struts his stuff as though the definition were pasted on his bedroom wall and he wants the entire human race to know it's untrue. Life has laughed at him plenty. Now he not only likes to have the last laugh, but wants to be the one to have the last laugh first. George worked as a janitor of the Hempstead Apartments until, the victim of a bus accident, he received a $3200 insurance settlement, with which he opened a dry cleaning business. He parlayed the one shop into several, then into a chain. As bigoted as Archie, George nonetheless counts professionally valuable white bankers among his favorite people to know, but has no need for honkies like Archie Bunker.

George's avoidance runs so deep that, although the Jeffersons move into the neighborhood in 1971, it isn't until 1973 that George Jefferson looms into view on screen. Before that memorable moment, only Louise, Lionel, and George's opinionated brother, Henry (Mel Stewart), cross the Bunkers' on-camera paths. When the Bunkers throw a going-away party for Henry, George refuses to attend. (He never set foot in a honky house and doesn't propose to begin at the bottom.) When he finally compels himself to make the overture, he does so with the firm intention of shouting his greetings from the threshold. Archie, while perfectly comfortable justifying his own prejudices, takes offense at George's. It doesn't help Archie's self-esteem any that George is an upwardly mobile shop owner, a white-collar black man on the move.

The few times that chance entices Archie and George to call truce, they might as well have mirrors, instead of heads, coming out of their necks. When George wants a place on the Republican county committee, he approaches Archie to sign the petition. George pleads a case of public-spiritedness, then admits that what he really wants to do is knock down a flower shop and put up a big cleaning plant. Archie, as public-spirited as the next man (if the next man happens to be George) agrees, in exchange for bargain cleaning rates. The deal is closed—until Archie's signature bounces because his voting registration lapsed, and George discovers that the district he's running for doesn't control the corner he plans to rebuild.

Lionel Jefferson (Mike Evans, whose driving someone else to audition led to his *All in the Family* part) has the most innocent countenance since Bambi's. The face can sink when he learns that his father ran for county committee not to better the world, but only to help his business. The face can radiate sincere concurrence when Archie says, "Familyarity breeds content," or when Archie implies that Lionel should hide, which Lionel politely clarifies, " . . . in the woodpile, Mr. Bunker?" Each time he relates to Lionel, Archie honestly believes himself to be proving a total lack of prejudice. Archie patiently explains to Lionel how blacks can't be happy in a white neighborhood, albeit whole bunches of them are "very decent people, as you probably know," and he extols their athletic superiority, attributable in Archie's mind to their greater speed, higher jumps, and resistance to bruising.

In the episode "The Jeffersons Move Up" (January 1975), George has become so successful that he bids goodbye to "Bunkersville" and moves with his family to an East Side Manhattan high rise. Of the four *All in the Family* principals, only Edith appears in this episode, in a tearful opening scene set in Louise's kitchen. The rest of the half hour introduces the cast of mid-season entry and *All in the Family* spin-off *The*

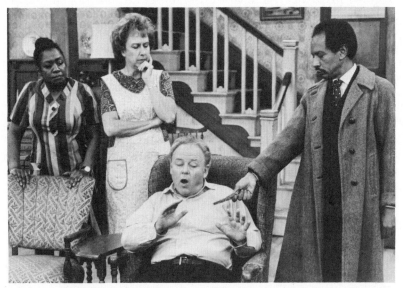

Archie and Edith with Louise (Isabel Sanford) and George (Sherman Hemsley) Jefferson.

Jeffersons, and takes place in the new apartment. Celebrating the magnitude of his relocation, George darts from one to another of his pristine bathrooms, four in all, flushing each sequentially—an appropriate echo of Archie's one flush, upstairs no less, in the neighborhood George has left behind. Such numbers, if ever dumped on Archie's ears, would greatly increase his misery. To him, fate struck cruelly enough when the Jeffersons moved onto his block, endangering property values; but to see the Jeffersons "moving on up" (their show's theme song) only reminds Archie that he's going nowhere, something he had less reason to face before he met the Jeffersons.

In 1973, another set of neighbors pulls up stakes, giving rise to the rumor that Puerto Ricans will buy the house. Backing Archie's effort to spare the neighborhood further change is none other than Henry Jefferson. The new neighbors turn out to be the Lorenzos who, though not Puerto Rican, bang several more dents into Archie's constantly beset bunker. As the first regular additions to the *All in the Family* cast, they stretch plot dimensions and possibilities, bringing, as Betty Garrett (Irene Lorenzo) observed, "new ideas the Bunkers have never known." Among these ideas are an Italian man (Frank Lorenzo) who loves cooking, and his Irish wife (Irene) who would rather work a forklift. Said Norman Lear of their inclusion, "Those characters came right out of the newspapers. I've been reading about the phenomenon of men learning to cook well. You read about men doing needlepoint. And women doing carpentry and masonry." Because Irene also happens to be devoutly Catholic, she represents a challenge to another of Archie's prejudices, Archie being no cheering fan of the Pope.

Vincent Gardenia, as Frank Lorenzo, came to the role by way of an earlier *All in the Family* part, as a wife-swapper whose ad Edith answers thinking it's simply for friends ("The Bunkers and the Swingers"*), and with decades of experience in

---

*Rue McClanahan played the wife in this episode, Lear having remembered her from a 1969 Off-Broadway production of *Tonight in Living Color.* Later in the same week, he cast her as the neighbor in *Maude.*

his father's Italian-language theater company, two Obies, and a Tony for Neil Simon's *The Prisoner of Second Avenue* on Broadway. (When accepting the award, he made the speech in Italian to "thank the Italian community and especially my father.") Like Frank Lorenzo, he showed considerable talent at home as a gourmet cook.

Sada Thompson, with a Tony for *Twigs* under her belt, came to the role of Frank's wife—but didn't stay. Giving the reason that she missed her family and the New York stage, Norman Lear squelched talk of dissension on the set. Reported *The Hollywood Reporter,* "she quits TV after a career of one and a half minutes, and that will be expunged when her replacement, now being chosen, reports for work the week after next . . . [Said Lear], 'Thank heavens she came to me early enough. Had we made a couple of shows with her it would have been impossible.'"

Thompson went on to play Kate Lawrence on *Family** (1976–1980), a domestic show of hugely different stripe, while Betty Garrett stepped into Mrs. Lorenzo's shoes. Garrett's background combined major singing and dancing roles in musical-comedy movies (*Words and Music, My Sister Eileen, Neptune's Daughter, Take Me Out to the Ball Game*) with Broadway (understudying Ethel Merman in *Something for the Boys* to starring in *Call Me Mister*), dancing with the Martha Graham company, and performing with Orson Welles' Mercury Theatre. Garrett knew Lear from the days when he acted as press representative for *Call Me Mister,* days when, coincidentally, Rob Reiner's father Carl was in the cast. She knew Jean Stapleton from *Bells Are Ringing,* and Carroll O'Connor from having appeared in a play he wrote. She and writers Don Nicholl, Bernie West, and Mickey Ross were good friends.

Betty Garrett (Mrs. Larry Parks offstage) assumed her part uniquely familiar with people like Archie. Husband Larry—most famous onscreen as Al Jolson in *The Jolson Story* and *Jolson Sings Again*—testified before the House Un-

---

*In addition to the ironic similarity in the names of the shows—*Family* and *All in the Family*—is the fact that *Lorenzo* is Italian for *Lawrence.*

American Activities Committee in 1951 that he had belonged to the Communist Party, which resulted in ten years of blacklisting by the U. S. movie industry. Already victimized by McCarthyism, Garrett wasn't one to be bullied by bellowing Archie Bunker.

Coincidentally, Parks, just like Frank Lorenzo, loved to cook, while Garrett "never gave it a second thought until one of my young sons came home from dinner at a friend's house and said that things were really strange over there. 'Do you know that his *mother* does the cooking?' And I'm pretty good mechanically. When the kids were growing up, they brought me all their toys to fix. And then I tried my hand at all kinds of repairs around the house when Larry was out of town and found it wasn't so difficult after all...."

Both Frank and Irene fly in the face of stereotypes.

The Bunkers and the Lorenzos: Frank (Vincent Gardenia) and Irene (Betty Garrett).

Frank lives to emote, to stop and smell the flowers, to crack incredibly stupid jokes because silliness is fun. Irene wears her gray hair in a long braid, fixes phones with a tool kit carried in her purse, spots scam aluminum-siding salesmen by their faulty use of technical terms, gets a job operating the forklift at the place where Archie works, and bests him in a game of pool. Archie can't stand admitting that pool is her game more than his, and resorts to any excuse for solace— from a bad back to having Frank's Sicilian curse on his head ("Archie Is Cursed"). To Archie's frame of reference, Irene is considerably worse than Frank Lorenzo. To him, Frank reflects badly on men by pursuing "woman's work" hobbies, but at least in comparison to him, Archie feels more manly, while Irene is living proof that the best man for the job is frequently a woman.

When Vincent Gardenia left *All in the Family* for Broadway in 1974, story lines changed to have Frank forsaking retirement to return to saleswork on the road, increasing the focus on Irene and the women's lib angle (and redoubling the pressure on Archie). Recalls Garrett:

> We never really got to explain too clearly where Frank had gone. There was very often a line in the show where Edith would ask about him, and I'd say "Oh, he's fine. He'll be home from the road next week," or something on that order. But during cutting, to make the time come out right, the line always managed to get cut because it wasn't necessary to the plot.
>
> I think at one point there was even talk about dispensing with Frank in some more permanent way. Of course, because Irene was such a good Catholic, we couldn't get a divorce, but maybe he could have died. Anyway, they were going to build a little romance with me and Stretch Cunningham, an interesting older woman/younger man thing. Then another thing that came up was the possibility of my having a crush on a priest.

But essentially, Irene's function in *All in the Family*'s life was to complicate Archie's. As Edith's confidante and friend, she frankly confronts the ways in which Edith shortchanges herself by knuckling under to Archie's male chauvinist demands. On other occasions, she introduces the voice of Catholicism into the Bunker inner sanctum—sharing it with Edith, defending it before the twin siege towers of Archie and Mike. When Mike contemplates not having children, she produces a clipping from Alistair Cooke that changes his mind. Irene's the sort who'd keep such clippings—while Archie hangs himself up on wondering who cares about the opinions of Alice the Cook.

In the episode "Archie and the Kiss," Irene presents Mike and Gloria with a reproduction of Rodin's famous, steamy sculpture, which to Archie is plainly indecent. Ultimately, Archie is forced to consider that the piece may be art—in one of the few scenes that shows him clearly aware of being inadequate, out of his depths, and the only outsider in the group.

Betty Garrett remained with *All in the Family* until 1975, then turned up as Mrs. Babish in 1976 on *Laverne & Shirley*. In the same year, Archie makes the fleeting acquaintance of Dr. Wynell Thatcher (Vinnette Carroll) while in the hospital for gallstone surgery ("Archie's Operation," parts one and two). Despite the brevity of their contact, Dr. Thatcher nonetheless makes a permanent impression on Archie when she, a black woman from the West Indies, is the donor for Archie's transfusion. Who woulda thought! Archie, none too thrilled to hear which blood was bused into his veins, learns to live with it, without so much as having to fight the urge to chant voodoo spells.

A year later, Archie finds definite advantage in his integrated bloodstream, when admitting to it gets him out of membership in the KKK ("Archie and the KKK," parts one and two). Emmy- and Obie-winning actress, writer, and director Vinnette Carroll (former director of the Ghetto Arts Program and the Urban Arts Corps; Sojourner Truth in CBS's *Sojourner* and *We the Women;* appeared in the movie *Up the Down Staircase;* conceived and directed Broadway's *Don't Bother*

Me, I Can't Cope, a Tony nominee; Tony nominee again for *Your Arms Too Short to Box with God;* recipient of an NAACP Image award, and the Black Filmmakers Hall of Fame award) had at first been announced as a regular who would move in with Gloria and Mike.

Instead, it's Archie and Edith who take a boarder. With Mike and Gloria living in the Jeffersons' old house, and Archie temporarily laid off as well as swamped by hospital bills, they accept the intrusion to raise quick cash. Teresa Betancourt (Liz Torres, previously of TV's *Ben Vereen...Comin' at Ya* and *Phyllis; The Ritz* on Broadway; her own nightclub act; and, like Jean Stapleton and Vinnette Carroll, an actress in the movie *Up the Down Staircase*), the outspoken nurse from the hospital, answers the "for rent" sign. Pronouncing his name "Mr. Bonkers," she talks back to Archie in a mangled English he finds unbearable, though he is hardly Henry Higgins. She sneaks her boyfriend in one evening, expecting the Bunkers to be elsewhere. She says *breasts,* setting Archie to cringing. Despite himself, Archie develops a measure of tolerance living with her, even growing fairly paternal. He suggests that she say not *breast* but *chest,* an idea to which she promptly warms up, offering him chicken chests with chiz. This sets Archie to cringing again.

Shortly after Torres' departure in 1977, the Bunkers become, by stages, parents again, with the arrival of Stephanie Mills (Danielle Brisebois) in 1978. Age nine when she started, Brooklyn-born Brisebois already had six years of solid showbiz experience to her credit: commercials, TV dramatic roles, singing in the chorus of *The Saint of Bleecker Street* with the New York City Opera Company, and a 40-minute cabaret act of singing, dancing, and playing the piano—an act with which she became the youngest performer ever to solo in a New York City nightclub. Her Broadway appearance as Molly, the youngest orphan, in *Annie* ("You're Never Fully Dressed Without a Smile") made a strong impression on Norman Lear, and led to the creation of Stephanie on *All in the Family.*

At first, Edith's ne'er-do-well boozer cousin Floyd Mills

(Marty Brill, later Ben Slack) drops Stephanie off for a visit, then doesn't bother to return. Edith and Stephanie take to each other right away. Archie, craving few things less than a child underfoot, balks—causing Stephanie, defensively streetwise from years of frightened vulnerability, to give him a taste of his own stubborn peevishness. But when Floyd reappears, attempting to leave Stephanie with Archie and Edith in exchange for ready cash, Archie reaches deep into his pocket. He wants better for Stephanie than Floyd's rotten influence and a series of rooms in fleabag residence hotels.

Over the seasons, Stephanie and Archie learn to love one another. In some ways, Stephanie more than anyone forces his notions to bend, as when Archie discovers that she's Jewish and agrees to raise her accordingly—then later joins the synagogue so that Stephanie can enroll in their religious-instruction program. Archie, it seems, is no match for a smart little kid. Like Edith, she can't argue at what he perceives to be his level, so that, as with Edith, he often resigns himself to grimacing and caving in. When, in the latter years of the series, Edith takes a less active part in stories (at Jean Stapleton's request), Stephanie readily picks up where Edith leaves off, bending Archie easily to her will. Recalls Brisebois,

In the beginning, Stephanie may have been how I was, in a sense. For instance, I was from New York, and I spoke New Yorkese. In fact, before *All in the Family,* I took diction lessons to get rid of the accent. Then I had to get it back to play Stephanie. Also, they made her kind of bratty, and I was a little bratty at that age. And she was uncomfortable, living in a new place and not sure if Archie liked her. She was a sad little kid when she started on the show.

But then, I think she was one of the only people who was actually able to get to Archie, get him to soften up. I had him in the palm of my hand. I could make him do anything I wanted. Stephanie was really smart, really shrewd. But she didn't abuse her gift. She cared a lot about people, and all she really wanted was a happy life.

The character was never really described to me. But that's
how Carroll and I developed her together.

Outside the house, most familiar to viewers among Archie's friends is the gang at Kelcy's* Bar. Since neighborhood
bars generally provide, along with the beers, bunkers away
from home, Archie can accept the surroundings as extensions
of his living room. Bunkers, after all, stand as shields in a
battle, not sinkholes in a void. *Stifles* and *dummy ups* aside,
Archie thrives on the right kind of noises—his. To defend
himself in life's battle, Archie beefs to listening ears. By 1976,
with Edith increasingly busy at the Sunshine Home and the
Stivics moved down the block, Archie finds Kelcy's compara-
tive bunker quotient greatly enhanced. In October of 1977,
he buys the bar ("Archie Gets the Business," of which parts
one and two form a one-hour episode; and "Archie's Grand
Opening," the half-hour part three), a decision as natural as
his choice of names—Archie's Place (later, Archie Bunker's
Place).

Even though the bar is open to the world, and thereby to
such dangers as robbery ("Archie and the Editorial," "Superbowl Sunday"), to Archie the bar offers people whose demands on him are limited but who do him considerable good.
While most visitors to 704 Hauser have been Edith's friends
or relatives, hippies seeing Gloria and Mike, politicians,
criminals, or cops, the regulars at Archie's Place are Archie's
longtime pals. It's like having them over to the house, but
better. When they visit the bar, they have to pay for the beer.

The Kelcy's cohorts (from the Latin *cohors*, an enclosure)
are "regular guys" of the sort one bowls with, drinks with, and
joins lodges with—able to accept their fates with a modicum
of bellyaching, and readily accepting of fellow sufferers prepared to share their gripes. The bond conjures up army ties,
but then again, so does the cast. Quintessential "regular guys"
fill the various roles: Allan Melvin as Barney Hefner and Billy
Sands as Nick echo their earlier portrayals as Henshaw and

---

*Unaccountably, the bar is named Kelcy's, but it's owner, according to closing credits,
is Kelsey.

Archie's Place opens in 1977, with Archie enthusiastic and Mike and Edith concerned.

Paparelli in *The Phil* (Sergeant Bilko) *Silvers Show* (1955–1959), and Billy Sands and Bob Hastings present a certain déjà vu of "Tinker" Bell and Lt. Elroy Carpenter, respectively, on *McHale's Navy* (1962–1966). Danny Dayton, as Hank Pivnik, brings a touch of the rackets (*No Questions Asked* and *Guys and Dolls*), the army (*At War with the Army* and *Which Way to the Front?*), and the ring (*Requiem for a Heavyweight*). Scott Brady, as Joe Foley, has the stalwart disposition of an aging Fifties adventure hero, underscored by Brady's string of Western and other movie credits (*Canon City, He Walked by Night, Johnny*

Scott Brady, a regular at Kelcy's, as he appeared in the 1954 movie *Johnny Guitar*. **Seen here with Sterling Hayden.**

Guitar, Mohawk, Black Spurs, The Maverick Queen, Crooks and Coronets) and his TV lead in the title role of *Shotgun Slade*.

Jason Wingreen (a founding producer of the esteemed Circle in the Square Theatre as well as a veteran of *Armstrong Circle Theatre, Philco TV Playhouse, Climax,* and the first *Playhouse 90,* and with recurring roles on five series before joining *All in the Family*—from *The Untouchables* to *The Long, Hot Summer*) comes aboard as bartender for a "one-shot" at the end of the sixth season. The plot for "Edith's Night Out" required that nobody in the bar recognize Edith. Since Kelsey knows her, Kelsey misses the episode, and Wingreen fills in. He becomes the regular bartender, Harry Snowden, in short order. As Harry, he adds immeasurably to Archie's life, teaching him humility at regular intervals along the way.

Bill Quinn (of *The Big Story, Mr. District Attorney,* and *Gang Busters* radio fame as well as Broadway and the screen, and most recognized by TV viewers at the time as Mary Richards' father on *The Mary Tyler Moore Show*) arrives in 1978, portraying the blind Mr. Van Ranseleer, barstool philosopher. Amazingly, Archie scarcely patronizes him at all, generally listening attentively to whatever advice he gives.

A bar chum and regular guy to end all regular guys is former football star Steve (Phil Carey) in the episode "Judging Books by Covers." Carey, veteran of rugged movie roles (*Pushover, Port Afrique, Wicked As They Come, The Great Sioux Massacre*) and TV series (*Tales of the 77th Bengal Lancers, Philip Marlowe,* and *Laredo*), portrays a man whom Archie regards as a model of masculine virtues—this at a time when Archie swears that one of Mike's intellectual friends is gay. Comes the

Bill Quinn—(Mr. Van Ranseleer) on *All in the Family* and later, on *Archie Bunker's Place.*

Allan Melvin—Sgt. Pulaski in "Archie in the Lock-up" and Barney Hefner on *All in the Family* and *Archie Bunker's Place.*

revelation: Mike's friend is straight, but Steve is a homosexual. Said President Nixon of the episode, "That was awful. It made a fool out of a good man."

Barney Hefner (Allan Melvin) goes beyond bar chum to be Archie's best friend, down-the-block neighbor, and president of the lodge (The Kings of Queens), though his first appearance is as Sgt. Pete Pulaski in a one-shot role. "Then," says Melvin, "through the magic of television, I came back a couple of weeks later as Hefner." Melvin launched his career doing voices and impressions, which led to his winning the Arthur Godfrey talent show, doing a nightclub act, and appearing on Broadway. Then, in addition to portraying Henshaw on the Bilko series, he played Sgt. Hacker on *Gomer Pyle, U.S.M.C.* and Sam the butcher on *The Brady Bunch.* As Barney of the hangdog rostrum, he mopes even when he's happy, which often he is not.

Barney's dog Rusty leaves surprises on Archie's lawn, causing Archie to accidentally back over the pooch with his cab. Barney's perpetually dissatisfied wife, Blanche (Estelle Parsons), leaves, with other men, periodically. Estelle Parsons —political activist, one-time commentator of the *Today* show, star of Broadway (multi-Obie winner and sole performer in the one-woman tour de force, *Miss Margarida's Way*) and the movies (*Rachel, Rachel, I Never Sang for My Father, Watermelon Man*), and winner of the 1967 Best Supporting Actress Oscar for *Bonnie and Clyde*—initially enters Archie's world as Dolores, whom he knew (in the Biblical sense) in school ("Archie's Secret Passion"). In this episode, he's terrified that she'll reveal their past indiscretion. But she doesn't, because she's forgotten it entirely; the experience hadn't lasted long

Estelle Parsons (Blanche Hefner) won the Oscar as Best Supporting Actress for her role in *Bonnie and Clyde* (1967). Seen here with (left to right) Gene Hackman, Warren Beatty, Faye Dunaway, and Michael J. Pollard.

Billy Halop (center) as one of the Dead End Kids.

enough to remember. Returning as Blanche Hefner, she im-
pacts significantly on episodes inspired by her absence (when
Archie tries to fix Barney up with Boom-Boom Turner in
"Reunion on Hauser Street" and with a rich widow in "Barney the Gold Digger"), and upsets Archie at least as much as
she does Barney when she happens to hang around. (In
"Weekend in the Country," a fight over a Monopoly game
lands a disgruntled Archie in bed with Edith and Blanche.)
Blanche represents that rarity in *All in the Family*—the person
who fully lives up to one of Archie's stereotypes. Comments
Allan Melvin, "It was a great concept, this wife who was so
flagrantly sexually involved with everyone who came through
the door—the window cleaner, the exterminator, whoever,
and Blanche was off and running!"

   Originally as a character named Barney, then as Archie's
crony and boss, Bert Munson, Bill* Halop (Billy Halop of the

---

*"Bill" Halop in some *All in the Family* credits, "Billy" in others.

Dead End Kids) adds the proper balance of Depression-era Lower East Side New York to Archie's surroundings. Munson owns the cab fleet for which Archie moonlights. For someone like Archie who hates excursions into enemy territory, there are pleasanter ways to pick up change. But to writers, Archie's part-time job illustrates the extent of his economic predicament, and how hard he'll work to relieve it; as well as introducing endless options for Archie to meet people he would never otherwise know.

Most prominent among these is Sammy Davis, Jr. whom Archie one day picks up as a fare. Davis leaves his briefcase in Archie's cab, then has to stop by Hauser Street to reclaim it and thank Archie ("Sammy's Visit"). Archie, filled with admiration for Sammy Davis, Jr., warns his family in advance that Davis has a glass eye and they'd better not embarrass him by noticing it. But when Davis arrives, Archie becomes so nervous that he makes the slip himself, asking whether his distinguished visitor would like cream and sugar in his eye.

Archie falls all over himself paying compliments which only reveal his deep-rooted prejudice. Davis does a Lionel—nodding graciously to whatever Archie says, but responding in double-edged courtesies. On the subject of Archie's racism, Davis concedes, "If you were prejudiced you'd go around thinking you're better than anyone else in the world, Archie. But...I can honestly say you've proven to me that you ain't better than anybody." Archie beams, oblivious to the tribute's second meaning. Then, elated that Davis has agreed to be photographed with him, Archie goes white-r when Davis plants a big, wet kiss on his cheek. Archie's plans had not included grazing the oral membrane of a one-eyed black Jew.

Sammy Davis, Jr.'s, guest spot on *All in the Family* resulted from his months-long campaign for the opportunity. A devoted fan, he had rearranged nightclub appearances when possible to begin only after *All in the Family* ended. He taped the show, and plugged it unsolicited: "*All in the Family* has turned the heads of the nation. It is exposing some of the ills of today's society and doing it in good taste via humor and entertainment. I just wanted to be part of it all."

Carroll O'Connor on the set with Sammy Davis, Jr.

Lear's initial reaction to writing a role for Davis was negative, only because a big-name performer would skew the emphasis of the program—like having Bob Hope play a plumber, or Lucille Ball a nurse. (You wouldn't see a nurse and a plumber; you'd see superstars Hope and Ball). But "we worked for months and finally came up with a story [by Bill Dana] that could include Sammy and still be realistic," Lear announced in January 1972. However, "Sammy's appearance will by no means set a new precedent for future shows. He's our first and last big star and he was fantastic."

Said Davis, "When Norman called and said I could do the show I was so excited I was speechless. As the day drew near to report for rehearsals, I got more excited and nervous. I was up at 7:00 A.M. for an 11:00 A.M. call. My wife thought I was ill. I'm a late sleeper and not known for being prompt, but on this special occasion I was 15 minutes early. It was a thrill which can only be compared to my first big break in show business."

Carroll O'Connor returned the favor in March of 1972 by hosting a Friars Roast honoring the entertainer, on which occasion he kidded that the Friars had wanted Moshe Dayan as their first-choice one-eyed Jew, but had to settle for Davis instead.

One of Archie's most voluptuous cab fares, Beverly La-Salle ("Lori Shannon"), makes another sort of contact with Archie's oral membrane when he gives her mouth-to-mouth resuscitation ("Archie the Hero"), only to discover the woman is a professional female impersonator. Once he controls his horror, Archie actually finds himself liking Beverly, whose aid he enlists to play a practical joke on a friend ("Beverly Rides Again"). A recurrent character, Beverly is beaten to death on Christmas Eve (which we hear about rather than see) for being a transvestite, in the two-part, one-hour "Edith's Crisis of Faith." The senseless murder so grieves Edith that she momentarily loses faith in God, and Archie, though a bigot, is forced to consider this end product of bigotry.

Death physically crosses the *All in the Family* Bunkers' threshold twice—when Uncle Oscar, never seen on camera, sheds the mortal coil upstairs ("The Saga of Cousin Oscar"); and when Bernard Bernstein (Jack Gilford) breathes his last, on the Bunkers' sofa ("Archie Finds a Friend"). In the first instance, Oscar mooches like a lord in life, then, despite relatives in sixteen cities, sticks Archie for the price of his send-off to eternity. Archie, hoping for a discounted casket or at least a floor model with nicks, coughs up the bulk of his bank account, $600 plus; undone by Undertaker Whitehead's (Jack Grimes) uncompromising funerary sales pitch. One of Archie's decent streaks springs to light. For all his resentment, he shoulders the burden. He may not be the perfect relative, but in this, he beats the other fifteen cities, no contest.

Bernard Bernstein, on the other hand, is a totally sympathetic character. Played by Jack Gilford, forty-year veteran of comic clubs, movies, and Broadway and professional sweet-face on such shows as *Get Smart* (as a twinkle-eyed crook) and *Taxi* (as Alex's irresistibly cute dad), Bernstein inspires friendship and trust. When he invents a remote-control doorbell ringer, Archie envisions it will be a gold mine. Archie wants to invest; Edith resists; Bernstein demonstrates it, discovering new flaws which he's certain can be remedied. But Bernstein's heart fails him in the excitement of the moment, and Archie and Edith must deal once again with the cruelty of death.

In each case, some critics wailed that death shouldn't furnish breakthroughs for situation comedy. But in the department of last gasps, undertaker "Digger" O'Dell broke the ground as early as 1949, as a regular (though short-lived) TV character on *The Life of Riley*. What *All in the Family* did that *Riley* hadn't done was to explore the mixed emotions and frank realities involved.

Infidelity—a staple of situation comedy—several times arises on *All in the Family*, and receives the same treatment of humor tempered by understanding. Archie discovers Denise (Janis Paige), a waitress at the coffee shop he frequents. Janis Paige, the gifted movie, television, and Broadway musical-comedy star (*Pajama Game, Here's Love, Mame*), presents a face and figure entirely too appealing for Archie to ignore, particularly when the lovely creature shows a definite interest in him. Flirtation is in the air and Archie, feeling slighted that Edith spends too much time at the Sunshine Home, lets the guys goad him into seeing how far he can go. He gets as far as Denise's apartment and a long kiss ("Archie's Brief Encounter," part one); panics, bolts, and runs back home to Edith. Being suspicious, she confirms her fears and moves into the Sunshine Home for round-the-clock duty, whereupon Archie has to swallow his pride and convince Edith to return ("Archie's Brief Encounter," parts two and three, presented as a one-hour special).

The first of these episodes (September 22, 1976) coincided, historically, with *Playboy*'s interview of Jimmy Carter, and Carter's revelation that he'd been faithful to his wife in practice but at times had committed "adultery in my heart." Comparing Carter's statement to the *All in the Family* episode, Sander Vanocur wrote in *The Washington Post* that Edith's pained expression "causes us more anguish than anything that could ever be said by a man who wants to be president... [Norman Lear] has made an important breakthrough in treating sexuality on television with a fidelity that bears some resemblance to how it affects our lives."

The previous year, Mike nearly falls prey to temptation of a similar stripe in "Gloria Suspects Mike," with Gloria pregnant and a student he's tutoring (Bernadette Peters, Kewpie doll Broadway star of *Dames at Sea* and *Mack & Mabel*) coming on to him. But Mike, like Archie, refrains from succumbing, and Bernadette Peters went on, in real life, to star in Norman Lear's series *All's Fair*, and to conquer Broadway several times over.

In later years, Alvin Klemmer (Theodore Bikel), the butcher, comes on the scene carrying a torch for Edith as a means to draw her out of the bunker and into a greater consciousness of herself. Bikel, distinguished Vienna-born folksinger, actor, Academy Award nominee (*The Defiant Ones*), and founder of the Tel Aviv Chamber Theatre and the arts chapter of the American Jewish Congress, crops up more than once. Noted Dwight Whitney in *TV Guide* in January of 1979, Klemmer would "be in for greater prominence, depending on how well the stories work." In "A Girl Like Edith," aired January 14, 1979, Klemmer tells Edith he found his true love. Edith invites the couple to the house. Klemmer's sweetheart Judith acts nothing like Edith, but could be a dead ringer for her visually. According to the closing credits, Giovanna Pucci plays the part (*Giovanna* being Italian for *Jean,* and *Pucci* being roughly the Italian equivalent of Jean Stapleton's married name, *Putch.*)

More in keeping with Edith's style than the sparking gent she brings home unawares are the senior citizens she welcomes gladly; and if they spark a little on the side, she just wishes more power to them. Veteran players Nedra Volz as Aunt Iola, Ian Wolfe and Merie Earle as the Hoopers, and Burt Mustin and Ruth McDevitt as Justin Quigley and Jo Nelson, Mike and Gloria's "adopted grandparents," provide a comedy breakthrough less heralded than sharp language and slurs, but easily as important. Rarely before them did older people appear in TV comedy series as people with their own

Klemmer the butcher (Theodore Bikel) shows a more than friendly interest in Edith.

lives who happened to be older—not sages; not laxative pushers in commercials; not bossy grandpappy Amos of *The Real McCoys* nor meddling Uncle Tonoose of *The Danny Thomas Show.* These elders enjoy nothing more than to live and let live—though they wish the system would let them live better. Through them, *All in the Family* explored such issues as the senior citizens on fixed incomes who suddenly find themselves shoplifting to eat, and the way senior citizens forfeit federal benefits when they marry instead of living together.

The man whom Archie most happily brings home, Stretch Cunningham (James Cromwell), shakes things up beyond Archie's wildest dreams. At first mentioned only as a goofy, goof-off worker at the plant, Stretch in time assumes flesh and blood form. James Cromwell, son the distinguished film director John Cromwell, stepped into the role when a friend gave him the name of *All in the Family* casting director Jane Murray. Recalls Cromwell:

> She showed me later in her little black book all the actors she'd seen for Stretch. Under "tall actors." Must have been a hundred names, and she'd gone through them all that week, eliminating them one by one. Too skinny, too fat, out of town. I was the last person she called, and I wouldn't have gotten the role if I hadn't happened to ring my answering service that day, which I seldom do.
>
> Playing Stretch was great. The character was made in heaven, because he had this reputation of being the funniest man Archie ever met. So the audience knew him already, and the writers wrote wonderful stuff for him, right from the beginning. I look at the character now and I don't know where I got him from. I guess I got him from Art Carney, because people said, "Are you doing Carney?" I never set out to copy, and I never watched his show that much though the character was dear to my heart. I guess my way of doing someone from the Bronx is very much like him.

Stretch's part was built up when it looked like Carroll O'Connor might be leaving *All in the Family*. O'Connor stayed, and soon after, Lear offered Cromwell leads in *Hot L Baltimore* and *The Nancy Walker Show*. When each of the two series folded, Cromwell could have returned to Archie Bunker's side—except that Archie had already buried him (and was shocked to discover Stretch had been Jewish) in the episode "Stretch Cunningham, Goodbye."

It's a funny thing about Stretch. In life, he nearly presides over Archie's doom. In death, he gives Archie the surprise of his life. Friends will do that to you—every time.

Making Scenes

> "No shows on TV are more heavily
> rewritten than Yorkin and Lear's."
> —Time magazine, 1972

All in the Family exceeds the sum of its parts to the degree that many of its best parts never meet the eye. Like the tip of an iceberg, the net result of a single script scarcely reveals the mammoth structure that set it afloat. Like a flawless Swiss watch, an All in the Family script began not with a shoebox of raw materials and a blueprint, but with the well-trained watchmakers who agonized over every detail.

A fastidious screenwriter/watchmaker himself, Norman Lear frequently worked like a dervish, nervously picking his head until his wife bought him a hat to preserve what remained of his hair. Sometimes he'd work around the clock, sleeping on a cot he'd moved into his studio office. As chief watchmaker of All in the Family, Norman Lear produced, oversaw, and rewrote (and wrote such episodes as "Meet the Bunkers" and "Archie Gives Blood") in the early months of All in the Family's life.

When CBS first advised Norman Lear in the late autumn of 1970 that All in the Family would be scheduled for January of 1971, the cast from the pilot was reassembled, a production team hired, and Don Nicholl brought aboard as story editor.

The cast needed stories to perform; the production team, something to produce. As Don Nicholl has described the response to these pressing needs, "If we were lucky, we had three scripts ready when we went on the air...We were writing week by week until the last minute. The first 13 weeks were a very hectic period. It was very exciting because what we were doing was so new to American television, but also very hard. Norman was writing very hard at that time...We were all writing tight to the wire."

Lear's writing background, comparable to that of so many who wrote for the show, had its roots in TV's Golden Age—and went on to launch another. As Bud Yorkin has expained, "All the great comedy writers came from a certain tradition. They were able to write for some terrific performers and learn the trade." Apprenticing under the best watchmakers around, they had mastered the skills that set them apart from assembly line stiffs.

Emmy-winner Milt Josefsberg, for instance, is said to have logged more years on more number-one-rated TV and radio programs than any writer in broadcast history. This statistic represents some thirty-plus years as a writer, script consultant, or producer with Bob Hope, Lucille Ball, Milton Berle, Danny Thomas, and as a longtime writer for *The Jack Benny Show,* while Josefsberg's Emmy-winning *All in the Family* partner, Mort Lachman, was head writer and producer for Bob Hope's specials for more than two decades. Before writing for *All in the Family,* Emmy-winner Hal Kanter wrote for Bob Hope's radio show, served as producer-writer-director of *The George Gobel Show,* and later, as executive producer of *Julia.* Emmy-winners Bob Schiller and Bob Weiskopf wrote individually on radio for *Duffy's Tavern* and *The Jimmy Durante Show* (Schiller), Eddie Cantor and Fred Allen (Weiskopf), and as a team on TV for Danny Thomas, Lucille Ball, Red Skelton, and Flip Wilson. Before becoming an Emmy-winning writer and story editor with partner Bernie West, Michael Ross held the positions of program editor for *Caesar's Hour* and comedy supervisor for *The Garry Moore Show* (on which, in addition, Ross and West performed sketches as a comedy team). Emmy-winner Mel Tolkin, as head writer for *Caesar's Hour,* cut his comedy teeth with the legendary writing team that included Woody Allen, Mel Brooks, Neil Simon, Carl Reiner, Selma Diamond, Gary Belkin, Mike Stewart, and Larry Gelbart.

From the more recent tradition of *Tony Orlando and Dawn,* Doug Arango and Phil Doran brought the finer points of "high heel and Puerto Rican jokes," becoming story editors and subsequently head writers of *All in the Family.* Rob Reiner, in addition to his experiences on *All in the Family*, came with writing skills honed as a member of the improvisational groups The Session and The Committee, and, on TV, as a writer for the Smothers Brothers. With partner Phil Mishkin, Reiner contributed such *All in the Family* stories as "Now That You Know the Way, Let's Be Strangers," "Flashback—Mike Meets Archie," and "Flashback—Mike and Gloria's Wedding." Independently of Reiner, Miskhin wrote or cowrote such stories and scripts as "Mike's Problem," "Cousin Maude's Visit," and "Archie Sees a Mugging."

So great ran the concentration of Emmy-winning writing talent that in, for instance, *All in the Family*'s ninth season, Milt Josefsberg and Mort Lachman were up for an Emmy for production, and three out of four comedy-writing nominations went to *All in the Family* writers: Bob Schiller and Bob Weiskopf for each of two episodes, "Edith's 50th Birthday" and "Cousin Liz" (story by Barry Harmon and Harve Broston), and Mel Tolkin and Larry Rhine for "Edith's Crisis of Faith" (story by Eric Tarloff). In all, eight separate *All in the Family* episodes from that season garnered Emmy nominations—in other words, one third of the season—with awards going to Lachman (executive producer) and Josefsberg (producer) for Outstanding Comedy Series and to Weiskopf, Schiller, Harmon, and Broston for Outstanding Writing in a Comedy Series ("a single episode or a regular or limited series with continuing characters and/or theme"), as well as to Carroll O'Connor for Outstanding Lead Actor in a Comedy Series, to Jean Stapleton for Best Outstanding Lead Actress in a Comedy Series, to Rob Reiner for Outstanding Continuing Performance by a Supporting Actor in a Comedy

Series, and to Paul Bogart for Outstanding Directing in a Comedy Series ("a single episode of a regular or limited series with continuing characters and/or theme").*

Writing partners constitute one of TV comedy's most common phenomena. Sometimes, one of the two is stronger at jokes, the other at plots; or one writes better for men, the other, better for women; or one types and the other doesn't; or perhaps, as Bob Weiskopf has observed, "There seems to be a feeling that if you put two people in a room you get twice as much fun on paper." Whichever combination causes sparks to fly in a given pair, the combustive energy, by extension, can only build as pair becomes foursome, group, and gang.

A quick glance at the writers and their staggering credits can lead to the easy image of a comedy genius, or genii, hunched over a typewriter trying jokes and crumpling paper, à la those inner-sanctum scenes on *The Dick Van Dyke Show.* Indeed, the crafting of most scripts involved such moments, but beyond those, the unseen bulk of the iceberg told the real tale: of the need to hatch sufficient concepts and scripts to complete each season; of the compulsion to polish and per-fect; of the rewrites that took years, and continued right on through rehearsal and shooting; of the pool of talent repre-sented by writers, story editors, script consultants, story con-sultants, script supervisors, performers, director, producer, et al., who all had a hand in the final look of the scripts. Noted Bob Schiller, "Titles don't mean a damn thing. Everybody on a comedy show writes."

Ideas, those essential building blocks of any script or story, came from writers, staff, newspapers, and freelancers. When director (and later, producer) John Rich saw a news piece about rising meat prices and people lining up to buy horse meat for human consumption, it became a key thread of the episode "Edith's Conversion." When women were asked

---

*In the same ceremonies, Lear's first writing partner, Ed Simmons, took an Emmy for Outstanding Writing in a Comedy-Variety or Music Series for an episode of *The Carol Burnett Show,* and Sada Thompson, the gal who pulled out of an ongoing *All in the Family* role several seasons earlier, won Outstanding Lead Actress in a Drama Series for *Family.*

The Stivics, nine days overdue.

for baby-shower recollections to incorporate in "Gloria Is Nervous," Betty Garrett came up with a favorite: "My husband had a habit of never putting the toilet seat down, and when I was about nine months pregnant, just about to give birth, I got up in the middle of the night and went in and I didn't turn the light on. I sat down and fell in the toilet, then couldn't get out. My husband came in and we almost got divorced because all he did was stand there and laugh. I said that it made me so mad—and they used something like my anecdote in the script. But the censors didn't like the idea of falling in the toilet, so it became a bathtub, which isn't quite the same."

"Of course nothing comes easy," Lear told the *Hollywood Reporter* in 1972. "Material is our lifeline. We have the best guys in the world that work for us on a steady basis all the time, but we're always looking for another idea, another writer. Any time one comes along, we're thrilled... We need ideas that can be turned into stories that can then evolve into scripts."

Each year, supplementing the thoughts of in-house sources, hundreds of original scripts sought the good fortune of acceptance by what may have been the greatest writers' showcase in the history of TV. At one point, an estimated 20 percent of submissions dealt with Archie discovering an unsuspected branch of his family tree—that he's Jewish, an Indian, a black, and so on—though this route never found favor with the people developing Archie. They came closest to the notion in *All in the Family*'s last season, when the Bunkers learn that Stephanie is Jewish in "Stephanie's Conversion" (by Patt Shea and Harriett Weiss, who also wrote "Edith Gets Fired" and "Too Good Edith," the final episode of *All in the Family*, and served as story editors during much of *Archie Bunker's Place*.)

Story editors, along with writing their own original scripts, talked with writers to elicit and assign story ideas, kept an eye to the balance of content and laughs, and oversaw the writing of every idea acquired from freelancers. Thereupon, noted Michael Ross during his tenure as story editor with partner Bernie West, "Most situation comedies in Hollywood are 10-to-5 jobs for the writers. But on *All in the Family*, there is a kind of community effort. Everybody stays with it until the final moment." This is because, like the opera that isn't over until the fat lady sings, a script qualified as completed only when the cameras stopped rolling.

Reported *Time* in 1972, "Whether a script originates with their staff or is one of the 60 percent that come from freelancers, Yorkin and Lear usually see that it gets torn to pieces. The story line acquires new twists, the dialogue is recast, sometimes new characters are added." By 1973, *The Washington Post* logged closer to 30 percent of the scripts coming in to *All in the Family* from outside sources.

According to Bob Schiller, "The scripts would come in,

and they would keep going through like a pepper mill. We'd just keep grinding them. Sometimes there were ten or eleven rewrites, and sometimes the stories change completely." Schiller once asked Lear, "What is the best you can conceive of a script coming in from an outside writer?" Replied Lear, "One where I would say, 'This will really rewrite well.'"

After the first year, Norman Lear, as executive producer, continued to consult on all levels but wrote pages only rarely. On the other hand, his tenacious commitment to rewrites never flagged: "When a writer says, 'I'd like to see Edith Bunker in menopause,' I know we can peel back layers of Edith and Archie. When I hear an idea like that, I'm like a dog hanging on to a bone. I'll hang on forever until the show is right."

An "SOS file" held material discarded from one show but of possible use in the future. Some lines belonged to two or three different episodes before reaching the air. Some scripts spent a year or more in reworkings. "The Threat," an episode about Archie's infatuation with the young second wife of an old Army buddy, was conceived in June 1971. Eight major rewrites later, it was scheduled for a February taping, then withdrawn from rehearsal by Lear for more polishing. By the summer of 1972 when it was finished, even the actors had become involved in the fine tuning of the product. The story "Edith's Crisis of Faith" took nearly three years.

Story conferences, held around an oval table with a tape recorder in the center, might generate eight to ten pages of notes—transcribed simultaneously in another room and ready for distribution at conference end. An average of six writers might be involved in a single show, with screen credit going to the writers of the first draft, even if the draft had been wholly rewritten. Initially, some credits required arbitration; after a while, with more than enough credit to go around, the issue essentially disappeared.

What never disappeared—rather, exerted palpable self-reinforcement—were the aggregate realities known as Archie, Edith, Gloria, and Mike. Said John Rich, comparing *All in the Family* to a novel more than a sitcom (which designation he detests), "We create the background for our characters, then we draw on the background for our stories. As we enrich the background, we enrich the stories that are possible to us." "Edith's Accident" with the peaches could provide the basis for the most banal and blithering throwback to dawn-of-Fifties domestic comedy—except that Edith's personality and relationship with Archie lift the episode into a totally different realm.

The reality, not the joke, reigned supreme, with the writers instructed "Don't write funny. Write real; it'll get funny. The characters will dictate the fun." Within the strictures of reality, the whole world beckoned. *All* of reality— constituting about 7000 percent more reality than traditional TV comedies generally embraced—disallowed precious little. Enthused Bernie West in 1974, "When you hear about other

The Stivics and the Bunkers, vintage 1975.

shows not being able to say this or that, it's nice to be with a show where we can be as free as we are. I'm not just talking about profanity either. It's the topics, the treatments, and the latitude we have to make things as funny and as true-to-life as possible. Other shows have problems."

Along with the freedom to be real went the obligation to be current. Mike and Archie argued about presidential primaries, developments in Vietnam, and Watergate. The news, not outdated headlines. Considering the shows that percolated for years, this mandate could conceivably constitute a tall order. Yet it wasn't unusual for episodes to wrap up mere weeks before airing. "We start the season a few scripts ahead," Michael Ross once observed, "but right now the script we're writing this week will be ready for shooting next week. It's hectic, but it also allows us to use a lot of topical humor."

Holding one finger to the pulse of the nation invariably spelled fun, instilling that sense of magicianship that intuits what the public wants before the public has a clue, and delivers it. *The New York Times* sat on each desk every morning. Yet the impulse shied from "what's the latest controversy?" The focus, always, came down to who Archie, Edith, Mike, and Gloria were. As Don Nicholl commented in 1973, "We'll be touching on the obscenity laws. We don't pick a subject and say, let's do that. We get into them because a character leads us into an area [as when] Archie walks in the door and says 'Watergate! I'm tired of reading about Watergate!'"

Topicality occasionally rebutted. In the summer of 1973, Ross and West penned a "run" in which Archie calls someone a Mick, then defends the slur by saying it's not wrong because, after all, he wouldn't mind if someone called him an American. The following week, attorney John J. Wilson, who represented John Ehrlichman and H. R. Haldeman, referred to Senator Inouye of the Watergate Committee as "that little Jap," then answered critics with the assurance that he'd have no objection to being dubbed "a little American." The Ross-West script aired, but without the run because, explained Ross, "it would have looked like we were copying Washington. It was life imitating art, and we beat life to it."

After a while, the *All in the Family* creative family's pumps were so primed that everyone came in talking, bubbling over with possible directions, incidents, and grievances. Not that everything led to a script, but the process proved rewarding. Says Lear, "It was like group therapy." Commented Bob Schiller, "We'd look into our own experiences. I call it plotting by Freud."

All in the Family writer Mel Tolkin had much the same to say about his head writing days for Sid Caesar two decades earlier: "Nearly all of us were in therapy and we often took out our anger in our script ideas. I realized later that we got a lot of laughs out of murders. In one Italian-movie satire, for example, Sid stabs his wife to death, and then, while he's mourning and carrying on, a shoeshine boy comes in to polish his shoes. Almost absentmindedly, Sid plunges the knife into the kid's back. Then, after he's arrested, Sid walks past the morgue attendants carrying off the bodies, and he also matter-of-factly knifes one of them. It was all done so preposterously that it wasn't offensive, but it gives you some idea of how we were venting our aggressions against each other—in our writing."

While *All in the Family* never relied on such slapstick story lines and comic violence stuck to the verbal, scripts certainly reflected a desire to work through life's aggravations. Writers may have found it therapeutic; the audience emphatically did. The jokes, it's been said, release our aggression without guilt. When Archie complains about a miserable rush-hour ride on the subway, viewers identify with him, hear their rage given voice, and realize that they can look as silly as Archie does if they take their disgust too far.

Lear's belief in therapy has extended to giving young writers $25 vouchers toward the cost of sessions. To the audience, whose bill he couldn't foot, he provided *All in the Family*.

To the cast and crew, Lear presented a series of consummately crafted scripts that underwent their own form of therapy—one that elicited the gamut of emotions from laughter to rage to tears as one after another beautiful piece of writing was torn apart and put together again.

Like the members of an orchestra receiving a score, each party had his or her own instrument to play. Even the London Philharmonic doesn't recompose Beethoven; but these musicians all had their suggestions to make. The conductor, whom they called the director, brought out the best from each instrument, blending the variant chords into one seamless harmony each week.

In early 1970, Norman Lear and Bud Yorkin had contacted *Colgate Comedy Hour* colleague John Rich, veteran director of *Gunsmoke*, as well as such classic comedies as *I Married Joan, Our Miss Brooks,* and *The Dick Van Dyke Show*, and the pilots of *Gilligan's Island* and *The Brady Bunch*. The native New Yorker had grown up in a home that "used to have a picture of Old Ironsides in our living room in Queens just like the one in the Bunkers' house." Lear and Yorkin asked whether Rich wanted to do an *All in the Family* season. He agreed to try two episodes, then five, then "I was hooked." As director, and later producer, of *All in the Family*, Rich brought his own relentless drive to the fore. Ears attuned and eyes opened to every detail, he set the tone for several remarkable years.

Speaking of one instance when John Rich helped her enhance the dimensions of a scene, Jean Stapleton revealed that in "Edith's Christmas Story," "Gloria finds out accidentally when we're alone in the kitchen that I've just come from the doctor and he's given me what seems like very bad news. When I did this scene the first time, I took the obvious tack I suspect any actress would instinctively take: I played it for self-pity and drama. John got me off that instantly. He told me it was all wrong, that my intent should be to comfort my daughter rather than feel sorry for myself. And that turned the scene all around. We'd all been afraid of being morbid before. But when it played that way, it wasn't morbid at all."

Indeed, any presentation depends as much on how the words are interpreted as on the words themselves. *All in the Family*, more than most comedy series that preceded it, and even than most in its day, drew strength from its willingness to pause mid-scene; to hold beats; to emphasize both comedy and drama with subtle gesture and facial expression. Edith, in the opening scene of "Archie's Operation," part one, compels herself to peruse a *Playgirl* centerfold because Archie, nervous in the waiting room, ordered her to read a magazine. Her essentially silent performance communicates volumes of human, funny reaction. Gloria, in the closing scene of "Gloria the Victim," also wordlessly conveys painful resignation when the men in her family demand that she not take her attacker to court.

Such acting finesse is often termed "theatrical." Yet when an actor performs in the theater each audience member perceives the moves from only one angle and one distance. On television, the camera—in this case, multiple cameras—can and must do more.

Just as *All in the Family* voiced some thoughts that TV comedy never touched before, it expressed unspoken humor, horror, and love by developing a comedically unprecedented vocabulary of camera shots and angles. As critic Marc Eliot observed, "The close-up had been used before in situation comedy, notably 'The Many Loves of Dobie Gillis.' However, it was Lear's use of that shot against an elongated background that included the diminished image of Edith . . . which gave an added sense of distance behind the close-up face of Archie." Without having had to invent the techniques it employed in this regard, *All in the Family* fundamentally altered the look of the home screen by bringing them to TV comedy.

On a purely practical level, there came the occasional piece of business that had to happen for a plot to work, even when the odds defied its happening. In "Archie Is Cursed," for example, Betty Garrett as Irene Lorenzo had to demonstrate her prowess at pool. "But," recalls Garrett, "I can't shoot pool and could barely hold the cue stick. Rob was my coach but I didn't do very well. They almost gave up but finally managed to get one shot of me at the table with the stick in my hands."

A running gag in the series concerned Barney Hefner's dog, Rusty, who left a repeating trail of surprises on Archie Bunker's lawn. Says Allan Melvin, who portrayed Barney,

"The inside story is that Rusty kept changing his breed. He started out as a little reddish dog. He was Jean Stapleton's own dog, originally. Then we got a bigger dog, and finally he was a dog who weighed about 30 pounds. In one scene, I had to hold him. He got heavier and heavier with each take, until I accidentally dropped him. Poor dog ran off and hid. We couldn't resume till we got him back, which wasn't easy."

Week after week, words and their renderings came together under the director's keen eye. A typical week in the life of *All in the Family* might have begun with a reading and discussion of the following week's script. Problems would arise; criticism and comment would be offered. Over the next few days, the writers would apply these to the script. On the same morning, the current week's script would be read, discussed, and rehearsed. Pieces for the current script continued to be reworked on a daily basis as needed. At any point during the week, anyone might contribute new lines, particularly Carroll O'Connor, a top flight ad-libber (for instance, his/Archie's description of Irene Lorenzo as "the queen of the women's lubrication movement"). In O'Connor's case, the running gag had it that as soon as he saw a script, he hated it, finding at once what was wrong with it and insisting on changes. He's been known to refer to scripts as "outlines." But he also instinctively knew how to slip inside Archie's character, and not just remark on the things Archie might say, but in fact to become and then speak as Archie. Says Lear, "Carroll O'Connor was the best writer for Archie we ever had."

Others spoke up too—Rob Reiner almost as vehemently and as often as O'Connor; Struthers and Stapleton not as much. On "Chain Letter," for example, Jean Stapleton wondered whether Irene Lorenzo, the voice of sanity, would plague her friends with chain letters. Betty Garrett agreed that Irene more likely would be against chain letters than be the one to send them. The writers modified the script.

After two more days of staging, rehearsal with props, and line rehearsals, a run-through in the rehearsal hall would lead to several more hours of cuts, additions, and changes in the script—the cap on the ritual Betty Garrett described as the

A key script element: needling Archie. Here, he doesn't know what's worse—the fear of hepatitis, or getting his shot from a black doctor (Robert Guillaume).

session when "the writers come in and line up against the wall like a jury to see what we've done."

Ken Lynch, who appeared in more than one *All in the Family* role, recalls rehearsals as having been "quite relaxing in an intensive kind of way. The writers were always there, and I, like so many actors, would make suggestions if a speech was a little uncomfortable. And I've noticed down through my career that writers are good. They're good people. They listen and try to accommodate you. It's not like they figured each word a diamond and absolutely too good to change."

Adds Allan Melvin, "The chemistry was very good between everybody, and there was a lot of give and take. Norman Lear, who was always the guiding factor through *All in the Family*, allowed the freedom of expression that a lot of shows don't. Here, everybody contributed, took what they wanted. I think the characters grew as a result of that. I think there was a kind of homogenizing of people into real family groups as a result of that, too."

When scenes required everyone's working into the wee hours, objectivity became more of a chore. The story is told that Bob Weiskopf, leaving a late-night session on *Maude* with a script to rewrite before morning, complained to partner Bob Schiller about the actors' lack of enthusiasm. Schiller advised, "Have a little compassion. They were up till four o'clock in the morning. They're tired." Replied Weiskopf, "They're actors. Let them act not tired."

Throughout, players without many lines did a lot of sitting around. Sally Struthers and Betty Garrett, who became instant soul mates, talked and giggled so much together that people finally told them not to sit together.

Once in a while, a scene or story that tied up neatly and cleverly on paper would get to the floor and suddenly not have a real conclusion. Then someone, or ones, would say, "What happens? What does the plot add up to?" and an end would take shape in the doing. One of John Rich's favorites: when Archie and Jefferson, thoroughly frustrated that they cannot get through to each other, square off in a crescendo of escalating raspberries.

The next revised script would go around and the cast advanced from rehearsal hall to studio—from, initially, a tiled room with no windows in which, after a whole day, perspective was hard to judge, to an area so cold that people joked about how CBS must keep black-market beef hanging from the ceiling. In fact, it had to be kept cold because the lights on the set beat down so hot. The permanent sets of living room and kitchen might or might not have been joined by sets that needed building for a particular show, as, for example, the voting booths and registration paraphernalia used on "Election Story." Such sets, costing several thousand dollars to construct, were frequently not used again.

An early-morning dry block with props segued into a camera run-through with complete wardrobe, ensuing script revisions, and director's "notes" (suggestions and comments) for the cast. Such days ran as late as they had to. The following morning, starting as early as it had to, brought more notes, a run-through, makeup, wardrobe, and finally, the taping of the episode.

"Now, in all of that process," Norman Lear has explained, "the actor is heard from a great deal, the director is heard from a great deal, and the writers are heard from again and again."

Indeed, the taping of an episode in no way implied its completion. For a 24-minute program (leaving the balance of the half hour for open, close, credits, and commercials), two separate tapings were held before live studio audiences—with time in between for further rewrites, revisions, and fine-tunings.

The line for tickets to the 300-seat facility began around 3:30 P.M. for the first (5:30) taping, also known as the dress rehearsal. The people on line had written for their tickets way in advance. Rehearsals inside might continue as late as 5:15. Immediately preceding taping came warm-up, during which Norman Lear, John Rich, or another *All in the Family* heavyweight jollied the audience. John Rich, for example, enjoyed publicly confiding, "You keep us honest. We don't have the arrogance to use a laugh track." One of Lear's favorite warm-up stories involved a scathing, denunciatory postcard received after the menopause episode. Written on the card in another hand were the words: "Please don't pay any attention to this person. This person does not know where it is at. Signed, the Postman." (Lear had a ritual, verging on superstition, of warming up the audience for each of his new series—a habit he's compared to always wearing the same socks when he flew his missions during World War II).

Cast members, announced by whoever did the warm-ups, acknowledged the wild ovation—inevitable anyhow, but encouraged along by such accolades as "the best actor in America, Carroll O'Connor!" Sometimes they hugged and kissed each other. When O'Connor and Reiner campily embraced, it was a source of audience hysterics.

Once the show began, the director ascended to the control booth, from it orchestrating camera shots and in general commanding the troops by means of mike and earphones to cameramen and floor director. The audience, for its part, discovered such tricks as watching the monitors overhead to catch action obscured by cameras and crew movement.

Each show taped straight through. Said Rich, "When we're working before an audience, if we stop and back up, we lose momentum. We do our repair work afterward." Afterward generally meant a phenomenon described by *Time* magazine as a "ruthless rehash session"—led in the first year by Bud Yorkin or Norman Lear and later, by others. The session might run hours, with cast members who were not immediately involved sitting around on bleachers, and crew breaking for dinner. The second taping, slated for 8:00 P.M., incorporated the results of these notes, a system often compared to out-of-town tryouts for Broadway plays. John Rich: "We're doing a play a week and we're trying to be entertaining every minute. We don't have a Hartford or a Boston for tryouts."

The crew could tell as soon as they came back from dinner whether changes had been extensive: If the meeting hadn't ended by the time the second audience filed in, plenty had transpired which required learning in a hurry. The 8:00 taping reflected changes, reinterpretations, and further rewrites. Any lines fluffed in both tapings could be covered by pick-ups later.

"We live dangerously, then our audience tells us what is possible," John Rich has explained. One time, in a 5:30 taping, Edith referred to a Christmas card depicting the "Prince of Peace driving a blue convertible." The line drew laughs but also commentary during the break. Someone suggested softening the remark. Another line was offered: "The Three Wise Men driving a blue convertible." Edith delivered this line at the second taping, receiving the same laugh. After the show, Lear told the audience what had transpired, and asked for their feelings. After a 20-minute rap, they voted for "the Prince of Peace," then Lear decided to use the softer line anyhow. For the same laugh either way, why hurt feelings?

This feat was accomplished at a point when it might seem that nothing remained to be done. John Rich said that "after we finish a normal day, which would choke a horse, we go to the editing for another whole day. Yet most people don't even realize it's edited—that an *All in the Family* episode is assembled from the best pieces of two tapes* and any pick-ups that follow... [there are] 70 or 80 edits per show."

In fact, *All in the Family*, and specifically John Rich, pioneered in the videotaping of situation comedies.† This was not for art's sake, but as an economy measure, because in the beginning, there wasn't much money to go around. Back then, videotape did not lend itself to close editing, nor did CBS have the facilities. So John Rich found Al Collins, a Hollywood technician and former Milton Berle gag writer, who had the necessary machinery in his apartment. Even after CBS acquired the capacity, Rich continued to edit his tapes chez Collins, reasoning that "they can match the equip-ment, but not the price."

At first, no one believed the results John Rich obtained. What he did, no one did: "We forced the machinery to do what we wanted. They hadn't thought about intercutting speeches..." Editing could run right up to air date.

In May of 1974, John Rich, having overseen every one of *All in the Family*'s first 85 episodes, announced that he was (understandably) "tired," adding, "I'd like to move on to something new" (notably *On the Rocks*, *Benson*, and the pilots of *Barney Miller*, *Newhart*, and *Amanda's*—Bea Arthur's ill-fated Americanized version of the British sit-farce *Fawlty Towers*). Under his overall supervision as producer and/or director, the series earned six Emmys for its 1971–1972 offering, and

---

*Including laughter. *All in the Family* didn't use a laugh track. The reactions you hear, the audience genuinely provided.

---

†NBC's 15-minute *The Jonathan Winters Show*, 1957, is considered the first videotape show in the country.

two more for the 1972–1973 TV year.

That summer, Carroll O'Connor differed with Norman Lear—not for the first time, but the worst time—and said he was leaving the show. In the past, when scripts conflicted with O'Connor's sense of what Archie Bunker would or should do, he refused to perform them. One involved Archie, a black man, and a pregnant Puerto Rican woman who was giving birth in a stalled elevator. Another concerned Louise Jefferson standing under mistletoe, and Lionel suggesting that Archie might kiss her. When such script differences couldn't be resolved, explosions were not unknown.

O'Connor particularly resented the mistletoe scene, which he thought inappropriate, unArchie, and destined not to work. When nobody offered to remove it, it bothered him that his judgment could be treated so lightly. He prepared to leave *All in the Family*. As O'Connor told *Playboy*, "I'm the star of the number-one show on TV. I carry 75 percent of every episode. If I were somebody like Jackie Gleason, they'd all be ordered out on the street."

The difficulty, to some degree, lay in the fact that Gleason produced and created as well as starred in Gleason's programs. In the case of *All in the Family*, O'Connor had to share these honors with Norman Lear. Elsewhere O'Connor had said, "His [Lear's] idea of comedy, I think, is at variance with mine, and we've disagreed over material from the very beginning of the show over what made naturalistic comedy. I had one idea; he had another. But my ideas prevailed...if there is a battle and I keep winning, one of us keeps winning, there are hard feelings. And I guess that's the best way I can put it." Yet another way he put it: "When Norman picked me up from what was supposed to be Nowhere Land, I was further along in my profession than he was in his. It was really a question of who did what for whom."

The particular incident was settled by the deletion of the mistletoe reference, along with a favorable contract renegotiation. Other conflicts loomed on Lear's horizon. Early in 1974, Redd Foxx had chosen to withdraw from *Sanford and Son,* with the result that he had to be written out of nine episodes until he decided to return to the show. In July of 1974, O'Connor, similarly, walked.

He filed suit against Tandem, looking for an amount in the neighborhood of $65,000 back salary, "clarification" of his contract, and—so rumor has it—his name above the title. Lear got a court order preventing O'Connor from perform-ing in other capacities for the duration of the litigation. Meanwhile, O'Connor's refusal to return meant that the first episodes of the 1974–1975 season had to be shot without Archie. Said Lear, people "sat for half an hour...waiting for Carroll to walk through the door."

Instead of an intended four-parter about inflation, the writers devised a scenario in which Archie went off to a convention in Buffalo, disappeared, and would die there or not, depending on what O'Connor ultimately decided to do. Lear told reporters, "If we make three shows and he has not returned, we'll have reached the point of no return and the character of Archie will be irretrievably lost to the series."

When O'Connor strode onto the set to speak his line— the last line of the episode "The Longest Kiss"—the audience went wild, because it meant that he and Lear had reached an accord.

Asked later what might have happened to Edith had Archie departed, Jean Stapleton ventured that she could easily marry another bigot who had different dimensions than Archie. As to other possibilities, "I'd like to see a black workman who went to high school with Edith be incorpo-rated in an episode or two, as a friend of hers, with terrific rapport between the two. I'd even like to see Edith and a black man in a romantic situation...a mature interracial romantic relationship."

In September of 1974, members of Local 45 of the International Brotherhood of Electrical Workers struck CBS. O'Connor refused to cross the picket line: "I've been a trade union man all my life. I cannot work with strikebreakers." Informed that Lear disapproved, O'Connor remarked, "Nor-man's tack, and you may quote me, seems always to be to question my sincerity and my goodwill and to imply that my

Archie and Gloria.

actions are against the best interests of the cast and company of *All in the Family*." When the strike ended and the picketers resumed work, so did O'Connor—in the first episode of the inflation four-parter. In it, Archie goes on strike.

In 1975, Sally Struthers wanted more time to work on feature films. Seeking release from her contract, she advised Tandem that she wouldn't be appearing for rehearsals. The writers, enthusiastic about a new plot direction in which Gloria becomes pregnant, grieved. Tandem, charging breach of contract, got an injunction against her working elsewhere. The issue went to arbitration. Reported *Variety:* "The arbitration decision not only ordered her to refrain from working in TV or radio until after all the first-run segments of *All in the Family* are completed, but also in the event Tandem should continue her contract for the pact's remaining two years. She is further to refrain from working on other entertainment media while *All in the Family* is in production."

A trend was thought to be afoot, with strong measures demanded. In addition to O'Connor and Struthers on *All in the Family* and Redd Foxx on *Sanford and Son*, Ralph Waite of *The Waltons* and reportedly Alan Alda and Wayne Rogers of *M*A*S*H* had reconsidered their contracts at inconvenient junctures. The tactic, according to CBS-TV president Robert D. Wood, amounted to a "gun-at-the-temple, to-hell-with-the-contract...wild-eyed attitude of 'meet my demands or I'll bring everything to a screeching halt'...The notion that a contract is just a scrap of paper to be torn up is fast gaining ground...We must be prepared to drop a regular from the cast of a series, or start a new season with reruns, or even go so far as to substitute a different program at the last minute."

Lear, addressing an American Film Institute seminar in 1977, summed up the phenomenon in gentler terms: When a network takes a chance on a risky new series, it pays as little for the property as possible. If the series fails, everyone accepts it in relative stride. But if the show goes gangbusters, people expect to see it reflected in something more concrete than the public's adoring eyes. The actors want more money. The producers want to give it to them. The network is perfectly delighted to stick to the terms of the original contract. "So at the moment at which everybody shoud be breaking out a bottle of champagne, that's the moment, the way television is structured, that everybody becomes instant enemies."

In Struthers' case, "Two years after I finished the show, I never saw another check. For a while I thought it was so unfair. I was green when I signed, I had no legal representation; we thought the show wouldn't last." In O'Connor's, "apart from CBS president Robert Wood and his successor Robert Daly, the top men never did—not in my presence—express any pride in the show."

Storm clouds gathered, burst, abated. The skies cleared. *All in the Family* went on. Along with contract resolutions, what restored some sense of calm to the set was the dual arrival of

Mort Lachman and Paul Bogart. Said O'Connor, "With Mort, all the personalities seemed to mesh." Of Bogart, who had not previously directed TV comedy, people spoke in glowing terms of his talent and supportiveness, and O'Connor had known him since the golden age of prestige TV drama. Though others had directed various episodes during John Rich's tenure, and others continued after his departure, Bogart stayed with Archie Bunker even after *All in the Family* became *Archie Bunker's Place.* Starting his career as a puppeteer-actor with the Berkeley Marionettes in 1946, Bogart became, by the early years of television, a celebrated director of important TV dramas along the lines of *The U.S. Steel Hour, Kraft Theatre, Armstrong Circle Theatre, Hallmark Hall of Fame,* and *The Defenders.*

Among the standout episodes while Bogart directed *All in the Family* is "Edith's 50th Birthday," the making of which argues eloquently for the whole *All in the Family* system. The idea, initially, had been developed for Ann Romano (Bonnie Franklin) on *One Day at a Time.* Then, as a story emerged, people began to feel that if rape is indeed a crime of violence against women of all ages, the message would come across more effectively with Edith Bunker as the victim. A new script evolved and was introduced in the customary fashion.

After everyone read over the upcoming week's script, attention turned to the week at hand. The script consisted of only the first half hour—the attempted rape and Edith's escape. Some felt the jokes tasteless, among them lines delivered at the scene of the party (next door at Mike and Gloria's) that the characters didn't realize bore on Edith's unfolding misfortune.

During the reading, the performers strained to keep their tempers while making their points. When they returned the next day, having talked it over among themselves, they declared that they wouldn't be doing the show unless something radically changed. Norman Lear came in with a woman from the rape crisis center and explained why it was important to do the show. Its importance wasn't disputed, but people argued the dialogue. Lear agreed that the episode needed another half hour to explore the incident's full effect. This the cast accepted, on the understanding that the second half would be developed for shooting in a few more weeks.

David Dukes, selected to play the attacker because he looked clean-cut and unthreatening—demonstrating the fact that no one is safe simply because a stranger "looks okay"— had already worked with Lear on other projects (holding contracts for the ill-fated series *Lovers* and *The Night They Raided Minsky's*). To Dukes:

> It was fascinating to watch the rewrite. The fights about that show were intense because it obviously meant so much to everybody. I don't care what joke you will give him, Carroll O'Connor will rewrite it. He and Rob basically work that way. Then their objections opened the door for Sally and Jean, who also had things to say, though Jean is the greatest diplomat. She doesn't rewrite until something absolutely isn't working, and she'll literally stand on her head to make it work.
>
> The thing I learned watching Jean, which was an astounding experience for me because she's a total professional, is that she didn't gripe. She was a very important television star at this point, and she certainly had the power to insist. But she just made it work. The whole show worked because of her. I could have done the most brilliant performance in my life, but if she hadn't created the reality, we would have had nothing. The audience looked at her. I was the force. But she was *it*.
>
> She and I choreographed the physical business. We had to push down, struggle, I had to rip her dress. You choreograph it all carefully, particularly any shoves. If I remember right, we had a little struggle until I knew we were in position and I could push her. I would just sort of do the move with no force on her at all, and she would do the fall.
>
> And I definitely remember our being very concerned about the cake she was going to hurl in my face when she escaped. How much force to use, whether she would break my nose, and how hot it would be. We really dwelt on the heat, because it was supposed to come out

of the oven, and there was steam coming out of the oven, so in our minds it was hot. The prop man said, "Hey, I put smoke in the oven. Just smoke. There's no heat." Then we felt sort of silly, because we should have known.

The crew's reaction when we did the camera block-ing was very interesting, because they just couldn't be-lieve what we were doing. Then Paul Bogart told us there would be no stops at the time of taping. No time for repositions. We had to go straight through. If we gave the audience any time to settle and talk to each other, we'd lose the tension. He decided five cameras, three booms, so we could cut right on the floor without breaks.

The 5:30 taping was one of the more amazing theatrical events of my life. The audience didn't know what the story was going to be, and at that first taping there weren't even any rumors. I remember coming in, passing myself off as the detective, and then when my character determines that Edith is alone, he locks the door. And the audience sort of murmured, "Ahg, aww, he's the rapist. This is going to be really funny." I went over to her, and they were ready for jokes. There were a couple of little laughs but the thing was that they didn't know whether it was an actor doing bad jokes, or what, actually. Then I did something, some moment came, where I made it definite that we weren't going for jokes, that we were deadly serious.

For the first and only time in my career, the audi-ence growled. Deep, guttural stuff. I've played villains before, but I never had an audience growl and really hate. They despised me. Consequently, whenever she would say some Edith line, like offering me a cup of coffee, they would just laugh outrageously because there was such tension. It was the essence of comic relief. It was real edge-of-the-seat time.

When we finally got to the scene in the kitchen where she slams the cake into me, knees me in the groin, and escapes, the audience stood up and cheered. They stamped on the bleachers. That was the only hold time we had, because she had to exit out the door, go behind the set, and get ready for her entrance. So we had to hold while she got into position. At the 5:30 taping, it was the one thing we had to reshoot, because the audience was still screaming. You couldn't hear the dialogue. Same at the 8:00 show. They had to hold until the audience got quiet.

I had no idea the audience had such a tremendous identification with Edith, such a feeling for her. I must say that I'd gotten so involved in trying to make each element work that I forgot about who Edith was until the audience's reaction. And I suppose what I learned between the 5:30 and the 8:00 tapings was that what we had done was evidently right. It worked the way we meant it to.

Much as John Rich moved on to other challenges in 1974, Bud Yorkin and Norman Lear found their attentions increasingly drawn to other projects. As their empire grew, Yorkin became executive producer of *Sanford and Son*, as well as coproducer of *Maude, Good Times,* and *What's Happening!!* Lear involved himself in a succession of spin-offs beginning with *Maude,* although, noted *The Washington Post* in 1977, "Lear is legendary for staying close to his shows, even after eight of them are on the air and most of them are big hits."

The same year, *New Times* confirmed that the whirlwind of activity known as Norman Lear "doesn't actually write his nine shows. He doesn't have to. The *auteur* in television is like the Great Clockwinder theory of God. He dreams up an idea, creates a concept, sketches it out, then lets others fill it in... but it is always Lear who has the final say on what goes into his shows. It's not as if he has some kind of giant lazy susan with nine typewriters set up on it, and he rotates from one to another, one for each show. He goes from one set of *writers* to the next set, keeping his eye on them."

The great watchmaker set all sorts of clocks in motion, in a decade (and a medium) that would bear his imprint ever after.

Making Waves

"You would have to have something no less than the size of the Chinese army to carry out every idea that Norman has."
—Martin Mull

Martin Mull once described Norman Lear's creative process: "He gets an idea at breakfast for a film, and if he has a second cup of coffee, we're gonna have two television shows out of that, and a novel, and if he stays around long enough to pick up his own check, which he probably would, we're gonna have a play on Broadway." Mull knew such things firsthand, having appeared as wife-beater Garth Gimble on Lear's *Mary Hartman, Mary Hartman,* then as Garth's twin brother talk-show host Barth on the program's subsequent spin-offs *Fernwood 2-Night* and *America 2-Night.*

The rest of the world knew too, having witnessed the result of Norman Lear's ideas. In a few short years after *All in the Family*'s debut, Lear had influenced all of TV comedy and dominated much of it, to the extent that by 1975, critic Michael J. Arlen wagered, "it's probably a good bet that roughly a hundred and twenty million Americans watch Norman Lear comedies each week—which adds up to a total of roughly five billion viewers each year."

The name of the game was part style per se, part stylish spin-offs. Said critic Marc Eliot, "The social pinprick is Norman Lear's stock in trade." Said others, he belongs in the book of *Genesis* with all the other begats (as in *All in the Family* begat *Maude* which begat *Good Times;* begat *The Jeffersons* which begat *Checking In* and *E/R*).

As Lear proved—and as others had done long before Lear, notably *The Andy Griffith Show* and *The Bill Dana Show* when they spun off from *The Danny Thomas Show*—spin-offs offer certain immediate leverage. Presumably, the public has already taken the character to heart—which is to say, nobody ever attempted to spin off *My Mother the Car* with *My Uncle the Hubcap*. Also, the newer show can follow its parent in the schedule, enjoying the reinforcement of an excellent lead-in.

A strong spin-off debuts in excellent shape. On the other hand, as the great age of failed spin-offs in the mid-Seventies bore out, there are no guarantees. The beloved *Mary Tyler Moore Show* set free two of its finest creations in their own series, *Rhoda* and *Phyllis*. Neither quite lived up to its provenance, though *Rhoda* managed to last a respectable four years. The brilliant *Barney Miller* gave *Fish* his own show, which went belly-up, though two of its players (Denise Miller and Barry Gordon) eventually re-emerged dating on *Archie Bunker's Place*.

Some Lear spin-offs worked, but they weren't the only arrows in his quiver. Nor can arrows alone win the battle. They have to hit the target, which is what Norman Lear in the early Seventies unfailingly did.

As closely as Norman Lear is linked with spin-offs in the popular imagination, Tandem's second TV triumph came not in the form of an *All in the Family* scion, but rather as an adaptation of the BBC's *Steptoe and Son*. England's *Steptoe* revolved around a sullen Cockney rag-and-bone man and his lazy partner son. Producers Lear and Yorkin developed it into *Sanford and Son* with writer Aaron Ruben (*The Andy Griffith Show; Gomer Pyle, U.S.M.C.*), translating the Cockney experience into the black world of Watts. The new vehicle, starring Redd Foxx as Sanford and Demond Wilson as son (Lamont), first aired as a midseason entry on Friday, January 14, 1972.

**Fred Sanford (Redd Foxx)
wearing his original wardrobe, on display
at the Movieland Wax Museum, Buena Park, California.**

In ensuing weeks, Fred Sanford picked on his son, his son's Puerto Rican friend ("Now you gone and got Puerto Rican all over our truck!"), and his Aunt Esther (who'd as readily shout him down as beat him up). As David Marc wrote in *American Film,* "Although there had been black sit-coms before, never had the characters broken so free of both traditional stereotypes *(Amos 'n' Andy, Beulah)* and honkyization *(Julia).* Instead of watermelon jokes, Lear offered jokes about watermelon jokes." The show hit big.

Sanford became Yorkin's responsibility as executive producer and director, with Ruben producing in addition to writing. Lear remained closer to *All in the Family* and, by September 1972, *All in the Family*'s first spin-off, *Maude.*

Introduced as Edith's cousin in an early *All in the Family* episode, Maude Findlay promptly captured the fancy of

CBS's Fred Silverman, who felt the character could carry her own show. The much-married Maude (Beatrice Arthur) of Tuckahoe, New York, rebutted Archie at every turn. She had money, he didn't. She talked women's lib to his male supremacy. For viewers who complained, "When are you going to make fun of a Democrat the way you mock Archie the Republican?"—Maude stood condemned by her own mouth on a regular basis. As the series made clear, whether a blue-collar bigot says, "You Jews make the best doctors" or whether a starry-eyed liberal does, it's still a sweeping generality and therefore, a prejudice.

Just as *Sanford and Son* was Yorkin's baby (with Aaron Ruben producing), *Maude* became Lear's (with Bob Weiskopf and Bob Schiller producing); and with *All in the Family*

All in the Family produced several hit LPs as well as a card game and a board game.

stronger than ever, the two men bustled in different directions while still working in tandem. Consultation might take
the form of rushed huddles in the studio parking lot, or of
one sending a script to the other, then calling for a "what do
you think?". By never duplicating each other's efforts, they
consistently multiplied their output. By the end of September
1972, *Time* projected that "Yorkin and Lear's profits from
their three shows this year could reach $5,000,000." Adding to
that, their income from books *(The Wit and Wisdom of Archie
Bunker, Edith Bunker's* All in the Family *Cookbook),* records (a
single of the theme song, and an *All in the Family* LP which
rose to the top ten within weeks of its release), and other
merchandising rights along with new project offers, "their
Tandem headquarters is the hottest TV production office in
Hollywood."

Meanwhile, others attempted to tap what they perceived
to be Tandem's surefire formula. ABC, which had twice
turned down pilots for *All in the Family,* briefly toyed with a
pilot called *The Neighbors* on the heels of *All in the Family's*
success. Reported *Variety* in February 1971, *"The Neighbors*
eschews the bigotry angle of [All in the] 'Family' and the
explosive language that goes with it, concentrating instead on
the ideological clashes between a family of hard hats living
across the street from a liberal psychology prof with his wife,
an exponent of Women's Lib." The former have a daughter;
the latter, a son. For the gist of the plot, consult *Romeo and
Juliet.* In September 1972, a Saturday-morning cartoon series
entitled *The Barkleys* premiered. It presented a sort of Archie
and Edith Bunker as dogs. The grousing father, Arnie, drove a
bus, but he didn't drive it far. *The Barkleys* only lasted a year.

Over in England, Johnny Speight resumed *Till Death Us
Do Part* for a seven-week stint (a length not uncommon for
British TV) after a four-year breather. The initial avatar, to
which Lear had bought adaptation rights as the springboard
for *All in the Family,** was a huge success when it first aired.

---

*A German version, *One Heart and One Soul*, premiered in 1974. Its Archie equivalent,
reminiscent of Adolf Hitler, went by the name Adolf Tetzlaff.

Since then, Speight's play, *If There Weren't Any Blacks You'd Have to Invent Them,* had been shown in 17 countries, including the United States, won numerous awards, and received scads of congratulatory letters, among them one from the U.S. Commission on Human Rights. Also since then, Lear's *All in the Family* had aired on the BBC. British viewers questioned the meanings of such words as *dingbat* and *terlet,* and in general wondered why Americans thought the show controversial. Compared to their own Alf Garnett, Archie seemed a perfect gent. But Speight complimented *All in the Family* as "the best American comedy show I've ever seen. The writers have gone as far as they can in the time spot." When *Till Death* returned in 1972, original cast intact, it reached an estimated 24 million in the British Isles, making it Britain's most successful program. When a movie version entitled *The Garnett Family* arrived on U.S. shores in 1973, it furnished a fascinating curiosity piece but hardly overshadowed Archie.

In January 1973, ABC tried a novel tack. If you can't find another *All in the Family,* find another Archie Bunker in real life. Locating a Las Vegas resident of that moniker, they staged a billboard campaign in which their Archie said he'd rather watch *Here We Go Again, All in the Family*'s time slot rival. Commented Lear, "I've seen the ratings, and I'm happy to see that Archie Bunker watches 'Here We Go Again' and that the rest of America watches 'All in the Family.' " Lear had a point. *Here We Go Again,* starring Larry Hagman, bowed out in June.

While others busied themselves trying to mine or undermine *All in the Family,* Lear and Yorkin preferred to explore previously untapped areas of contemporary interrelationships. When they created *Sanford and Son,* Bud Yorkin had told interviewers, "one of our major concerns was not to make *Sanford* look too grim. The *Steptoe* set in England was dark and gloomy; we took pains to make ours poor but not depressing." At the same time, Norman Lear had a notion in the back of his mind to see what a deeper level of poverty might yield in the way of a "real black ghetto family show."

Good Times, essentially fitting the description, spun off from *Maude* in February 1974. Esther Rolle, who had played

Thelma (BernNadette Stanis), Florida (Esther Rolle), and James (John Amos) in *Good Times*.

Maude's maid Florida Evans, here lived as Florida Evans with her husband and three children in the Cabrini-Green housing project on Chicago's South Side. Their life was a constant struggle to keep their heads above water, maintain their values, and yet appreciate life's "good times." Having the best of times in this series, Jimmie Walker as oldest son J. J. became an overnight sensation with his catchword "dy-no-mite." The series struck a common chord overseas as well as nationally, with other countries buying scripts and producing their own versions of the show.

In January 1975, Lear struck pay dirt again by taking a black family to the opposite economic extreme. *The Jeffersons* (cocreated and coproduced by Michael Ross and Bernie West) spun off from *All in the Family*, giving George Jefferson (Sherman Hemsley) his own show, and introducing TV comedy's first prominent interracial couple (Roxie Roker and Franklin

Cover as their in-laws, the Willises). Slotted in the CBS Saturday evening half-hour between *All in the Family* at 8:00 and *The Mary Tyler Moore Show* at 9:00—a space occupied until a few months earlier by *M*A*S*H*—the series fell comfortably into one of the most golden lineups in the history of television. *Time*'s Lance Morrow found George Jefferson to be "entrepreneur, black bigot, a splenetic little whip of a man who bullies like a demented overseer, seldom speaks below a shriek and worships at the church of ostentation," and the public found him so much to their liking that Lear had another major hit.

Other good news accrued to *All in the Family* in the year *The Jeffersons* spun off. From an effort that virtually squeaked through a hole in network programming in January of 1971 to be scheduled for Tuesday nights, 9:30–10:00, *All in the Family* had moved in September of 1971 to the lucrative Saturday 8:00–8:30 slot.* Wrote *The Washington Post* in June of 1975, "This fall, an advertiser who buys a one-minute commercial will pay $125,000. This is TV's highest priced minute."

Before 1975 rolled to a close, *All in the Family* reruns had entered the daytime lineup, pitted against NBC's *Another World* (in the process, bouncing CBS's *The Edge of Night* all the way over to ABC). Norman Lear, despite the additional revenue thereby engendered, had reservations. As a prime-time show, *All in the Family* allowed three minutes for commercials; as a daytime half-hour, it would have to be cut to make room for six. A CBS spokesman said Lear could do the cutting, but Lear responded that "It is enormously destructive to the intent of the original show, and I think it is a terrible crime against all the people who worked so hard to make the original show... It isn't the same show we made when you take three minutes out of it." He suggested that whatever money CBS might lose by omitting the extra commercials, CBS could

---

*Originally, CBS announced that the move would be to Mondays at 10:30. After NBC and ABC arranged their schedules to counter-program, CBS pulled a switch—in part, to combat NBC's promising new *The Partners* starring Don Adams, fresh out of *Get Smart*. CBS instantly took firm hold of Saturday night.

simply pay that much less for the reruns. CBS didn't go for it. Ultimately, when Lear felt his insistence would deprive others of income from their work, he let the show air with cuts.

Along with *The Jeffersons*, the advertising clout, and the reruns came three more Lear entries in 1975 alone. With *One Day at a Time*, *Hot L Baltimore*, and *Mary Hartman, Mary Hartman*, Norman Lear became undisputed ruler of the air-waves. *One Day at a Time*, coming out in December, starred Bonnie Franklin as Ann Romano, TV comedy's first single, divorced heroine. Ann raised two socially active teenage daughters as rationally as possible, while trying hard to maintain some normal social life of her own. Various plot ideas sprang from the things Lear heard his three daughters say. The show enjoyed high ratings—at a time when, to have another top series, Lear sat largely in the position of having to beat out himself.

Hot L Baltimore, launched in January 1975 and based on the award-winning Off-Broadway play of the same name, centered around activities in the sleazy Hotel Baltimore (so run-down no one ever repaired the "e" in the hotel's neon sign). Developed with Rod Parker (the other executive producer of *Maude*), it dove into sexual innuendo the way *All in the Family* and *The Jeffersons* had braved racial material. The public, apparently more comfortable hearing about bigotry than prostitution and homosexuality, did not embrace *Hot L Baltimore.* Insiders suggest it could have done better had they not been forced away from the original script, and had ABC—which finally had a Lear property—not been so timid about selling it to the stations: "We have A and B and C, and, oh that's right, we have something about hookers and gay guys. Are you interested?" Followed by, "Gee, Norman, we can't sell *Hot L.*"

A Lear battle with the networks that reached its accord *outside* of the networks arrived in the form of a gutsy, satirical, five-shows-a-week soaper, *Mary Hartman, Mary Hartman.* Violence and famine, omnipresent by virtue of TV and radio news, provided a background counterpoint hum to the booming day-to-day cacophony unreeling in Mary's mind. A "typi-

Mary Hartman (Louise Lasser) with Gore Vidal on *Mary Hartman,*
Mary Hartman **(1976).**

cal housewife," she placed more faith in TV than in real life,
about which her priorities were confused. When a maniac
slaughtered the Lombardis, their three children, two goats,
and eight chickens down the street, Mary marveled, "What
kind of a madman would kill two goats and eight chickens?"
But when her sister noticed her floor's "waxy yellow buildup,"
she registered genuine concern. In other episodes, a child
prodigy preacher accidentally electrocuted himself with a
television in the bathtub; Mary's grandfather found fame
exposing himself as the Fernwood Flasher; a coach drowned
in the bowl of chicken soup that Mary brought to cure his
cold;* and Mary was institutionalized. A highlight of the
latter came when Mary discovered that she and fellow nearly
comatose inmates enjoyed the distinction of being a Nielsen
family. As Louise Lasser described her character, "She survives in a world that may not be worth surviving for."

CBS fronted $100,000 for the first few episodes, then

---

*Coach Fedders' memorial service, held in Mary's kitchen, became a highlight of the
season. The inspired staging came about because there wasn't enough money in the
budget to build a mortuary set, and Mary's living room hadn't been constructed yet.

expressed doubts about the direction being taken and pulled out. When neither of the other two networks signed it, Lear in a sense created his own network—selling the series himself to 128 local stations around the country, and demonstrating for the first time that a national hit could exist and thrive outside the three-network system. Lear enjoyed, along with the coup, the freedom: "We realized we could paint our own mural our own way. There was no program practices man standing over anybody's shoulder, and our own taste ruled what we could do and what we would do."

Mary Hartman, Mary Hartman drew a fanatical following, along with vocal flak. Fan clubs formed; the *New York Post* published daily plot synopses; *The Village Voice* described the marriage scenes as being what Ingmar Bergman tried to do in *Scenes from a Marriage,* only better. Opposed were protesting picketers and letter writers, for instance a *Soap Opera Digest* reader who demanded, "How in the world can anyone put such a filthy, vulgar show on the air at 3:30 P.M. for grown people to be exposed to all the filthy talk Mary Hartman stands for, to say nothing about the children coming home from school? What is our country coming to? This is the reason so many teens are dope addicts, VD carriers, and drunks. My goodness, let's clean this filth up. I'm a grandma and this show makes me sick."

To the series' first director, Joan Darling, this wasn't far from the point: "My goal with that show was that it should be on at 4:30 in the afternoon and people would laugh, and then at six o'clock they'd watch the news and get a little uncomfortable."

By no stretch of the imagination did *Hot L Baltimore* and *Mary Hartman, Mary Hartman* constitute Lear's first experience with making network and newsworthy waves. *All in the Family* broke that ground for him, and before it, *Till Death Us Do Part* broke the ground in England. When the latter came back in 1972, some audience members went wild over the number of *bloodys* in a given episode (*bloody* being, technically, an irreverent allusion to Christ's blood shed on the cross); and a comment about the Virgin Mary and the pill caused

Mary Whitehouse, general secretary of the Viewers and Listeners Association, to denounce the show as "obscene, blasphemous and a calculated offense to a great many viewers." When BBC network chairman Lord Hill apologized for the joke, Johnny Speight remarked, "If that's the state of affairs, I will refuse to write again for the BBC." Within a few weeks, the stars of the series appeared in a special edition of the series at the London Palladium. The queen mother and other members of the royal family attended.

That same year, U. S. televison writers, speaking for the Writers Guild of America, told Senator Sam Ervin's committee* that broadcast executives heavily censored scripts. David W. Rintels, head of the Guild's censorship committee, testified that they allowed "laughter but not tears, fantasy but not reality, escapism but not truth…75 million people are nightly being fed programs deliberately designed to have no resemblance at all to reality, nonsense whose only purpose is to sell snake-oil and laxatives and underarm deodorants… Writers by the dozens report that they have written characters who are black and have seen them changed to white. They have written Jews and seen them converted to gentiles. They have proposed shows about South African apartheid, Vietnam, old folks, mental disease, politics, business, labor, students and minorities; and they have been chased out of studios."

Lear, in the same context, indicated a certain freedom CBS had permitted him with regard to taboos, yet "we dealt recently…with the subject of impotency on the show. It was very difficult to get the program made, even at this late date, but when it was made the reaction from the public was incredible. Even those people who felt that perhaps the subject was too adult for the time period, which, by the way, only the network controls—they were excited by what happened in the house—by the fact that when the show was over children were asking questions, and they were forced to

---

*Hearing before the Subcommittee on Constitutional Rights of the Committee on the Judiciary of the United States Senate, 92nd Congress.

answer, the parents were forced to answer questions and conversation was taking place in the homes where conversation in many cases had become kind of a forgotten art.

"What I mean to say is that I think the public has been for so long underestimated, and whatever success we have, I owe to the public who understood the show in the first place."

Responded Senator Ervin, "I think the American people are more intelligent than some of the broadcasters and some of the politicians think. Your series about Archie Bunker shows that because the American people have accepted it."

Lear reacted to questions of taste by pointing out that he'd made an absolute habit of hearing out legitimate protests; that when people wrote multipage letters commenting on themes and treatments, they did not go unread into the wastebasket; that he and his writers regularly consulted with religious leaders, crisis counselors, and so forth when sensitive issues arose as potential stories.

He felt, further, as he stated on the occasion of winning the 1972 Broadcaster of the Year Award of the Independent Radio and Television Society: "The so-called adult themes that television is currently dealing in are themes for which the American people have always been ready. We in television simply weren't trusting the people…to accept or reject as they saw fit…We, especially in the media, must start to trust the American people more. And to do that, we must begin to trust ourselves."

He believed, ultimately, that if viewers thought he overstepped his bounds, they had only to "reach out and turn to another channel; I'll get the message." But what he did not appreciate were network censors who, in their zeal to ensure viewers' not changing channels—a move which can only lead to sponsors reallocating advertising dollars—inclined to press the panic button too freely. The clichéd network warning of "this has to go or there'll be a tremendous knee-jerk reaction in Des Moines" did not appeal to Lear, who knew Des Moines, and had greater faith in its tolerance quotient.

With *All in the Family*, censors worried about such words as *Mafia* and *smart-ass*, which they ordered out, and such matters as Mike's impotence (when he feared for his academic standing), Joey's genitals (when Archie diapered him), and a confrontation between Mike and Archie about whether God exists—which Lear kept in. Lear readily admits that the censors sometimes raised valid points, or sometimes created an atmosphere in which he changed things for the better even if they were wrong in their objections.

In some instances, when considering extremely sensitive material, he'd bounce the concept off the network in advance, to avoid investing time and money preparing a piece that would not air. On occasions when he deeply cared about doing subjects that the network didn't want to touch, and when lawsuits were threatened, he took the position that they could back a truck up to his house and take it all away; he'd still have his family and his typewriter. They generally did not back the truck anywhere; they backed down.

Once, the Mushroom Industry Action Committee faulted an episode in which Archie, having eaten mushroom stew, hears that three people were just hospitalized and one had died from bad mushrooms. The MIAC requested but did not get a disclaimer to the effect that "there has been no known illness to anyone in the United States from the consumption of canned or bottled mushrooms." They were, however, promised deletions in the rerun, and a spokesman thereupon concluded: "While there are still implications in it with which I object, at least we as an industry can go on from here without the specter of Archie's contrived malady."

Sometimes members of the viewing public raised their voices and pens in protest. On *Good Times*, VD among the young stirred up notable controversy. On *Maude*, Maude drew condemnation for, in one episode, calling husband Walter (Bill Macy) a "son of a bitch" and, in another, for weighing the merits of having an abortion. She reluctantly decided against having the baby, drawing a reported 24,000 letters of protest to the network, and outraging some viewers so thoroughly that they threw themselves down in front of the cars of William Paley and Norman Lear.

In the racial department, some critics argued that Archie's bigotry encouraged bigotry; that *Sanford and Son* merely updated *Amos 'n' Andy;* that J. J. Evans on *Good Times* presented a questionable stereotype; and that George Jefferson of *The Jeffersons* was no more flattering to blacks than Archie was to whites. Not easy issues to negotiate. To avoid black shows is to ostracize black performers and issues. To do them, yet spare the performers themselves as the subjects of jokes, is to engage in another form of racism, and moreover, to risk criticism for having created another *Julia*. To do them as Lear did them is to invite such charges as exploitation and stereotyping. But Lear answered that "in a sense, I feel I'm black myself...I know what it's like to be treated as an inferior, because I'm Jewish." Besides which, black writers, as well as cast members, contributed to the scripts.

For his part, Carroll O'Connor asserted, "if I felt for one moment that this show was doing any harm, I'd drop it like a hot coal. I can make a goddamn good living without *All in the Family.*"

A study instituted in late 1974 had different views on the subject of harm. Hard-hitting series like *Kojak* and *Police Story* were determined to have outlived their usefulness. According to the researchers, violence wormed its way into our diet with the angst-ridden pressures of Vietnam. Others feared it had gotten out of hand. A 1974 movie of the week, *Born Innocent*, portrayed a young girl's (Linda Blair) brutal victimization by other girls in a detention home. Subsequently, the identical crime was duplicated by a real group of youngsters.

A 1975 ABC inquiry concluded that viewers, finally through with Vietnam and Watergate, longed to return to traditional values, while the Federal Communications Commission (FCC) recorded a jump in viewer complaints from approximately 2500 in 1972 to some 33,000 in 1973—a 1200 percent increase. Congress pushed the FCC to pressure the National Association of Broadcasters (NAB) to do something. What they did—by imposing the "family hour"—required broadcasters to keep "adult"-themed programs off the air between 7:00 and 9:00 P.M. This meant, in terms of Lear's offerings, considerable movement into less remunerative slots. *All in the Family,* for example, switched in September 1975 from Saturday at 8:00 to Monday at 9:00 (opposite NBC's *Monday Night Movie* and ABC's *Monday Night Football*).

Lear, along with other interested groups, sued. So did Alan Alda, Mary Tyler Moore, and Carroll O'Connor, charging "self-regulatory censorship which restrains free speech and ideas in violation of the First Amendment." Hollywood's three largest unions supported them by calling for an injunction against the "family hour because its repressive atmosphere has a chilling effect on the creative community."

Reported *The Boston Globe,* "The networks and the FCC denied, ineffectually, that the 'family hour' was involuntary. ABC, CBS, NBC and the National Assn. of Broadcasters have found by polls that the idea is popular and they plan to continue...[even though] the writers, producers and performers who opposed the 'family hour' are among the most

Gloria and Mike—either going to a Marx Brothers film festival while Archie may have disappeared from town and from the series (1974)... or expressing their opinion on the "family viewing hour."

vigorous supporters of better, tougher, more thoughtful television. Norman Lear's *All in the Family, Maude, The Jeffersons,* and other shows are popular entertainment, topical and sometimes unsettling, but they are about the real world. And although they do little obeisance to the rituals of conventional morality, their underlying themes are honesty, decency, candor and brotherhood."

In November 1976, district judge Warren J. Ferguson ruled in Los Angeles that the "family hour" violated the freedom of speech as guaranteed by the Constitution. Testimony had revealed that broadcasters had been threatened with the denial of license renewals unless they complied. Said Ferguson, the "desirability or undesirability of family viewing is not the issue," but "censorship by government or privately created review boards cannot be tolerated."

The ruling, though not universally welcome, brought relief not only in the industry, but to many a critic who pointed out that under the "family hour," TV had been generally sophomoric and insipid for two hours a night—while the other 22 hours acted under an unintended mandate to embrace whatever crime looked most marketable.

All in the Family sailed in November 1976 from the Wednesday at 9:00 slot (having moved there in September 1976) to Saturday at 9:00. Before it were *The Mary Tyler Moore Show* at 8:00 and *The Bob Newhart Show* at 8:30. TV has rarely seen so solid a 90 minutes.

Viewers' tastes, however, had new dishes to sample. "Relevant" TV comedy gave way to racy "T&A" at one end of the spectrum, and quieter humor at the other. The change came in part when ABC, at the end of the 1974–1975 season, showed unexpected muscle, edging out CBS—after 20 consecutive seasons—as number one in the ratings game. CBS and NBC panicked, one result being a sudden resistance to letting new shows establish themselves with time. When *All in the Family* had entered the fray in 1971, the system more or less guaranteed a minimum of 13 weeks followed by 13 weeks of reruns. No longer. Even *All in the Family*, had it debuted in 1976, might have found itself hamstrung into extinction.

What ABC had that CBS lost—aside from the number-one spot—was Fred Silverman. A *Time* magazine cover story dubbed him "The Man with the Golden Gut," a reference to his uncanny ability to zero in on viewers' inmost desires. Lear called him "a showman, perhaps our P.T. Barnum. Freddie is decisive, courageous, and smart—all are rare in television." Credited during his CBS stint with everything from *Green Acres* to *Maude* to *Hee Haw* to *The Autobiography of Miss Jane Pittman*, Silverman went over the wall to ABC in 1975. There he acquired *Charlie's Angels, Three's Company,** *Laverne and Shirley, Happy Days*, and *Soap*. CBS lost 15 stations to ABC; NBC lost six.

By the end of the 1976–1977 season, ABC had the four top-rated shows in the nation. The top two, *Laverne and Shirley* and *Happy Days*, hailed from Garry Marshall, a self-proclaimed sentimentalist who crafted comedy "in the tradition of Norman Rockwell." At the time, *Laverne* star, Garry's sister Penny, was married to Rob Reiner—making Garry Marshall his brother-in-law.

At this point, Lear was associated with T.A.T. Productions as well as Tandem. T.A.T. produced *Mary Hartman, Mary Hartman* and other properties independent of Bud Yorkin. The name derived from the Yiddish phrase "tochas affen tish," meaning "derrière on the table," or "be honest and get to the bottom of things (even if it means embarrassing ourselves)." In 1976, T.A.T. brought forth *All's Fair*, about a conservative congressman (Richard Crenna) and his substantially younger, liberal, photographer girlfriend (Bernadette Peters). The show lasted less than a year. Lear's *The Dumplings*, about an overweight couple who adored each other and the whole wide world, didn't make it through three months.

Lear's *The Nancy Walker Show*, with a strong cast that included Nancy Walker, William Daniels, and James Cromwell, ran from September to December 1976. His *The Baxters*, an audience participation novelty in which actors

---

*Developed and produced by *All in the Family*'s Don Nicholl, Mickey Ross, and Bernie West, and based on the British comedy *Man About the House*.

presented a situation comedy about controversial issues—nursing homes, homosexual teachers, and so on—invited the studio audience to discuss what they'd seen after the show, *as part of the show*. The concept, while intriguing, never attracted a large following.

In 1977, Norman Lear sprung *Fernwood 2-Night* as the summer replacement for *Mary Hartman, Mary Hartman*. Starring Martin Mull as host Barth Gimble and Fred Willard as his second-banana stooge Jerry Hubbard, it did to talk shows what *Mary Hartman, Mary Hartman* had done for soaps. *Fernwood* dared to satirize everything—from bad amateur acts to a Talk-to-a-Jew call-in spot to the doctor who found, by dressing one group of rats in leisure suits and the control group in simple sports jackets, that leisure suits cause cancer. The summer show came back as *America 2-Night* in April 1978, this time purportedly from Alta Coma, California, "the unfinished furniture capital of the world."

All That Glitters developed from Lear's wondering how different the world would be had God created Eve first, then whipped up Adam from her rib to give her a playmate. Its sex roles reversed, *All That Glitters* became, in 1977, the first series on commercial TV to focus essentially on questions inspired by the feminist movement. Women held top production posts. One, Virginia Carter, had been local president of the National Organization for Women before becoming a vice president of T.A.T. Despite *All That Glitters'* interesting premise and lively cast (for instance, Linda Gray just before *Dallas* and Gary Sandy just before *WKRP in Cincinnati*), the series didn't take hold.

In 1978, Rue McClanahan of *Maude* starred in Lear's *Apple Pie*, which debuted September 23 and went off the air within weeks. In another show, Bea Arthur of *Maude* landed in Washington, D.C., to finish out the term of a deceased congressman, and husband Walter (Bill Macy) tagged along. Two episodes into the series, Bea Arthur bowed out. The script became a second pilot, *Onward and Upward*, in which a black football pro (John Amos, formerly Florida's husband James on *Good Times*) replaced Maude. Disagreements between

(Left to right, standing) Mike Binker, Dick Libertini; (seated) Jack Gilford, Dabney Coleman, Rue McClanahan, and Caitlin O'Heaney in *Apple Pie.*

Amos and the producers brought a replacement for Amos—Cleavon Little, who once played a housebreaker on *All in the Family*—and a title change, to *Mr. Dooley*, then *Mr. Dugan*. When Lear screened the *Mr. Dugan* pilot for members of the Congressional Black Caucus, they expressed concern that the characterization was too harsh. Lear withdrew the series because "it just wasn't happening with the kind of importance and dignity that the first black congressman on TV should have."

CBS claimed that they would make the decision as to its suitability. Lear declined to deliver the program. The old, familiar lawsuit noises reared their ugly tonsils. The resolution came about when the black football-star-turned-congressman became a white football-star-turned-university-president (Bill Macy). Otherwise, the script didn't greatly change. As *Hanging In,* the series ran four weeks.

All in the Family became *Archie Bunker's Place* in the fall of 1979; *Sanford and Son,* which in 1977 turned into *The Sanford Arms* (minus Redd Foxx and Demond Wilson), yielded *Sanford* in 1980 with Redd Foxx. *The Jeffersons* (still one of the most successful comedies in syndication) spun off *Checking In* in 1981, with maid Florence (Marla Gibbs) managing a hotel staff, and Larry Linville (of *M*A*S*H*) and Liz Torres (of *All in the Family*) as her coworkers.

Esquire announced in March 1984 that "Norman Lear returns to prime-time TV after a five-year hiatus" with the series *A.K.A. Pablo,* network TV's first all-Hispanic prime time series. About a young Mexican-American stand-up comic on the rise, it earned, in *People,* such nicknames as *All in the Family Eats Frijoles* and *Maude Goes Mexican.* Its star, Paul Rodriguez, had been spotted by Lear while doing warm-ups for TV studio audiences. Lear invited Rodriguez, and Rodriguez in turn "took a shot and asked him to come over to my parents' house in East L.A. for a laugh, and he came." Prior to that, as the son of migrant farm workers, Rodriguez had suffered the indignities Lear's shows fought: "As a teenager in Los Angeles, I learned what it is to be a Mexican and be kicked around by the police. Because I wore a bandana and drove a Chevrolet that was lowered in the rear and because there were dice hanging from my mirror, that made me a murderer, right?"

A.K.A. Pablo beat out the competing *A-Team* in Los Angeles and Chicago, and the *National Examiner* wrote that, according to a top political analyst, "Rodriguez has what it takes to enter the political ring and win a presidential election by the year 2000 ... the time and the motivation to build a strong political base with his acting career."

A.K.A. *Pablo* was canceled after six episodes. Today, Rodriguez jokes, "I like to think of myself as the man who ruined Lear. After my TV series folded, he went into pretzel sales."

In 1984, Lear wrote and served as one of the two executive producers of *P.O.P.* Its salesman hero (Charles Durning) somewhat resembled his father, and its magazine publisher heroine (Beatrice Arthur) took after his wife. The pilot aired during the summer lull in August, but the networks never picked up the series.

In the final analysis, someone's going to up and ask why Lear lost his touch. But the question seems to be neither how, nor if. Lear held office longer than any of the presidents his shows ridiculed, and ran a consistent platform right along. When public imagination sought a new platform, Lear moved on to other challenges.

The industry had changed. Networks no longer gave shows enough time to catch hold. A show that didn't draw ratings in its first or second week frequently had no third week to turn things around. As Mark Fowler, the just-retired FCC chairman, commented in 1987, "Television is just like any other appliance—it's a toaster that produces pictures instead of toast."

Critic Marc David has noted, "So clear were the Lear trademarks of generational conflict, frank political allusion, and controversial plots that he emerged as the first sit-com maker identifiable to the public." On the scope and scale he accomplished, to date he also remains the last.

Archie Bunker's Place

"All in the Family will close up shop
after the coming 1976–'77 season."
—*New York Daily News,* June 1976

"...will not be back next fall."
—*New York Daily News,* January 1978

"...almost certainly will go off
the air after this season."
—New York *Newsday,* December 1978

When Archie Bunker forges Edith's signature on a home mortgage to be able to purchase Kelcy's bar ("Archie Gets the Business," parts one and two as a one-hour special), he sets their marriage back about a century, but he buys his series a five-year lease on life. Edith, though furious, forgives him at Mike's insistence. Jean Stapleton, the actress behind Edith, proved less pliable. As dearly as she loved her show and her character, she wasn't ready to

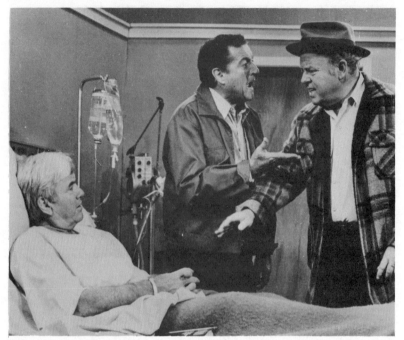

When Kelsey (Frank Maxwell) is ready to sell his bar, Harry (Jason Wingreen) and Archie debate buying it.

shuffle and stifle for another five years. The exodus of principals had, in fact, already begun.

At the start of the 1977–1978 season, Tommy Kelsey suffers a heart attack and decides to sell his business. Archie and bartender Harry acquire it jointly, with Archie intending to play it safe by retaining his job on the loading dock. A month into the season ("Archie's Grand Opening"), Archie manages to antagonize Harry and Carlos at the bar (they both storm off) and Mr. Sanders, his plant boss (inspiring Archie to brush Sanders off), whereupon Archie becomes a full-fledged saloonkeep full-time.

Reported the *New York Post,* "If the new locale works with viewers, that's the way it will be all season. If not, they'll shift Archie back home. Sally Struthers has been written out of the first three episodes because she's making a movie for ABC, 'Battered' with Dennis Weaver, but the rest of the family are on hand." Actually, even the early fall 1977 episodes shift from the pub to 704 Hauser, with the "Edith's 50th Birthday" rape episode, on October 16, interrupting the tavern-based stories, and with a flashback to Gloria and Mike's first date set on home base in December of that season.

In January 1978, Norman Lear's office flatly declared that he would wrap up the series at the end of the season. To fill the void, Carroll O'Connor proposed returning for occasional Archie-and-Edith specials that would not include Mike and Gloria, since Rob Reiner and Sally Struthers had already advised that they wouldn't reprise their roles, having other projects to pursue.*

By February, *The New York Times* quoted Lear as saying "I think it's time to move on. When Rob and Sally leave, the show is going to lose three of the important relationships that make the program what it is—between Archie and his son-in-law; between Archie and his daughter; and between the kids. We've had eight good years. It's time to let others compete for that half-hour. The entity we call *All in the Family*, the song that leads into it, that particular location in Queens, will be gone. But if Carroll and Jean want to do a show called *Archie and Edith,* I wish them a long and happy life."

CBS favored continuing Archie. Robert Daly, president of CBS Entertainment, asserted that "from a legal standpoint, we have an option that we can exercise on *All in the Family.* Contractually, Norman Lear does not have to be involved. We are willing to do the show with Jean Stapleton and Carroll O'Connor. We feel that the program can run without Rob Reiner and Sally Struthers. While Norman Lear is taking the position 'enough is enough,' we have a contract and think the program is important to CBS." But a spokeswoman for Norman Lear confirmed that "Lear has said that the series is finished. If O'Connor or Miss Stapleton return to the screen, it will have to be in other properties."

---

*Rob Reiner held a contract to star in and produce *Free Country* (which he and partner Phil Mishkin created) for ABC; and Sally Struthers signed with CBS to have a program created for her, while maintaining her interest in doing TV movies (among them *The Great Houdinis* in 1976 and *And Your Name Is Jonah* in 1979).

The Stivics and Bunkers, vintage 1977. Joey is played here by Jason Draeger.

In March 1978, Mike accepts an offer to teach in California. Archie, vehemently opposed, can't stop him. To make matters worse, George Jefferson sells his house out from under the Stivics, compelling them to move back with the Bunkers for the weeks preceding their departure.

The final episode of the season, a major tearjerker, has Mike declaring his affection for Archie, and Archie embarrassed by his own tender feelings for the Meathead. Archie tells Mike to take care of Gloria and Joey. Mike assures Archie that these are two things he'll never have to worry about. There's no escaping the authenticity of this goodbye.

Of the taping, Sally Struthers told *People,* "I feel the way you do after you'd been to a friend's funeral. The weeping has stopped, but you're not adjusted to the loss. I have to get used to not seeing these people who were my friends—my best friends—the last eight years...[Carroll O'Connor] saw me through an engagement, dates, boyfriends. He always disapproved of them because he thought none of them was good enough for me. Just like my own father would have." *People* added that Rob Reiner didn't cry on the set, but broke down on the freeway driving home; Norman Lear left the set to get sunglasses in order to cover his eyes; and the sobbing, sniffing, and rustling hankies of the studio audience recorded on the tape.

True to their dire warnings, Struthers and Reiner left the series at season's close, but *All in the Family* held its own. O'Connor and Stapleton agreed to come back. The show would keep its name. For the moment. In the weeks leading up to the Stivics' move, the end was fixed as not far off. The *New York Post* announced that "the final show has already been planned for next year. It will have Archie and Edith retiring from the bar and going off to California to join Mike and Gloria."

In June, newspapers carried the story that Carroll O'Connor's production company would develop five pilots for CBS, one of them a one-hour drama in which he would star should *All in the Family* fold its tent. But if *All in the Family* fared as in the past, and CBS asked him, he would stay with it because "I probably wouldn't play a better role as long as I live. There's no sense in walking out on that."

Also in June, precedent was shattered with the announcement that *All in the Family* would no longer be taped in front of a live audience. Now an episode could be done on a scene-by-scene basis, not necessarily in sequence, more the way movies are made. Economy was served. So were the people involved. Writers could rewrite at a saner pace than the previously allotted mad dash between 5:30 and 8:00 tapings. Actors wouldn't have to commit whole scripts to memory at one time. Nor would they have to strive for the tricky balance of playing simultaneously for the cameras and for a live audience—a maneuver which, some say, was responsible for the loudness with which dialogue sometimes seemed to be delivered. The idea was O'Connor's, as was a new shooting schedule—a four-day week rather than five.

Lear had always been partial to the element of playing for a live audience. But Lear, as *The Washington Post* reported in September 1978, "technically... has retired from television production and is off independently working on movie projects. 'I have not seen an episode of the show made this year,' Lear insists. 'I have not read a script. I'm into other things. In order to make the break complete, I didn't even call to say 'good luck' at the beginning of the season.' "

Lear's handpicked replacement, Alan Horn, later told *TV Guide,* "CBS had taken the position that, with or without Sally and Rob, the show was a fine ratings performer. It was Norman who felt it was a natural stopping place. Well, I didn't think so, and Norman deferred to me. *All* is the flagship of the fleet as far as I'm concerned." Horn added that the departure of Struthers and Reiner might lead to new directions for Edith: "Edith would grow in stature. She would now become capable of standing up to Archie. That alone would give us a new dimension."

In October 1978, *All in the Family* entered its ninth season, with 19 Emmys and a Peabody Award under its belt. Its future was still up for grabs. In December, Archie and Edith visit Mike and Gloria in California in the two-part "California Here We Are," but contrary to earlier prognostications, they aren't retired and they don't relocate. Yet, within a week and with the show ranking number one in the week's ratings, Jean Stapleton revealed that she didn't expect to do another season: "Nobody's coming back as far as I know. It's our last year. No one has even discussed our tenth year. If there is a discussion, I'm quite certain I wouldn't do another year." When Tandem was asked the same question, a spokes-woman answered that Stapleton wanted to quit the previous year and "so did Carroll O'Connor. Norman Lear swore last year would be the last year. Carroll and Jean were talked into one more year and I believe CBS will try to talk them into one more year again."

In December 1978, then-producer Milt Josefsberg re-marked, "When I came here in 1975 I was told it would be the last year. I've heard that every year since. Eventually, it's going to come to an end."

The season that began in the autumn of 1979 shook up several longtime favorite series: Gary Burghoff left *M*A*S*H*, Michael Learned returned to *The Waltons*, Mike Evans re-placed his erstwhile replacement, Damon Evans, on *The Jeffer-sons*, and Archie and Edith were back, but *All in the Family* was not. Their show, now called *Archie Bunker's Place*, involved Edith in occasional episodes only, had Stephanie sitting in for Mike and Gloria as the kid at home who keeps Archie hopping, and Murray Klein (Martin Balsam) joined the cast as

Martin Balsam (Murray Klein) becomes a co-owner of the bar in *Archie Bunker's Place*.

Archie's Jewish liberal intellectual partner at the bar. The theme song remained, but as an instrumental—no more Archie and Edith at the piano to sing the words.

Bronx-born Martin Balsam, a distinguished veteran of every form of the medium, came to the role with an Oscar (best supporting actor in *A Thousand Clowns*), a Tony (*You Know I Can't Hear You When the Water's Running*), an Obie (*Cold Storage*), a career comprising movie classics from *On the Waterfront* and *Twelve Angry Men* to *Psycho* and *Catch 22,* and a long list of TV credits going back to the home screen's earliest prestige dramas (among them *Actors Studio, Studio One,* and *Playhouse 90*) and nine months on the soap opera *Love of Life.*

Murray Klein comes aboard when Archie expands his operation to include short-order food service and former partner Harry disapproves of the plan. Archie's worst fear becomes his only salvation. Murray buys out Harry as part owner, much to Archie's dismay. Archie endeavors to talk Murray out of the purchase, explaining to him, "A Jew and a gentile don't have a Chinaman's chance."

As Archie's partner, Murray puts him on the spot in ways Mike never could; allows him to stew in his own juices; lets him flounder on the ropes; insists on showing Archie the light, in various metaphysical variations of locking him in a dark closet with only one match to strike. Far from sponging on Archie as Mike did, Murray controls a goodly number of purse strings, which to some degree control Archie. Where Mike, in effect, used to say "Do it my way," Murray smiles and says, "If you won't take my advice, try it your way and fail. And when you come crawling back, expect a few concessions to be in order."

With the expansion of Archie Bunker's Place, the place becomes less Archie's bunker than ever. Archie learns, perforce, to coexist and compromise—not just with Murray, but with his Puerto Rican kitchen help, Jose (Abraham Alvarez) and Raul (Joe Rosario), and with Veronica Rooney (Anne Meara), his sharp-tongued Irish Catholic cook.

Anne Meara, most famous as half the husband-and-wife comedy team of Stiller and Meara, includes scriptwriting and

Broadway and movie parts among her credits, as well as starring roles in TV's *The Corner Bar* (a forerunner of Archie's) and *Kate McShane* (a breakthrough prime-time drama featuring a woman lawyer in the lead). Veronica provides a principal source of friction in Archie's new life, along with her gay nephew whom she obliges Archie to hire. Meara gives a particularly touching performance in the episode concerning Veronica's bouts with a drinking problem.

Though deeply moving, Veronica's agony pales in any consideration of TV's cruelest traumas when compared with another from *Archie Bunker's Place*'s 1980–1981 season. The death knell first tolled in April of 1980, when Norman Lear announced that Edith would shortly die. Stapleton, feeling that the possibilities of the character had essentially exhausted themselves, and wishing very much to pursue other stage and screen vehicles, went on record as absolutely wanting out. From a story point of view, it made no sense to work plot after plot around an invisible off-camera Edith. On the other hand, a widower Archie would free script potential enormously.

The nation sent up a wail to the heavens well in advance. A Save Edith Bunker Committee emerged, issuing fervent pleas. Newspapers published eulogies and memorials. Jean Stapleton cautioned against disproportionate mourning: "It's like talking about something that really doesn't die. Edith still exists in the imagination...We must encourage people to realize that Edith doesn't die because she never really lived. You can't kill something that's an idea, can you?"

Someone suggested that as long as Edith was going to die, perhaps Jean Stapleton should appear on the show one last time—to expire. But mercy prevailed, and the decision was made not to be ghoulish. In her honor, Tandem Productions created a $500,000 Edith Bunker Memorial Fund to further the cause of the ERA and women's rights.

Five years earlier, when McLean Stevenson pulled out of *M*A*S*H*, producers Larry Gelbart and Gene Reynolds chose to write him a permanent exit. We last see his character, Colonel Henry Blake, ecstatic to be discharged and bound for home. Handshaking. Hugging. Kissing. Farewells. Then the episode ends, with the shocking news that his plane never made it. Henry Blake was shot down over the Sea of Japan. Many an audience member, outraged and bereft, charged that Henry really didn't have to die. But Gelbart and Reynolds had their reasons. *M*A*S*H* opposed the horrors of war. Surely needless death, no rarity for soldiers, heads the list of horrors. Nobody *has* to die in war. Plenty of people do.

When Edith dies in the autumn of 1980, no controversial issues weighed in the balance. Not death on the battlefield. Not the transvestite Beverly LaSalle being beaten to death ("Edith's Crisis of Faith"). Not Paul the Jewish activist being blown up in his car ("Archie Is Branded"). Not for the first time, crisis befalls Edith Bunker, and viewers' emotions are drained. But in this case, Edith isn't mourning, and Edith isn't a victim—unless to the exigencies of story development. She succumbs to a stroke in her sleep, leaving troubles behind. The victims are Archie and Stephanie, who hurt too much to acknowledge hurting at all.

Archie contemplates the bleak prospect of facing life without Edith.

The episode begins with the funeral long over. Stephanie wants to visit the cemetery. Archie ignores the reality, insisting that forgetting is the best way to get on with life. He won't sign the death claim on Edith's insurance. He sleeps on the sofa, complaining the mattress upstairs always made him squirm. Friends urge him to grieve. He refuses. Only in the last scene, when he happens on one of Edith's slippers, does Archie break down and give vent to his sorrow: "You had no right to leave me that way, Edith, without giving me just one more chance to say 'I love you.'"

The issue here, in no way controversial, is eloquent in its simplicity: Good people die in peace as in war. Loved ones must grieve before they can go on.

Recalls Danielle Brisebois, "Everyone was upset making that episode. Edith was part of the show, a definite part of all the characters, and she affected their lives. So in the show, we had to cry, and it came very naturally. It was an instant reaction—for everybody. After the show, Carroll came back to my dressing room and said that I'd done a really good job. That's always stuck with me. Everything Carroll told me, I remember and treasure. I couldn't have had a better teacher than Carroll."

In ensuing episodes, Archie's broken heart begins to heal. Stephanie's problems draw Archie into situations Edith's presence used to help him escape. Moreover, with Edith gone, and Gloria and Joey 3000 miles away, there is no one around but Stephanie for Archie to love, while Stephanie has not a soul in the world but Archie to love and be loved by.

Stephanie's wealthy Grandma Harris (Celeste Holm—Oscar winner for Best Supporting Actress in *Gentleman's Agreement,* and star of Broadway musicals ranging from *Oklahoma* to *The King and I*) occasionally shows up, telling Archie how to rear Stephanie, or trying to take her away by legal means. But the courts decide in favor of Archie as the most appropriate and loving legal guardian. Eventually and reluctantly, Ms. Harris admits that Stephanie's lucky to have him.

Just as Archie concentrates on Stephanie the love once spread out among three, he seems now to save for Barney

Hefner the abuse he once divided between Edith and Mike. Says Allan Melvin, "Barney grew, as a lot of characters did on the show, out of the doing of it. Experimenting, trying things. I'd been with the character on and off for years on *All in the Family*, then as a regular on *Archie Bunker's Place*, by which time there existed between Carroll and myself the sort of relationship that I imagine existed between Jackie Gleason and Art Carney. The kind of bantering, fairweather friend situation that existed between Kramden and Norton. One day Archie and Barney would be real buddies, then they'd have an argument and be at each other's throats. This was really the growth of Barney. Barney was the brunt of Archie's spleen. Archie would take everything out on Barney, and Barney would rebel occasionally."

Barney's expanding role and widening web of misadventures increasingly entangle Archie—when Barney falls off a barstool and plans to sue; when Barney's boarder (Don Rickles as a whining hypochondriac) dies mid-gripe; when Bar-

Don Rickles guest stars as Barney Hefner's whining boarder, on *Archie Bunker's Place*, 1982.

A new woman enters Archie's life in 1981: his eighteen-year-old niece Billie (Denise Miller), seen here with Stephanie Mills (Danielle Brisebois).

ney's engagement to a hooker-turned-waitress (Sheree North) leaves Archie pale. "Of course," sighs Melvin, "the wedding never comes off. It was a real tearjerker for Barney. He never quite scores. He's the lonesomest guy in town." And he runs up record-breaking tabs at Archie Bunker's Place.

Early on *Archie Bunker's Place,* Ellen Canby (Barbara Meek), a black housekeeper, joins Archie's household to give a hand with Stephanie. Archie has come a long, long distance since the 1971 day when the Jeffersons moved next door and he rebelled against blacks living in the neighborhood.

In May 1981, Archie's niece Billie Bunker moves in. Explains O'Connor, "There were too many older people on the show. We needed younger people to attract a younger audience. We tried getting girls into the bar, but that didn't work. We finally decided Archie should have a teenager living in his home." Denise Miller (formerly of Sears catalog modeling stints and the series *Fish*) and four other girls tested with

.

O'Connor for the part of the young charge into whose personal life Archie feels bound to intrude. Handpicked by O'Connor, Miller as Billie the liberal is soon hitting Archie on everything ranging from politics to sex to how to raise Stephanie, and defying him on general principle just to prove she won't be ordered around. When she starts dating Archie's accountant, Gary Rabinowitz, their relationship becomes the focus of several episodes. (The nephew of Archie's attorney Rabinowitz, Gary is played by former child star and recording star Barry Gordon).

Philosophically, it's business as usual at 704 Hauser. Psychologically, paralleling changes at the bar, business undergoes renovation. Not one liberal syllable exists that Archie has yet to hear spoken. But—just as Murray does at the bar—a

Archie gets into trouble with Reggie Jackson *twice*—**first, by having an accident, then by saying all the wrong things.**

new set of incentives prompt Archie to give a fairer listen.

As compared with *All in the Family*, the Archie of *Archie Bunker's Place* doesn't become a liberal, or even the "closet liberal" conservative critics start to call him. But he opens his mind to ideas kept out by "case closed" some years before, while he finds himself fighting other conclusions that used to be easy jumps. When Stephanie is cut from the softball team for being a girl, Archie confronts the coach demanding that she get equal rights. When bigots bomb her temple, Archie at first orders her to stop attending services—then relents, and joins the temple's committee to end the attacks. When he learns that Mr. Van Ranseleer refused during the McCarthy era to testify as to whether he was a Communist, Archie opts not to let it destroy their friendship. When rumors fly that Archie and Mrs. Canby are having an affair, it amazes him that people can be so quick to label what they don't understand. He even has the sensitivity to regret the delicacy of Mrs. Canby's position and to quit his lodge over their insult to her; the Archie of a decade ago might have fumed exclusively in self-defense. When Sammy Davis, Jr. returns to Queens to visit Archie's saloon, Davis sees how much Archie's intent has softened. Then Archie refuses a friendly kiss on the cheek— because this time, he wants to kiss Davis.

When Archie resumes dating, Katherine Logan (Yvonne Wilder)—originally Barney's lady through a computer dating service—particularly captures his fancy, with the feeling being entirely mutual. But she's Puerto Rican, which he hadn't realized, and he's more of a bigot than she ever dreamed. Archie first encounters Katherine's brother in his pub, takes one look and mistakes him for a numbers runner, then instructs him to hit the road. Katherine's family invites Archie over for dinner—cultured, educated people whom Archie desperately tries to please by, for instance, bringing a bottle of tequila and wishing them "bonus aires." He learns Katherine's father has retired from his job at a bank, assumes he worked as a security guard, and asks if he got to keep his uniform. When informed that the job had been vice-president, Archie presses with jovial camaraderie that obviously this all happened in Puerto Rico. No—comes the answer—it was Broad Street, Philadelphia.

Katherine's father calls Archie "thoroughly obtuse." Archie accepts it as a compliment. He hasn't a clue that these Puerto Ricans have thoroughly outclassed him. When they can't stand any more and instruct *him* to hit the road, he confides to Katherine that his "feelings are a little hurt." Later, Katherine appeals to Archie either to turn his brains around or kiss their relationship goodbye. Archie agrees to give it a whirl.

There is no whole new Archie on *Archie Bunker's Place*. After all, the same Archie Bunker who bungles the meeting with Katherine's family is the Archie who, in 1977, doesn't discover Stretch Cunningham is Jewish until the moment he walks into a room to deliver the eulogy ("Stretch Cunningham, Goodbye"), then proceeds to insult the mourners with his every inept effort to show respect.

Archie 1981, like Archie 1971, never means to hurt anybody. He is just innately scattershot in struggling to defend his own, two of whom, in 1982, fly home to roost. In September, Gloria and Joey (played here by Christopher Johnston) move in because the Meathead ran off to a commune with another woman. Archie prepares to set the clock back a few decades by supporting Gloria and her child. Gloria ultimately persuades him that she's got to become her own— as opposed to his own—person with her own place, her own job, and not accidentally, her own series. *Gloria* spins off as a short-lived story about Gloria, Joey (now Christian Jacobs), and her crusty old boss, veterinarian Dr. Willard Adams (Burgess Meredith). *Gloria* followed *Archie Bunker's Place* on Sunday nights, winning its time slot for a while, but didn't fare well enough to stave off cancellation.

In 1983, *Archie Bunker's Place* followed *Gloria*—into the out basket. O'Connor wrote in *TV Guide* that the call came the same day he paid his income tax, with Bud Grant, president of CBS Entertainment, venturing that O'Connor might say the decision was his should the end indeed be inevitable, and O'Connor (taking a leaf from Murray Klein) preferring that

CBS stew in its own juices: "Why invite blame—sour the friendship of a cast and staff who would have to find new jobs, not to mention a TV audience loyal enough after 13 seasons to keep *Archie* 26th in the standings?"

Norman Lear suggested a few new tacks to shake up viewers and restore the former cutting edge to the plots. In a glaring May-December liaison, Archie could take a much younger wife, then wrestle with guilt, embarrassment, insecurities, and the shock of his nieces and friends. Farther on, Mike could enter a handful of episodes.

Many a vein beckoned, untapped. But CBS tipped its hat and bid adieu. *Archie Bunker's Place* received its foreclosure notice, and O'Connor received a note from his agent—how about portraying Khrushchev in a miniseries?

Esquire later reported that the year CBS dropped *Archie Bunker's Place* (ranked twenty-sixth) and *Gloria* (ranked eighteenth), it renewed the shows *Alice* (forty-first) and *The Dukes of Hazzard* (thirty-fourth). The two lower-ranked shows, unlike Lear's, were supplied by Warner Brothers, at a time when former CBS Entertainment president Robert Daly happened to be Warner's chairman.

The Mary Tyler Moore Show ceased production, after seven successful seasons, in 1977. People choked back tears for weeks. In 1983, *M*A*S*H* scripted the end of the war at the close of season 11, the episode surpassing all antecedents to become the most-watched in TV history. *Archie Bunker's Place* went out not with a bang, but a whimper.

Danielle Brisebois advanced the wish that millions continue to echo: "They could have given us a better goodbye show. It was like a piece of chicken. They ate us up. Instead of cleaning the bone before they threw it out, they just threw it out with a lot of the meat still on it. *M*A*S*H* got a goodbye show. They should have given us one. I think we were as much of a landmark as *M*A*S*H.*"

There is, in every beginning, somewhere an end, and every idea potent enough to sway masses eventually has to stare back, part of history, at the very masses it swayed. Maybe Archie didn't change enough with the times. Maybe he did, too much. Or perhaps the times changed on Archie, who personally contributed to the change. Through the Seventies into the Eighties. From Richard Nixon's presidency to Ronald Reagan's. From the Love Generation to the Me Generation. Over 13 indelible seasons—those were the days.

Sticks and Stones

"I hate to hear talk about the show encouraging prejudice. Some people are always seeking justification for their attitudes and if they didn't find it in Archie, they'd find it somewhere else."
—Jean Stapleton

*A*ll *in the Family* opens at the piano, then out to bird's-eye overlooking Manhattan, then closing in, in, in to the Bunkers again. It concludes pulling out, out, out, back to bird's-eye. The camera, wordlessly eloquent, draws us into the microcosm from the cosmos. The image, instantly obvious, is that we are the family it's all in. The family it's in, and we're all in, is the family of man.

The theme song, nearer that of a Broadway musical comedy than a sitcom, has its words belted out on the air. (Though most sitcom themes have lyrics, you usually have to buy the sheet music to find out what they are.) Also more like

Broadway than television, the words are sung not by top-selling crooners, but by the characters themselves. The effect is one of establishing the characters by reflecting what's on their minds and hearts.

The song gives us them. The camera gives us us. Before an episode even begins, something valuable has been stated. The deceptively simple introduction sets the stage for what follows—a first in TV history—complex comedy plots.

Before *All in the Family*, a situation comedy traveled from square one to square one. Few things that developed in the course of an episode had any cumulative effect: A problem was either resolved in one show or blown to outrageous proportions, to be forgotten by next week. But *All in the Family* nurtured substance, subplots, and soap-opera continuity. Gloria suffers attempted rape in "Gloria the Victim." She reflects on the incident, years later, when Edith narrowly escapes an attacker in "Edith's 50th Birthday."

In another case of continuity, Archie wears the same suit to pay last respects to Cousin Liz in "Cousin Liz" that he wore to Stretch Cunningham's funeral. He discovers the yarmulke in his pocket.

Continuity lends texture when the cleaners used by the Bunkers are the Jeffersons, who buy a house in "Lionel Moves into the Neighborhood," and much later still, prosper enough to move away ("The Jeffersons Move Up"). In episodes interspersed between these, Archie's union goes out on strike ("The Bunkers and Inflation"), Archie becomes a nuisance at home ("Archie Underfoot"), driving Edith, out of necessity, to work for the Jeffersons in their cleaning shop ("Edith the Job Hunter") until Archie's union settles ("Archie's Raise"). When Mike can finally afford his own home with Gloria, the house they select is the one that belonged to the Jeffersons ("Mike Makes His Move"). George Jefferson makes it available to them on astoundingly attractive rental terms, in hopes of aggravating Archie.

Real people are like this. Events of their lives intertwine. *All in the Family* pioneered the most complex plots outside of *Masterpiece Theatre*, miniseries, and daytime soaps. (Evening soaps such as *Dallas* and *Dynasty* hadn't happened as early as 1971. Perhaps *All in the Family* paved the way for them, too.)

But forget equating complexity to complication. An inverse proportion operates here. The more real the people and their complexities—and the more interrelated their lives—the less convoluted the plots have to be. Far from straining and constraining, plot complexity becomes a liberating force. "Soft" comedy can be achieved, as opposed to "hard" with its spacemen, witches, or fellow humans of the sort described by Carroll O'Connor as creatures "whose mentality and behavior week to week remind us of nothing in the realm of our experience outside a sanitarium."

"Hard" comedy is frequently delightful, but not the only way for comedy to be done. "Situation" comedy, to which it is closely connected, is neither intrinsically wrong nor right. It is what it is: comedy derived from situation. The term, too freely applied to any structured TV comedy as opposed to a funny variety show, simply suggests fairly normal people reacting fairly normally to varied, often unusual, events. *The Adventures of Ozzie and Harriet* and *The Dick Van Dyke Show* offer such situations. Dave Nelson asks Ozzie's advice for a school editorial he's writing; Rob Petrie's son is embarrassed that his dad writes comedy for a living. Neither the incidents nor the characters' reactions to them depend on wackiness for their fun.

Neil Simon's theatrical (later, film) comedy *The Out of Towners* is pure situation. Substantial wackiness prevails. It's wonderful. But it's also not a broadcast situation comedy, to be sustained at the same frantic level week after week after week. When television seeks to sustain such frenzy, what we call sitcoms often incorporate another tradition of comedy entirely, the comedy of humours ("humours" meaning extremes of personality to the point of caricature). The form as practiced in the sixteenth century served up figures whose names were generic labels (e.g., Brainworm), and whose distinguishing motivational traits ranged from "sanguinity" to "bile" and "spleen." When television turned to the form, its figures included Lucy Ricardo (*I Love Lucy*) and Joan Stevens

(*I Married Joan*), whose character types come under the heading of deranged schizoid housewife.

Granted, Lucy's and Joan's situations varied from week to week. But their types dictated the stories; the plots were outgrowths of their types. Lucy's response to dipping chocolate in a factory, or trying to dance and sing at Ricky's club, is hilariously funny. But not fairly normal. Not very normal at all. The plots, while bizarre, are simple. Stuffing wet chocolate into your mouth and dress is no sophisticated maneuver. Once the audience gleans that Lucy equals zany, no further need for psychological setup remains.

All in the Family demands its setup. Lear had to insist on getting "all wet at once" in order to plunge into fleshing out the Bunkers and Stivics, and to liberate his plots away from dependence on burlesque story lines and unreal buffoons. Yes, Archie is a bigot. But no, Archie doesn't do bigot shtick. Were Archie a bigot the way Lucy is a housewife, he'd be grabbing a cross to burn on some lawn, then accidentally drop it on his foot, into Mike's face, into dinner—causing stew to fly up and onto his head—sending him backward into a mirror, which he would break, inviting seven years' bad luck. And Mike and Gloria would be brother and sister, and younger, so that Archie could step on a roller skate, sailing into the coat tree or the closet...

If anything, Carroll O'Connor complained when episodes seemed to sin in this direction. He favored human comedy with enough confidence in its integrity to steer clear of slapstick farce. A trained theatrical actor, O'Connor developed his Archie much as he might a towering figure of the drama. He built an Archie composite from nuances of movement and speech picked up hither and yon, from swagger to riveting stare to "youse people." Though O'Connor's voice is refined, with a touch of Brooklyn and the blarney, Archie's is closer to deese-dems-dose, in part influenced by a New York State supreme court judge whom O'Connor once heard speaking "exactly like Archie. His accent was pure Canarsie."

O'Connor's family background reflected advanced education: teachers and lawyers whose friends and partners included blacks and Jews, and a father who labeled talk like Archie's "the hallmark of ignorance." When O'Connor took on the Archie role, it was as an actor convinced of the worth of the project. Not because he *was* Archie—he wasn't—but because all around us, people were, and are, and a good actor faithfully reports people's emotions. "I don't have to share the feelings of my character to play them," he once said. "I'm not playing him to make people hate him or his attitude or to make them like him, either. I'm just playing his attitude as truthfully as I know how."

Peter Boyle, who played an Archie-like role as the title figure of the deadly serious 1970 movie *Joe* ("Forty-two percent of liberals are queer... the George Wallace people took a poll"), expressed sentiments that could apply to himself or O'Connor, Joe or Archie: "Let's cut out the two-bit Freud junk. First, playing someone you aren't is what acting is all about. Second, I can *understand* a guy like Joe. He's got every penny he ever saved sunk into his house, and a black family is moving in on the same block. He doesn't really hate Negroes, but he feels threatened... These days, you have to have money to be a liberal."

Archie Bunker need not be any more admirable than Stanley Kowalski (*A Streetcar Named Desire*) and Willy Loman (*Death of a Salesman*) to be real. But he must be impeccably rendered. Norman Lear, the directors and writers, and Carroll O'Connor made sure that he was. Raved Cecil Smith in the *Los Angeles Times,* "One of the wonders of the Western world is Carroll O'Connor playing Archie Bunker... one of the most meticulously made and exquisitely detailed performances that we've known in our time. His Bunker is as consummate a work of art as anything the County Museum boasts or that was buried with young King Tut."

Jean Stapleton, also stage-trained, turned in an equally staggering Edith. Her own voice modulated and precise, she managed for Mrs. Bunker a sort of spoken caterwaul. But Edith's persona follows Stapleton to the footlights only by choice—as during a summer-stock performance of *Hello, Dolly,* in which she stopped the show with an ad-lib during the title song: "Wow, wow, wow, fellas. Look at the dingbat now, fellas."

The fundamentally theatrical discipline of O'Connor and Stapleton—shared by a steady stream of others over *All in the Family*'s history—fits the set as much as the Bunkers fit their house. The rooms tend toward a Broadway real. With its stagecraft more in tune with a play than, for instance, the Stone (*The Donna Reed Show*) or Douglas (*My Three Sons*) dwellings, a sense of theater permeates *All in the Family*'s scenes. Donna Stone (Donna Reed) and Steve Douglas (Fred MacMurray) aren't not real, but neither are they towering figures. They belong in TV kitchens. Archie and Edith keep company with Hamlet, Falstaff, and Hedda Gabler.

What is made palpably clear by the noblest works of the theater is the absolute need for great characters, because through their being, mere words and broad issues take on the dimensions of life. Drama depends—in a nutshell—on the degrees to which people can hurt one another. The more real the characters, the more powerfully they project heart and soul of their crises, and the better we understand them.

Before *All in the Family*, moral questions comfortably found their place in TV sitcoms, but only when readily answered by unwavering moral law: don't cheat on exams; don't lie to your parents; don't wreck a street light to prove you're a whiz with a slingshot. Matters of politics, religion, and race—to which there are sides, facets, factions, and doubts—rarely arose, primarily because they were controversial, and to some minds, lacking in taste; but not incidentally, because few if any characters existed who were strong enough to address them. Real issues, like real people, are complex, and serious subjects dare not be treated too simply for fear the subjects themselves might seem trivialized or diminished. Therefore, Lucy never did a menopause episode; Wally Cleaver never grappled with impotence; and the biggest danger on the Stones' block on *The Donna Reed Show* was the Mitchell kid, Dennis the Menace.

In 1971, *All in the Family* leapt into sitcom's vast untapped unknown. With its character complexities, theatrical design, and overall high quality, it entered the fray uniquely

> **"**My real media heroes are producers, like David Wolper (*Roots*) and Norman Lear (*All in the Family*), who focus TV's enormous power on real problems....**"**
> —Betty Friedan, 1984, *Parade Magazine*

equipped. This time, Dad was no paragon of ethical conduct; Mom was no princess in pearls; the house was no picket-fence fantasy; and problems gnawed away unresolved. Shunning as material the age-old dilemma of what to do when the roast burns and the boss is coming for dinner, Lear plunged headlong into "subjects that matter and people worth caring about." The more serious the conflicts, he reasoned, the funnier the result: "My critics don't seem to understand that great humor always comes out of great pain. The shows I produce—like life itself—are tragicomedy."

As never before, a sitcom reflected the headlines: a swastika painted in error on Archie's door; a Jewish activist blown up in his car; a transvestite beaten to death; political demonstrations; surveillance and the invasion of privacy; women's lib; gay rights; handguns; the KKK. Personal trauma came to the center stage: breast cancer, rape, infidelity, drug addiction.

Treating the subjects not *as* jokes, yet with sympathetic good humor, *All in the Family* "took the audience and put it on the air," wrote Kenneth Turan in *TV Guide;* "changed the face of comedy forever...with a depth never seen before in any television series" said television historians Joel Eisner and David Krinsky; and "the tempests in the Bunker teapot" became, according to Don Shirley in *The Washington Post*, "America's most commonly shared artistic phenomenon."

Schools asked for study guides. Psychologists guided studies. Real-life drama took to comedy like chocolate to peanut butter—then pounced out of friendly TV tubes right back into real life again. In mirroring issues, *All in the Family* became one. Armies formed from left and right, taking positions along such battle lines as these:

A sitcom that's all sit and no com?

One objection ran that ugliness can exist without comedy trying to find it; that in fact the business of comedy is to make it go away. Proponents drawn to this camp questioned: "How much can people hurt one another? Ask Norman Lear. He's the pro." Bill Cosby, for instance, compared Bunker to a "junkie shooting up," something neither funny nor fun to watch. To Lucille Ball, the parallel more resembled the Colos-seum: "Years ago, the Romans let humans be eaten by lions, while they laughed and drank—that was entertainment. But I'm tired of the ugly."

Yet the other side answered that reality demands ac-knowledging ugliness, yowls and all. Our antagonists and tragedies don't require permission to be admitted into our lives. The Bunkers don't go looking for issues. Rather, issues find them. The Bunkers don't initiate; they react. Wrote Kenneth M. Pierce, "Archie Bunker is a bigot, it is said. Well,

Sound and Fury

Addressing another aspect of the ugly for an article in *TV Guide*, Max J. Friedman measured *All in the Family*'s decibel peak at 61 (experts consider 55 com-fortable; an outboard motor registers 90, a subway 100, a pneumatic hammer 120). This level occurred six times in the episode rated.

Iago was a murderer, but no one blames Shakespeare's *Othello* for that."

A breakthrough, or a throwback?

Nobody blames Shakespeare—claimed opponents—because Shakespeare clearly presented *Othello* as a tragedy, not a minstrel show. But to restore to the airwaves an insensitivity seemingly purged in the Sixties, to them bode ill for the future of sensitivity in general: Label your viewpoint any upbeat new motive you want, derision will still be derision. Wrote John P. Rocke in *The Washington Post*, "Let's not get so carried away with the new quest for ethnic authenticity that we accept a tasteless, low comedy like *All in the Family* as symbolic of the 'higher tolerance.'" Arnie Rosen, whose TV writing and producing credits ranged from *The Honeymooners* in the Fifties to *Get Smart* in the Sixties to *The Carol Burnett Show* in the Seventies, expressed concern that *All in the Family* had started "the same vicious cycle [of shows like *Amos 'n' Andy* and *Abie's Irish Rose*] all over again."

From the opposite ranks, in 1973 the American Civil Liberties Union bestowed on Norman Lear the Freedom of Press Award, singling out *All in the Family* as a TV "break-through...in terms of presenting life as it really is. In attacking controversial subject matters, in dramatizing the attitudes of the far right as well as the left, and doing this in terms of warm human comedy and drama, *All in the Family* has opened wide the boundaries of the small screen. It literally caused all television to take a hard look at itself and to commence updating the contents of other shows." Flip Wilson admired the program both on these grounds and artistically: "I like it because it's different. It's a pioneer show that opened the door for *Sanford and Son* and other series. Sure, I'm sorry the subject has to be prejudices, but they do exist and I look at the program from the standpoint of a comedian and artist."

If you laugh at something, it's a joke.

According to another argument, people can't be serious about anything they laugh at. Once they've laughed at a racial slur, they figure it's a funny word to use conversationally.

Said J. Fred MacDonald in *Blacks & Whites: Afro-Americans in Television Since 1948*, "If the wide approval of Flip Wilson and his self-deprecating style of comedy suggested the acceptability of exploitive racial humor, the programs created by Norman Lear and Bud Yorkin turned this suggestion into an industry." Stated Benjamin Epstein, national director of the Anti-Defamation League of B'nai B'rith, "We do not believe that it is possible to combat bigotry by laughing at a central bigoted figure who evokes the sympathy of the audience. We feel the show sanctions the use of derogatory epithets. When the program is over the listener has had a good time and he has enjoyed the bigotry of Archie rather than feeling a sense of revulsion." Rabbi Arthur J. Lelyveld, president of the American Jewish Congress, wrote that "it is teaching our children disrespect: disrespect for Archie and Edith Bunker, disrespect for blacks and Jews and Italians and people of Polish and other ethnic origins, disrespect for minorities and, essentially, disrespect for all of us: disrespect for man."

Went the counterargument: *All in the Family* laughs not at the words, but at the people who use them. Carroll O'Connor, on various occasions, noted that "most viewers realize Archie Bunker is a bigot. They're not really laughing with him but at him." "Black people can't like him but many like to watch him. It's the first time ever that they've been able to see a real white bigot—a lower-middle-class man who is their arch foe—

> 66 I've lived in the ghettos. I was brought up in the slums. You cannot tell me that a black hears the words 'nigger' or 'spade' for the first time from someone who's just watched Archie Bunker. 99
> —Michael Ross, 1974, quoted in *The New York Times*

in all his glory," and minorities seeing this can say, "What the hell have I got to be afraid of?"

Said Rick Mitz in *The Great TV Sitcoms,* "*All in the Family* gave us permission to laugh, which took some of the pressure off." Observed Roger Rosenblatt, reviewing *All in the Family* in *The New Republic,* "to make a joke of something is to kill it."

Can we talk?

Some argued that *All in the Family* opened Pandora's box: Subjecting these issues to public airing is no more than publicly picking scabs, letting old wounds fester all over again. But those favoring *All in the Family* applauded its "decontamination" of topics once thought too painful to discuss. They further felt that it challenged folks to quit hiding and take a stand.

In a sermon preached to the First United Methodist Church of North Hollywood in 1972, and later entered into the Congressional Record's Extension of Remarks, Dr. Kermit L. Long cautioned, "if we are wise at all, we will also be cognizant of the fact that the world, too, prepares the agenda for the church. Thus I have chosen to speak on *Jesus Christ and Archie Bunkerism* ... Some of us think there is more Christian gospel being preached from that program than from many churches and temples—if we get the message ... All of us have a mission, whether we stand in the pulpit, produce an *All in the Family* show, teach school, go to the office, go to the farm, or go to the plant. We all have the mission to bury bigotry once and for all. If you are not in the business of burying bigotry I don't give a hoot what you do, you are not doing what God is calling you to do in our time." Indeed, the age-old message of the sermon introduced no new concepts. But in using *All in the Family* as his vehicle, Dr. Long drew attention to the contemporary immediacy of his talk.

Revealed Senator Sam Ervin to Lear during a congressional hearing, "I will have to confess that I always enjoyed watching *All in the Family* because I think it presents so well and in such a dramatic fashion some of us people ... I think most people would rather talk about a controversial issue.

> 66 Bunker's and Stivic's analyses of President Nixon's actions in the Watergate affair, as far as I'm concerned, more than compensate for the removal of analysis by CBS elsewhere in its schedule. 99
> —Marvin Kitman, 1973, in *Newsday*

"I will have to state that the few times I saw it, I was astounded by some of the subjects you dealt with, because the discussion of those subjects has been taboo. However, they were presented with such a wonderful amount of humor that I think it is one of the great public services, not only in amusement, but also in the themes that you deal with— themes that concern us all."

Why are liberals always right?

Perhaps the most widely voiced bone of contention asked why, if *we* can talk, are *they* the only ones being heard? Such objections, in ongoing salvos, took the form not only of newspaper pieces, but of phone calls, letter-writing campaigns, and actions by special interest groups. Stop Immorality on TV awarded Norman Lear their Shield of Shame. Morality in Media urged followers to write to the networks, to Tandem, and to Congress. They felt Lear had far too large a podium to express essentially one-sided ideas. In 1977, the Church of God polled its million members to prepare a list of the shows "most offensive" in their portrayal of violence, sex, degradation, and the like. *Maude* nosed out *Soap* for the number one slot. *All in the Family* placed third. The group urged followers to boycott the shows and their sponsors' products. Commented *New York Daily News* TV critic Kay Gardella, "In a medium in which time is a premium, the Norman Lear-produced *All in the Family* is the greatest luxury item of all. Imagine having a 30-minute weekly comedy show to put over your political views..."

Conservatives, in the eyes of conservatives, came off on the show as crude, primitive, know-nothing fools. Their beliefs were presented as "intrinsically loony, prejudiced and anti-intellectual," argued William F. Buckley, Jr. Readers wrote to Kay Gardella that "the show is an arrogant affront to anyone who is not liberal." Why is Bunker the only have-not type treated to all-out abuse? asked Richard Adler in *Television as a Social Force.* "Who exploits Archie's bad taste for profit in TV? Who but Ivy grads, prepared for plunder by Scarsdale High SATs...? Are they really incapable, the lads, of grasping that their education costs five to ten times as much as his?" Al Capp lamented the show's one-sidedness by nailing the shoe on the other foot and suggesting a formula for "the left-wing Archie Bunker: The left-wing bigot refuses to go along with the government because it was the choice of the wrong people ...[His] purpose in life is to get a job on some human rights or fair practices commission—that pays him to poke his nose into the lives of people like Archie Bunker."

On the other extreme, but still opposed, stood Marxists disgruntled that Archie put workers in such a bad light. There he was, a conservative oppressor, instead of leading the revolution. Workers themselves had mixed feelings, from loving the show to despising it. An open letter to presidential candidates in the Teamster newsletter *Focus* (1972) assailed the show for characterizing American workers as bigots and slobs. Said Bob Kasen, editor of *Focus,* "The average worker is no dingbat...Maligned in public, he knows he's being made fun of by the so-called opinion-makers." In the same year, Vernon E. Jordan, Jr., executive director of the National Urban League, told the 16th Constitutional Convention of the United Steelworkers of America, "The Archie Bunkerization of the American working man is a myth fed by the media, by the enemies of both working people and black people, and by those who would roll the clock back to the good old days when blacks knew their place and unions weren't recognized...And to the degree that the general public is convinced that labor is selfish and bigoted, the labor movement will lose the moral standing and public goodwill it needs to succeed in its aims."

Yet *All in the Family* focused sufficient attention on the workers' plight that a phenomenon arose, not novel in itself but suddenly called "The Archie Bunker Vote." From the Honorable Michael Harrington (Massachusetts) of the House of Representatives came these words confirming the focus: "One healthy result of the Democratic primary elections has been that many of our commentators have rediscovered American working men and women, and their problems. It is ironic that it should have taken some of our national opinion leaders so long to recognize the very serious problems that beset those who work for a living in the United States...And the wholly one-sided and unfair manner in which the economic stabilization program has been administered has added even further to the worker's burdens...Symptomatic of this is the use of the Archie Bunker stereotype to describe those workers genuinely outraged—as they should be..."

Commenting on this development in *The Washington Post,* William S. White noted George McGovern's reaction to attacks on George Wallace. McGovern, liberal, said of Wallace's supporters, conservative, "It is not prejudice to fear for one's family or to resent tax inequities." Added White, "The senator now correctly sees Wallace as a symbol of frustrations going far beyond any race. Such a symbol, too, is Archie Bunker."

By the spring of 1972 (repeated in 1976), the nation witnessed an outbreak of bumper stickers, T-shirts, beer mugs, posters, and political buttons touting "Archie Bunker for President." "Archie Bunker Campaign Headquarters" popped up in stores like Montgomery Ward & Co. In the summer of 1972, Archie received a vote for the vice-presidency at the Democratic Convention. Partisans shared the views not of Bunker's creators, but of Bunker, and had no qualms about associating themselves with the image. They— as much as their liberal counterparts who'd vote for the likes of Pat Paulsen—"debased the electoral procedure" in the eyes of the *New York Post*'s Harriet Van Horne: "A few cranks and nuts will always waste their votes on self-seeking eccentrics."

Artifacts from Archie Bunker's 1972 "presidential campaign."

Neither Norman Lear nor Carroll O'Connor had sought any such conservative leadership. By no stretch of the imagination did they embrace it. *All in the Family* set out to present an essentially liberal viewpoint, with a conservative character who is generally wrong and a liberal character who is generally right *in their perceptions*. But Archie is accorded considerable sympathy, and Mike, certain scorn, for the way they've come by their philosophies. Droves of critics pointed out this particular reality as if to humble Norman Lear: "Ah ha! You don't even know who your own bad guys and good guys are." But Lear knew. He had to. He made them that way in the first place.

True, he did not grant both sides equal support; both sides were heard from, but not by virtue of equally cogent arguments. Despite numerous opponents rallying to the press, to the airwaves, and to Archie Bunker as a conservative figurehead, Lear undoubtedly had an edge, which reflected Lear's own leftist feelings. But the same can be said of a right-wing Al Capp cartoon. It is one's own feelings which one tends to express. To Lear's credit, he offered a measure of balance, but he never claimed to be fully impartial. He never asked to be mistaken for John Wayne.

Only bigots and hypocrites would call a spade a spade.

Some held that Lear asked to be mistaken for a liberal, but that all he really wanted to do under the guise of "freedom of speech" was exploit the right to be obscene. According to a 1976 editorial in *Advertising Age,* "Mr. Lear's shows tend more than others to rely on sophomoric seduction scenes, lots of talk-talk-talk about sex-sex-sex, the low humor of a drunk-with-fly-open, of a young lady stuffing her sweater with tissue paper, or another soon-to-wed lady telling all within earshot that she is two months' pregnant...[i.e.] a book of dirty jokes."

Observed Thomas Berger, in *The TV Guided American,* "with Archie Bunker we get a double payoff, so to speak. We are able to enjoy the ethnic humor, in one sense, and condemn it in another...The point is that we can get the forbidden pleasure of aggression against ethnic groups and the pleasure of aggression against the aggressor, and so get twice as much pleasure for our money—or time spent—and we come out smelling like the proverbial rose."

It's an excuse, not reality, charged many. Among them, Philip Wander described it in *The Journal of Popular Culture* as "A few statistics, a little righteous indignation, but no bodies, no malnutrition, no spittle dribbling down the chin of someone making a meal out of a can of cat food." A *Daily Variety* reviewer, in 1972, lamented that "they have softened the punch, taken away most of the sting, mellowed Archie," to which director John Rich replied, "If you stayed on racial themes every week, then it would be boring. Even a racist doesn't talk race all day long."

In direct contradiction of groups condemning any comedic use of the ugly, these dissenters worried that *All in the Family* wasn't ugly enough.

Leading their ranks, Laura Z. Hobson vented her misgivings in "As I Listened to Archie Say 'Hebe...,'" a lengthy piece (Lear called it a "novella") in the September 12, 1971

Sunday *New York Times*. Herself a pioneer in the battle of art versus prejudice—Hobson's courageous novels ranged from *Gentleman's Agreement* (about anti-Semitism) to *Consenting Adults* (about homosexuality)—she complained that *All in the Family's* bigotry wasn't harsh enough. Noting the use of *spade, coon, Hebe,* and *Polack,* Hobson found in the absence of *kike, sheeny,* and *nigger* a dishonesty that softened the threat of prejudice. She wondered whether if, consciously or unconsciously, the producer and network had rendered bigotry more acceptable by deodorizing it, and whether poorly educated viewers would know enough to see the error in, and feel superior to, Archie's basic shortcomings.

In researching the article, she contacted heads of major civil-rights organizations, read voluminous clippings, watched *All in the Family* with pen in hand, and attempted to reach Norman Lear by phone. He did not take her call because, as she reported in the *Times,* his public relations office invited her to California where Lear would run tapes "and spend all the time you might want in a personal interview about *All in the Family,* but he feels that this is too sensitive a subject to discuss on the phone."

Deciding that she had only wanted an answer to the one question—concerning the use of *sheeny, nigger,* and *kike*— Hobson declined the offer, which she construed as a subtle refusal to talk. Lear, unable to meet her on his turf, brought his case to her. His response, "As I Read How Laura Saw Archie...," appeared in the October 10, 1971 Sunday *New York Times*. In it, he asserted that *Hebe* isn't all so soft a dig to the man on its receiving end, which end he knew intimately. As to *sheeny, kike,* and *nigger,* Archie didn't use the words because they connote hate, and Archie doesn't hate; he fears. As to why Archie isn't a pillar of evil, most bigots aren't, and when they are, we know enough to recognize the danger. Perhaps—noted Lear—Ms. Hobson's idea of a bigot was someone who spat on minorities or raped them, but Lear insisted bigots came in degrees. If Hobson hadn't noticed the variations, "We are obviously aging in different wine cellars." Quoting Mrs. Fay Love of the Lutheran-affiliated social-service agency for children and families in Harrisburg, Pennsylvania, Lear underscored the value of depicting "a lovable bigot who helps us all to laugh at ourselves and view our own behavior with new insights."

Regarding the educational level of the audience and its ability to discern themselves in Archie, Lear had more faith in them than in Laura Z. Hobson. He questioned whether, in fact, her article had betrayed a certain prejudice against noncollege grads.

Bigotry is in the eye of the beholder.

Both Bill Cosby and Lucille Ball commented that Archie's hand could have been slapped more often and more obviously. Said Ball, "It's good to bring prejudice out in the open. People do think that way, but why glorify it? Those not necessarily young may not catch the moral. That show doesn't go full circle for me. You have to suffer a little when you do wrong. That prejudiced character doesn't pay penance. Does he ever reverse a feeling? I'm for believability, but I'm tired of hearing *pig, wop, Polack* said unkindly. Me, I have to have an on-the-nose moral."

Remarked Cosby, "Some watch the show and love Archie because they think he's right...Names have a tendency to stay. Names like *kike, nigger,* and the rest of them never seem to die. Archie says them in his home where in his mind it's safe. I guess what I dislike most about him is he never says what he does is wrong."

According to a *Variety* piece in 1972, "Depending upon who's watching, it can make prejudice look silly or justify it, or it can serve as a lightning rod for the overt hostility of some and the repressed anger of others." Wrote Robert Lewis Shayon, also in 1972, in *Saturday Review,* "*All in the Family* is America's barricades of the air. Every Saturday night the polarized armies in the audience clash on the program's battlefield, opposing their prejudices and hostilities, and coming away not a whit persuaded by the other side. The Silent Majority roots for Archie, the liberals for all those who oppose him."

Observations being one thing and cold facts quite another, studies were launched to determine who actually came
away from the show thinking what. In 1971, the *Philadelphia
Inquirer* asked of readers whether Archie reflected the mindset of the average blue-collar American. Over 61 percent said
he did. A 1977 report by the U. S. Civil Rights Commission,
entitled "Window Dressing on the Set: Women and Minorities in Television" determined that Edith Bunker "scoots into
the kitchen to fetch Archie a beer and rarely fails to have
dinner on the table by 6 P.M.," thereby providing an unaccepta-
ble stereotype. Said a coal miner, quoted by researchers,
"What I like about Archie is that he has his own chair. And
nobody can sit in it but him." Another diehard fan confided,
in the third year of *All in the Family*, "I don't like it anymore,
now that they're starting to make Archie look ridiculous."

1976 studies in Holland, where *All in the Family* enjoyed
enormous popularity when broadcast in prime time with
subtitles, found an "overwhelming majority" convinced that
Mike won out in quarrels with Archie. Respondents favoring
Archie, not coincidentally, supported strong parental author-
itarianism at home.

"Archie Bunker's Bigotry: A Study in Selective Perception and Exposure," presented by Neil Vidmar and Milton
Rokeach in 1974, examined some 400 adolescents in the
United States and Canada. Among the revelations: Of those
reporting that the show gave them insights into some of their
own prejudices (20 percent of the sampling), "55 percent
were low prejudice viewers and 80 percent were infrequent
watchers of the program." The authors posited three interpre-
tations, ranging from "the more frequently persons watch the
program, the less insightful they become about prejudice," to
"infrequent and low prejudiced viewers are more likely to be
persons who look for and/or report self-insights into prejudice." (They inclined toward the second possibility.) It further
seemed that high-prejudice adolescents favored Archie, and
disliked aspects of Mike, while low-prejudiced students had
the reverse response. Ten percent of U. S. respondents and 32
percent of Canadian saw Archie as the main character most

> **❝** Archie makes statements so ridiculous that nobody but a real bigot would go along with them. **❞**
> —Bernie West, 1974, quoted in
> *The New York Times*

often ridiculed; 46 percent of U.S. and 10 percent of Canadian believed Mike was; 35 percent of U.S. and 43 percent of Canadian found "nothing wrong" with Archie referring to members of minority groups as *colored, coons,* and *chinks.*

Ten years later, a Harris poll sought an element of correlation between people's politics and their favorite shows. The poll concluded that, for both Republicans and Democrats, the favorite TV show was *M*A*S*H,* followed, among Republicans, by *Dynasty, Star Trek, Hill Street Blues, Dallas, 60 Minutes, Magnum, P.I., Three's Company,* and *All in the Family;* and among Democrats, by *Dallas, Dynasty, Hill Street Blues, The Jeffersons, Star Trek, 60 Minutes, Knots Landing,* and *The A-Team.* In others words, Republicans—presumably the viewers more easily offended by the politics of *All in the Family*—watched it more than Democrats did, despite being its political kinsmen.

Thanks to over a decade of studies and statistics, we now know that we're still surprised by results of studies and statistics. *All in the Family* exerted monumental influence in terms of changing its medium. In terms of changing minds, perhaps it reinforced many more philosophies than it modified. In the Vidmar/Rokeach study, as indeed across the board, some people apparently got new handles on their old ideas from watching *All in the Family,* some had insights into mindsets alien to their own, and others saw precisely what they would have seen regardless of what actually cropped up on the tube.

The dictionary defines *influence* as "the act or the power of producing an effect without apparent force or direct authority." By inviting people to feel and to think, *All in the Family* produced a degree of its desired effect, along with responses it never desired.

When Don Shirley asked, in the Style section of *The Washington Post* in 1973, "What does it mean—the public thirst for the Bunkers and all the previously forbidden topics they discuss?" Rob Reiner answered, "It's doing nothing to change America."

Responding to the same line of questioning for *Playboy*, in 1972, Norman Lear said, "How much could I expect to happen from my silly little half-hour television show, when the entire Judeo-Christian ethic for some 2,000 years hasn't budged in the area of race relations? I don't think there's much impact."

Carroll O'Connor, lifelong Irish Democrat who has supported the American Civil Liberties Union, the Neighbors of Watts, Eugene McCarthy, and Edward Kennedy, and who in 1972 filmed a commercial for New York's Mayor Lindsay (asking that voters listen to him as an "old fashioned" American who believes in national security but not illegal, undeclared wars), surely derived clout from his portrayal of Archie Bunker. But as to the series exerting Pavlovian control for good or ill, *The Christian Science Monitor* in 1974 reported him unconvinced: "Borderline bigots pushed over the edge by *All in the Family*? That's a lot of baloney. I've been on college campuses—I have my M.A., you know—and a lot of academics are hairbrains who dream up issues. And who cares? I don't know what effect the show has had. Many people say good. A few bad. I don't know how to assess these judgments at all. It's more likely that the show hasn't had much of any kind of effect. I would guess not one way or the other."

For all of *All in the Family*'s unprecedented popularity— as when one-fifth of Americans viewed an average episode during the 1974–1975 season*—its influence outside of its

---

*In the spring of 1974, *All in the Family* ranked number one in evening TV programs, but *The Waltons*—a wholly dissimilar family offering, with decidedly different appeal—resided comfortably in slot number two.

own field remains something of a question mark. Concluded Philip Wander in 1975, *All in the Family* "may function as a giant ink blot in the media allowing us to read into the drama what we will."

So perhaps *influence* is the wrong word, and the question is one of impressions left behind. Edith would liken them to *Reader's Digest*'s "My Most Unforgettable Character." Images linger that stay with us always. Real people do this to us, without ever winning a public election, or walking off with the Nobel Prize for Peace.

This is how it happens that *All in the Family*, as the most popular program in Kuala Lumpur, elicits one Malaysian woman's observation, "Those white people are no different from us," and another's smiling comment, "If that's what America is all about, then I like it."

It is how Jean Stapleton can receive a letter in which "One woman wrote to me that her most glorious moment came when her husband started swearing while doing some work in the yard. He suddenly stopped. 'Good grief,' he said, 'I sound just like that ass on TV.'"

It is why Archie's chair, Edith's chair, and Archie's beer can occupy a place of honor on display at the Smithsonian Institution in Washington, D.C., as much a part of our national heritage as Abe Lincoln's stovepipe hat and George Washington's wooden teeth.

Ad appearing in *The New York Times*, April 29, 1972. The merchandise, long ago discontinued, is highly collectible today.

Knowing the Family

Any topical program runs the danger of becoming quickly dated. *All in the Family* for the most part escaped that fate. So strong is the story, so real are the people, that the episodes work even when occasional references elude the audience. Even so, *All in the Family* was designed to work with, rather than in spite of them, for which reason the following reminders are provided, particularly for the readers to whom the Nixon era and John Wayne were a long time ago.

Included too are salient small details that make up the characters' lives: Edith's cousins, Archie's boners, and the thoughts dropped in passing that contributed inestimably to fleshing out all of the family.

AB-negative: A handy description of *Archie Bunker's* approach to life, but also, his uncommon blood type in "Archie's Operation," part one.

American grafilthy: What Archie calls the obscene graffiti written on the walls of Stephanie's school in "Stephanie and the Crime Wave."

Applebaum, Wilson: Edith gives him as an example of a child who, as a result of premature toilet training, used to slide into the pot, then grew up to be a gambler ("Archie's Brief Encounter," part one).

Aquarius: Mike's sign according to "Archie's Civil Rights."

"Archie Bunker's Bicentennial Minute": When Archie praises the Statue of Liberty for its message and the nation for letting people come over to live in their own neighborhoods which outsiders don't dare enter, Mike refers to the oration as "Archie Bunker's Bicentennial Minute" ("Mike's Move"). The mid-Seventies Bicentennial Minutes were presented by CBS each night at the end of the first prime time show, and each related an incident from America's past that had occurred two hundred years earlier to the day. Charlton Heston presented the first. Others included Beatrice Arthur reading from the writings of John Adams (New Yorkers "pay no attention to each other, they talk very loudly, very fast, and all at the same time") and Jean Stapleton quoting Martha Washington on the storage of cherries ("then set them under a feather bed where one lays continually, for the warmer they are kept the better").

As the World Turns: According to what she tells loan officer Gordon Faraday in "Edith Versus the Bank," it's Edith's favorite soap opera.

Ass: What Archie threatens that God can turn Edith's jawbone into for standing in the way when Archie wants to kidnap Joey for the purpose of baptism, in "Joey's Baptism." This is Archie's perception of the Biblical story of Samson, supernaturally powerful man of God who slew some thousand Philistines with the jawbone of an ass.

Aunt Gertrude: Edith's "klepper" (kleptomaniac) aunt ("Edith Flips Her Wig").

Blockbusting: The practice of buying into a white neighborhood, at top dollar if necessary, and moving a black family into the home. With this, other residents panic and sell their homes for next to nothing. In "The Blockbuster," Archie nearly succumbs to a blockbusting realtor named Mr. Byrd.

"Blue Moon": 1934 Richard Rodgers and Lorenz Hart tune which, according to Edith in "Archie the Gambler," is the first song she and Archie danced to.

Boom-Boom: Mildred "Boom-Boom" Turner (Gloria LeRoy) works at the plant and sometimes doubles as a waitress at Archie's Place. Called Boom-Boom because, in Archie's words, she wears a steel-belted-radial brassiere. When Archie disappears on his way to a lodge convention in Buffalo, Mike suspects that he's run away with Boom-Boom.

Boomboom: What Edith calls what Archie calls number two in such episodes as "The Unemployment Story," part one.

Bracken, Peg: Author of such Sixties bestsellers as *The I Hate to Cook Book*, and in many ways an Erma Bombeck forerunner, Bracken is cited by Edith in "Archie's Aching Back." Archie complains that the meat isn't cooked enough. Edith says Bracken suggests meat is better when not well done. Archie retorts that Bracken "don't even like to cook."

Brief Encounter: Its title echoed in the title of the three-part "Archie's Brief Encounter," this bittersweet 1945 British film classic concerns two married people who meet at a train station café, become intensely involved, but must part to return to their own lives.

Bunkersville: What George Jefferson calls his Hauser Street neighborhood the day he moves to East Side Manhattan in "The Jeffersons Move Up."

California: According to Archie in various episodes, it's the land of fruits and nuts, and a bad place to be buried because of the earthquakes. The earthquakes, by the way, he believes to be St. Andrew's Fault. Archie would not be surprised by the

Cartoon Voices

Among members of Archie's gang who have done cartoon voices elsewhere on the tube are Allan Melvin as Drooper the lion on *Banana Splits* and Sally Struthers as the voice of Pebbles on *The Flintstones.*

1987 government survey which showed that one in three California men is arrested at least once before the age of thirty.

Chicago World's Fair spoon: What Archie eats his cereal with in several episodes.

Chisholm, Shirley (Shirley Anita St. Hill Chisholm): First black woman to serve in the U.S. House of Representatives (Democrat, N.Y., 1969–1983). In "Henry's Farewell," Louise quotes her as saying that she ran into more discrimination for being a woman than for being black.

Cleavage, Elder: In "Henry's Farewell" and elsewhere, Archie's rendition of the name of black leader, activist, and author Eldridge Cleaver.

Cosmopolitan Magazine: Under the leadership of Helen Gurley Brown (bestselling author of *Sex and the Single Girl* and the like) in the Sixties, *Cosmopolitan* changed its more conservative image to address the issues of the sexually liberated woman. Archie regards the publication with as much affection as Adam had in Eden for the serpent.

Cousin Henry: Edith's cousin who got so drunk at his mortgage burning that he set his house ablaze ("Mike Makes His Move").

Dear Abie: What Archie repeatedly uses as the name of a famous advice columnist.

Debt, Mike's to Archie: According to "Gloria and Mike's House Guests," by the time the Stivics have moved into their own home, Mike figures he owes Archie $2600. Archie calculates the amount at $3840.

"Drove the Shadows Away": According to Edith in "Edith's Friend," it's the song the band played when she and Cousin Roy danced at Steeplechase Park (qv). When he doesn't recognize the title, she sings it for him: "La la la la la drove the shadows away." He identifies it as "Love Walked Right In." The correct title is "Love Walked In," a big hit when Kenny Baker sang it over and over in the 1938 movie *The Goldwyn Follies*.

Duffy's Tavern: One of the all-time favorite shows of the golden days of radio, the hero of which was named Archie, "a typical New York mug" in the words of *Duffy* creator Ed Gardner, who was born in Astoria, Queens, within a few miles of the Bunker address. This Archie butchered English too: "I tink you've given me da mucus of an idea...." Archie's oft-quoted catchline was, answering the phone, "Duffy's Tavern. Archie speakin'. Duffy ain't here. Oh, hello, Duffy."

Duke: *See* LOOMIS, DUKE, and WAYNE, JOHN.

Edna: Edith's aunt who moved to Burbank when she was told she had six month's to live, fifty years ago, in "End in Sight."

Exercising his loopholes: Archie's justification for not declaring his cab-driving income on his taxes in "Archie's Fraud."

Faith: According to Archie's reverential pronouncement in "Mike's Pains," faith is "something that you believe that nobody in his right mind would believe."

Faye, Alice: The lovely leading lady of musical comedies of the Thirties and Forties (*In Old Chicago, Rose of Washington Square, That Night in Rio*) dances through Archie's dreams in such episodes as "End in Sight" and "Mike and Gloria Split."

Feltcher, the Reverend: Is the correct name of the clergyman Archie calls The Reverend Fletcher, upon saying which, he is invariably corrected, "The Reverend Feltcher," to which he invariably replies, "Whatever."

Fensil, Bummie: Archie meets him on a subway after not having seen him in 36 years ("Mike's Problem"); as a kid in the old neighborhood, he used to eat slimy things for money—e.g., flies and worms for two and three cents. The audience gets to meet Bummie, too, married to Archie's once-flame Dolores, in the episode "Archie's Secret Passion."

Fletcher, the Reverend: *See* FELTCHER, THE REVEREND.

Foggia, Italy: Where Archie was stationed with the 15th Army Air Force (same as Norman Lear) during WWII.

Groinocologist: According to Archie, the doctor Edith sees when she experiences mental pause.

Hail Moses: According to "The Man in the Street," Archie's idea of the Jewish equivalent of a Hail Mary.

Hauser Street: Archie bought his home there after the war for $14,000. The Bunkers live at the nonexistent 704 Hauser Street, in Astoria, in the borough of Queens, New York. Years later, Geraldine Ferraro represented the district in Congress.

Heatherton, Joey: When Mike and Gloria move out of 704 Hauser ("Teresa Moves In"), Edith replaces their broken mattress with one she describes as the kind Joey Heatherton has on TV. The reference is to sexy Heatherton's steamy commercial for Serta Perfect Sleepers, a scorcher in its time.

"Hi Mom. Hi Dad. Hi Rick. Hi Dave:" Gloria's greeting as she enters the room in "Grandpa Blues." A reference to that great granddaddy of familycoms, *The Adventures of Ozzie and Harriet.*

Hoffa, James Riddle (1913–1975?): President of the Teamsters Union 1957–1971; disappeared in 1975 and is generally assumed to have been murdered. In "Little Miss Bunker," Archie says that if the cops can't find a big person like Hoffa, they'll never be able to find a little girl like Stephanie.

Honor your parents: In "The Dinner Guest," Archie pegs it as one of the Top Ten Commandments, then guesses it's got to be right up there at number three or four. Edith correctly identifies it as being number five.

Jeanette: In the episode "Unequal Partners," what Edith wanted to name Gloria when she was born, after Edith's favorite movie star, Jeanette MacDonald

Jefferson, Henry: After Mike, Henry probably sails into Archie's attitudes more than anybody else in the first year of *All in the Family*. Favorite topics include whether Santa is, and Jesus was, black or white. Early on described *en passant* as Louise's brother, then more emphatically as George's—in any case, always Lionel's uncle—Henry refers to Louise as his sister in the episode "Gloria the Victim," though the closing credits list him as "Melvin Stewart: Henry Jefferson."

Jetty, Paul K.: Archie's idea of a rich man, in "Joey's Baptism." He means J(ean) Paul Getty (1892–1976), variously considered one of the richest and *the* richest man in the world.

Jimmy Carters: Archie's euphemism for teeth in "Archie's Brief Encounter," part one; so named for the toothy 39th U. S. President, whose own jokes about his ample mouthful included this attribution to Johnny Carson's Great Carnac: "The answer is: 60 minutes. The question is: How long does it take Jimmy Carter to brush his teeth?" (Philadelphia fundraising speech, 6/30/76). The Eighties equivalent of "Jimmy Carters" seems to be "Mary Lou Rettons."

Justice, Archie: The name of the Archie Bunker character in the original *All in the Family* pilot.

Kelcy's: The neighborhood "jernt" a few blocks away, of which the name on the window is clearly *Kelcy's*, while the owner's name, according to cast credits, is *Kelsey*. Archie later buys Kelcy's and converts it to Archie's Place. Among the regulars at Kelcy's: Joe Foley (Scott Brady) and Hank Pivnik (Danny Dayton); behind the bar at different times: The Bartender (Brendan Dillon), Kelsey (Bob Hastings), Harry Snowden

(Jason Wingreen). According to "Edith's Night Out," a sherry there sells for 70 cents a glass.

Kenny the Cockroach: Archie names him as he scurries across the kitchen, in "Gloria and Mike's House Guests."

King, Billie Jean, and Bobby Riggs: Cited by Irene in "Archie Is Cursed," when Archie tells her women don't belong in sports. An apt parallel. King has said of her adversary in the much-hyped 1973 match, "He claimed any man could beat any woman [at tennis], that the women's game was dull compared to the men's, and that there was no reason for us to get equal prize money...[the match] for him was the ultimate ego trip, a vehicle for a super hustler to carry off (he hoped) the ultimate hustle." King won over Riggs—as did Irene over Archie.

Kings of Queens: Not to be confused with that other men's club by the bus station, the Queens of Queens. Archie is a charter member of the lodge. Among other members are Barney Hefner, Hank Pivnik, and Harry Snowden. At one time, Barney is president of the lodge, and Archie is membership chairman. The phone number of the lodge is 555–4378.

Koumiss (variation of _kumiss_): An intoxicating fermented or distilled liquor originally made by the Tartars from mare's or camel's milk. Gloria learns the word to impress Mike in "Mike and Gloria Split."

The Last Supper: According to Archie in "The Dinner Guest," it was attended by the 12 opossums.

"Let me make this perfectly clear": A phrase used by Richard Nixon and subsequently ridiculed by large segments of the population. When Archie's nephew Wendell says it, prefacing a two-faced explanation in "The Insurance Is Canceled," Mike gibes, "Where have I heard that before?" Mike himself echoes Nixon when looking for his own apartment and unable to find one ("Mike Makes His Move"), he is accused by Archie of deliberately trying to prolong the gravy train. Mike explodes that he'll find a place no matter what. "You won't have Mike Stivic to kick around any more."

Lincoln, Abraham (1809–1865): During his term as 16th President of the United States, the Emancipation Proclamation decreed that slaves be free. According to Archie in various episodes, George Jefferson considers Abraham Lincoln a honky…and Archie thinks Lincoln signed the Declaration of Independence.

Little Emanuel: Forced to fire either Little Emanuel, Black Elmo, or Stretch Cunningham from the loading dock in "The Insurance Is Canceled," Archie picks Emanuel, the Puerto Rican. Emanuel, despite a bad leg, is his fastest worker. Elmo has perfect attendance. Stretch Cunningham is a jerk, but white. Since there are other whites who would miss the joke if Stretch were fired, and blacks who would sizzle if Elmo went, Emanuel, the only Puerto Rican, gets dumped.

Loomis, Duke: The man who saved Archie's life during the war in Foggia, Italy ("The Threat").

Malaprops: Verbal blunders caused by using for one word another sounding like it, were earlier found on such tongues as those belonging to Shakespeare's Dogberry ("Thou wilt be condemned into everlasting redemption") and nightclub comic Norm Crosby ("Congressmen made incisions that effect our lives").

McGovern, George (George Stanley McGovern): One of the first senators to oppose the Vietnam war, he ran in 1972 as the Democrat's presidential candidate against Nixon, the war, and spiraling defense spending. Mike volunteered time and donated money to his campaign ("Mike Comes into Money").

Marvin: The mouse that Edith and Archie can't get rid of in "Teresa Moves In."

Minnesota: Its desirability as a new home for the Stivics is questioned in "Mike's Move" because Mary Tyler Moore keeps losing her hat there, and Rhoda and Phyllis didn't like it enough to stay. The references are to *The Mary Tyler Moore Show*, set in Minneapolis. Its opening credits showed Mary tossing her hat in the air, and the series birthed two spin-offs when the characters Rhoda (Valeria Harper) and Phyllis (Cloris Leachman) relocated to star in sitcoms of their own.

Moon: What Archie did to the TV when the Rolling Stones were on ("Edith Versus the Bank").

Mustard: Says Archie, a substance capable of wrecking the rectal nerve if gotten in your eye ("Superbowl Sunday").

Muumuu: A loose-fitting Hawaiian dress, but when Amelia and Russell bring Edith one in "Amelia's Divorce," Archie claims it looks like gypsy underwear.

Octopus McMuffin: What Mike says he had at McDonalds for lunch to avoid having to eat octopus with friends for dinner in "Stalemates."

One: What Archie estimates Stretch Cunningham's IQ to be in "Archie Is Worried About His Job."

Plunger: In "Chain Letter," Archie refers to one as a Polish swizzle stick, and Mike says in fact it's a bigot's toothbrush.

Polish jokes: Archie figures they were started by the Mafia to take the heat off the dagos ("Mike's Pains").

Promptly at six: When Archie likes his dinner, according to Edith in "The Insurance is Canceled," "We're Still Having a Heat Wave," etc.

Pyronymphiac: What Archie calls Blanche Hefner in "Weekend in the Country," meaning nymphomaniac (a female sex freak) but thinking of pyromaniac (a maniac who sets fires). Actually, Archie unintentionally makes a cogent point. Sexually speaking, the lady plays with fire.

Queens, Kings of: *See* KINGS OF QUEENS.

Quinn, Hazel: The 78-year-old woman jailed for shoplifting a can of tuna in the episode "Edith Finds an Old Man."

Revenge: Advocated by Archie as a good way to get even; also, according to Archie, one of two things Sicilians are known for, the other being spaghetti ("Archie Sees a Mugging").

Radio Voices

All in the Family faces who were once popular radio voices include Billy Halop (Bobby Benson of *Bobby Benson and the B-Bar-B Riders*), his sister Florence Halop (Hotbreath Houlihan on *The Jimmy Durante Show* and Miss Duffy, replacing Shirley Booth on *Duffy's Tavern*), Bob Hastings (Archie on *Archie Andrews*), Ken Lynch (Tank on *Hop Harrigan* and the lieutenant on *Twenty-First Precinct*), and Bill Quinn (as a regular re-creating "real life" crime cases on *The Big Story*).

Richard: Edith's cousin Richard used to drink buttermilk and tie her to trees ("Stalemates").

Riggs, Bobby, and Billie Jean King: *See* KING, BILLIE JEAN and RIGGS, BOBBY.

Robinson, Bill, and Shirley Temple: Performed the famous stairway dance in the 1935 movie *The Little Colonel*. At the time Robinson, a black tap dancer, was 57 years old, and Temple was 7. When Archie says whites should only dance with whites and proceeds to give examples of popular silver-screen teams, Edith counters with these two ("Lionel Steps Out").

Rogers, Will (William Penn Adair Rogers): In "Archie's Operation," part one, Archie misquotes him as having said "I never met a friend I really liked." The actual quotation, closely identified with the beloved, homespun cowboy humorist (1879–1935) went: "I never met a man I didn't like." Understandably, Archie's way works better for Archie.

Room 822: Edith asks Archie what it means to him, and he thinks it's a TV show, confusing it with *Room 222,* the 1969–1974 TV series about an integrated high school. Fact is, it's the room in Hotel Atlantic City where the Bunkers spent their honeymoon ("Second Honeymoon").

Rosemarie: What Archie thinks Stephanie's name is. *See also* ROSE MARIE, under The Occasional Blooper (page 215).

Safe City: A top-security complex in Santa Monica, California, to which Archie has reveries of moving in the episode ("The Blockbuster"). Equipped with TV monitors in the lobbies, armed guards, and a 12-foot fence protecting it from marauders on the street. Mike compares it to living in San Quentin.

Shiboom: Archie's conception of *shalom* in such episodes as "Archie Finds a Friend," wherein Archie greets Mr. Bernstein with, "As youse people say, shiboom."

Sing Sing: The maximum security prison in Ossining, New York. Nick Howard is a plumbing assistant on work furlough from Sing Sing; is in for armed robbery; tried to hold up a pawnshop with a toy gun ("Prisoner in the House").

Sodom and Glocca Morra: What Archie says the world is turning into, in "Joey's Baptism." Sodom and Gomorrah were twin sin cities of Biblical times; Glocca Morra, however, a pastoral Irish village awash with the songs of skylarks, was created by lyricist E. Y. Harburg for the Broadway musical *Finian's Rainbow.*

Steeplechase Park: The Coney Island amusement park where Edith and Cousin Roy danced when they were younger, very fond of each other, and thought they were cousins by blood. Years later, in "Edith's Friend," Cousin Roy reveals that they were never blood relations, and asks Edith how things would have been had they known way back when. They dance. Edith panics and pretends a wrong number is a phone call from Archie. Roy leaves, and Archie never does find out how lucky he was.

Sunsweet: Archie's regular brand of prune juice.

Superburger with everything: Waitress Denise's nickname for Archie in "Archie's Brief Encounter."

Temple Beth Shalom: Archie's temple. He has to join in the episode "Stephanie's Conversion," when he discovers that Stephanie is Jewish and cannot belong to the temple nor take religious instruction there unless her guardians are members too.

Temple, Shirley, and Bill Robinson: *See* ROBINSON, BILL and SHIRLEY TEMPLE.

Tidybowl: One of the favorite TV commericals of the Seventies involved a tiny fellow sailing his boat in a balmy toilet tank freshened by Tidybowl. In "Birth of the Baby," part one, Archie's chief lodge potentate, Ed Bradley, says of Archie's constantly flushing toilet that the little man from Tidybowl wouldn't last long in the Bunker household. The little toilet man is referred to, also, in "The Commercial," when Edith has the opportunity to make a TV ad with the famous sailor, who is now going around to laundries tearing shirts.

Tony's Little Naples: Where Archie offers to take Edith after she's brought him to his knees on the issue of pantsuits, in "Edith's Night Out." Archie particularly extols its "veal scallo-peepee."

Twenty-two seconds exactly: In "Archie's Aching Back," the amount of time—according to Mike—that it takes Archie to belch after a bicarb.

UFO-CIA: What Archie says George Meany is the head of in "Grandpa Blues." He obviously has in mind the AFL-CIO.

Uncle Alex: The first Stivic to come to America from Poland. When he struck it rich in the United States, he sent money to bring Mike's father over. When he died, he left Mike $500, less $225 for back taxes.

Uncle Walter: Edith's uncle who broke his hip on his dog, then rolled out of the ambulance and into the bay, because he failed to answer a chain letter ("Chain Letter").

Urology: What Archie tells Edith he doesn't want the Reverend Fletcher (which see) pronouncing over him at his funeral, in the episode "Archie and the Quiz."

Wayne, John: Reference is often made to John Wayne on *All in the Family*. By the 1970s, many an ardent patriot spelled American "J·o·h·n W·a·y·n·e." Superstar hero of blockbuster war films and Westerns, "Duke" Wayne (1907–1979) spoke out for traditonal zeal and values, as in: "They keep bringing up the fact that America's for the downtrodden. But this new thing of genuflecting to the downtrodden, I don't go along with that. We ought to go back to praising the kids who get good grades, instead of making excuses for the ones who shoot the neighborhood grocery man. But, hell, I don't want to get started on that." In 1971, Wayne's unabashedly flag-waving special, *Sing Out, Sweet Land*, garnered a 37.7 Nielsen— the highest ratings for an NBC special that season.

"We're in the Oval Office": Mike's comment when he realizes that Gloria's employer, Mr. Crenshaw, has been taping their conversation concerning Gloria's dismissal from work ("Mike Faces Life"). A reference to the then-headlining revelations about Nixon's Watergate tapes

The Occasional Blooper

I t happens in the best of families. Under time pressure, with last minute changes, as well as the possibility of enriching a script by adding a new dimension to a character—or if only because a given writer wasn't one of the show's writers two or six or eight years ago—contradictions and downright errors do infrequently occur. For trivia buffs, here are six.

Archie's Brothers: Flabbergasted by Archie's convoluted attempts at courtesy toward Judaism in "Archie Finds a Friend," Mr. Bernstein asks him how he celebrates Brotherhood Week. Missing the implications of the question, Archie replies that he doesn't because he's an only child. But in "The Saga of Cousin Oscar," Archie talks about his sister Alma and his brother Phil, and in other episodes, he has a brother Fred, though the two are, admittedly, estranged during most of the life of *All in the Family.*

Chauvinism: In "Gloria and the Riddle," Gloria states that *chauvinism* is named after Chauvin, the prototypical stupid nationalist who thought women were no good. But if Chauvin had anything against women, history forgot. What history records is that Nicolas Chauvin, a soldier for Napoleon, was wounded seventeen times in service, was pensioned off with a miserably paltry pension, then spent the rest of his mangled life singing the praise of Napoleon's generosity. Therefore, throughout most of its life the term referred only to an extreme form of nationalism. It wasn't until the Sixties that people began speaking about "male chauvinism" to mean men's attitudes toward women who threaten men's territorial imperative by expecting equality. Soon after, people used "male chauvinism" and "chauvinism" interchangeably.

Chocolate Cake: When Archie finds out that Mike and Gloria are moving next door in "Mike Makes His Move," Archie shoves Mike's face into a chocolate cake. Mike raises his face, wipes off the frosting with his hand, and puts it in his mouth—a funny move that capitalizes on the image of Mike the glutton. But what he does next—something that presumably the camera wasn't supposed to catch—is spit the glop back into his hand. Evidently Reiner the actor hadn't Mike the character's lust for eats.

Foley, Joe: Scott Brady's regular role as a denizen of Kelcy's. Yet, specifically introduced as Joe Foley in the episode "Edith's Night Out," his character is billed "Mr. Benjamin" in the closing credits.

Maude's Husbands: In "Cousin Maude's Visit," she and Archie discuss the fact that she buried two husbands—Fred, who died of a brain hemorrhage, and Burt, who had a heart seizure. Yet in "Maude," Carol is identified as the daughter of Maude and her second husband, Chester, who was buried at sea on their honeymoon. Since Carol is a grown woman, it's not as though Maude only married him last week. Maybe Maude's been married so often, it's tough to keep the names straight.

Rose Marie: 1936 musical starring Jeanette MacDonald and Nelson Eddy. In "Alone at Last?" Edith says she saw the film seven times, and begins to recount it in meticulous detail, assigning to MacDonald the name Rose Marie La Flamme, and to Eddy, the name Jim Kenyon. Unfortunately, while the Broadway musical used these names, MacDonald's character was Marie La Flor in the 1936 version of the film, and Eddy's was Sergeant Bruce. Jeanette's name being *La Flor* (Spanish for *flower*) is such a significant plot device in the movie that if Edith had seen the film even one time, she wouldn't have made the error.

Nelson Eddy and Jeanette MacDonald in *Rose Marie* (1936)—a movie Edith doesn't know nearly as well as she thinks she does!

Family Quiz

The best reasons to watch *All in the Family* are for the stories, the ideas, the acting, the writing, and the humor. But there's always someone out there who wants to play trivia too, so for the benefit of the mavins, here's a quiz to test your mastery of Bunkerana.

1. In "Archie and the Quiz," when Edith takes the life-expectancy test for Archie, she figures he will live to be 63 years and four months. When he takes it, he loses six years. How old is he in that episode, and when was he born?

2. In the same episode, how old does Edith figure she'll live to be?

3. According to the episode "Maude," where was Gloria born, and why did Archie take Edith there by bus?

4. According to Edith in "Mike Makes His Move," what did Archie say when he carried her over the threshold of 704 Hauser?

5. In "Super Bowl Sunday," in which the guys are robbed at gunpoint at the bar and have to drop their pants, a banner proclaims the game being played. What does the banner say?

6. In "The Dinner Guest," Edith has prepared a special dinner for Mike and Gloria on the eve of their departure for California. But Mike and Gloria make other plans with the head of Mike's department in California. What's his name, and where will they be dining?

7. In "We're Still Having a Heat Wave," what does it mean if the tomatoes are squishy at Roselli's Market?

8. What color is Archie's beer can?

9. In several episodes, Edith identifies the ice cream concoction she was eating when she met Archie. What was it called?

10. When Archie thinks he's going to die in "Archie in the Cellar," what does he will Gloria?

Extra credit: In the same episode, on what does Archie get bombed?

Answers

1. In this episode, Archie is 51. He was born in 1924.
2. Edith computes that she will live to 84 years and six months.
3. Bayside Hospital, because the subway doesn't go to Bayside.
4. "Watch your head, dingbat, or you'll knock your brains out."
5. Dallas vs. Denver, Superbowl #12.
6. Professor Lyman King, whom they'll meet at the Oak Room of the Plaza, at 7:30.
7. It means that Mrs. Goldblatt was there ahead of you.
8. With few exceptions, a yellow-orange with red lettering.
9. A steamboat.
10. His armchair.
Extra credit: On the bottle of 100-proof Polish vodka that Mike and Gloria got from Mike's Uncle Casimir for their wedding.

Scoring: Score ten points for each correct answer (five each for two-part questions), and ten points for the extra credit answer. 0–20: Stretch Cunningham. Ya dope ya. 25–50: Dingbat. 55–80: Meathead. 85–110: A regular King of Queens.

People to Watch For

An actor or actress who worked out well in a small role in *All in the Family* often reappeared in a regular role later on, either on *All in the Family* or on another Lear series. Some performers, relatively unknown when cast in *All in the Family* roles, have since found fame and fortune elsewhere on television, the stage, and in the movies. You'll really have to keep your eyes peeled to spot some of them. Among the more prominent are:

Abraham, F. Murray: Plays an unemployment-office clerk in part one of "The Unemployment Story." Looking not at all like Salieri in *Amadeus,* he wears an orange shirt, rust tie, light-blue jacket, and has more hair.

Booke, Sorrell: Mr. Sanders, Archie's boss at the plant in a number of episodes, later became a hit as Jefferson Davis "Boss" Hogg on *The Dukes of Hazzard.*

Brennan, Eileen: The nervous secretary in "The Elevator Story" had a history of Broadway musical successes behind her (for instance, *Little Mary Sunshine*), and went on to play Kit

Flanagan (the mother of Tony Flanagan, portrayed by a young Rob Lowe) on *A New Kind of Family* and Captain Doreen Lewis on *Private Benjamin.*

Carey, Philip: Veteran hero of such movies as *The Long Gray Line, Pushover,* and *Springfield Rifle,* and the TV series *Tales of the 77th Bengal Lancers* and *Philip Marlowe.* He played a gay football star in "Judging Books by Covers." In 1980, he became Texas tycoon Asa Buchanan, a central character on the soap opera *One Life to Live.*

Conrad, Michael: Appears as Mike's Uncle Casimir in "Flashback—Mike and Gloria's Wedding," and went on to become a two-time Emmy Award winner for his portrayal of Sergeant Phil Esterhaus on *Hill Street Blues.*

Dukes, David: The same evening that David Dukes appeared on CBS as the would-be rapist in "Edith's 50th Birthday," he played opposite himself on NBC's miniseries *79 Park Avenue*— as a good guy, Mike the cop. Since then, he's excelled in the miniseries form (*The Winds of War, George Washington, Space, Kane and Abel*), as well as in film and on Broadway.

Gardenia, Vincent: Plays the swinging husband in "The Bunkers and the Swingers," then returns to *All in the Family* in the regular role of neighbor Frank Lorenzo.

Geary, Tony: Roger, Mike's intellectual friend whom Archie swears must be gay in "Judging Books by Covers," starred in the serials *Bright Promise* and *The Young and the Restless,* then hit the heights of soap stardom as half of the popular Luke and Laura team on *General Hospital* (for which he won an Emmy).

Glass, Ron: Appeared as the younger of two refrigerator repairmen in "Everybody Tells the Truth." Glass soon went on to starring roles in *Barney Miller* and *The New Odd Couple.*

Guest, Christopher: Plays Jim, the man responsible for bringing Mike and Gloria together, in "Mike and Gloria Meet." Guest's subsequent successes include the Rob Reiner movie *This Is Spinal Tap,* and as a regular on *Saturday Night Live.*

Guillaume, Robert: Checks Archie over for hepatitis in "Chain Letter," going on to play Benson in the controversial soap opera send-up *Soap*, to star in its spin-off, *Benson*, and more recently, to appear in print and TV ads for Phillips' Milk of Magnesia.

LeRoy, Gloria: Appears as Duke Loomis' wife in "The Threat," in several later episodes as Mildred Boom-Boom Turner, and played the part of Millie in Lear's short-lived (1975–1975) *Hot L Baltimore*.

Little, Cleavon: With Demond Wilson, he tried to rob the Bunkers in "Edith Writes a Song." He later turned up as Lear's *Mr. Dugan*, as Dr. Noland on *Temperatures Rising*, and as the sheriff in Mel Brooks' megahit movie *Blazing Saddles*.

Macy, Bill: The uniformed policeman in "Archie Sees a Mugging" went on to play Maude Findlay's husband Walter in Lear's series *Maude*.

Mandan, Robert: Mr. Morrison, lawyer for the city commissioner's son who mugs Archie in "The Taxi Caper." Mandan subsequently starred as Chester Tate on *Soap*.

McClanahan, Rue: Brought in to play the swinging wife in "The Bunkers and the Swingers," she was cast later the same week as neighbor Vivian on *Maude*. Subsequent starring roles include Ginger-Nell on Lear's *Apple Pie*, and Blanche *The Golden Girls*.

McEachin, James: Mr. Turner, insurance examiner, in "Archie's Fraud," as well as Solomon Jackson, the black Jew that Archie tries to recruit into his lodge during their "absentee membership drive," in "Archie the Liberal." In 1973, McEachin assumed the lead in the TV series *Tenafly* as private detective Harry Tenafly.

Morrill, Priscilla: Katie Korman, the TV personality who interviews Edith when Edith saves a life at the Sunshine Home, in "Mr. Edith Bunker"; Edith's classmate Sarah in "Class Reunion"; Bernice, the delivery-room nurse when Joey is born ("Birth of the Baby," part two). Priscilla Morrill subsequently appeared regularly on *The Mary Tyler Moore Show* as Lou Grant's wife Edie, and on *Newhart* as Stephanie's mother.

Patrick, Dennis: Seen on *All in the Family* as Mr. Scanlon, aluminum siding salesman, in "Archie's Contract," and as the bigoted Gordie in "Archie and the KKK," Patrick is remembered as the blackmailed executive in the 1970 movie *Joe* and as Vaughn Leland on *Dallas.*

Peck, Ed: The chiseler at the telephone in the IRS office ("Archie's Fraud") and the cop ("Archie's Contract"), filled the title role in the short-lived 1951 action series *Major Dell Conway of the Flying Tigers.* In the late Seventies, he became a favorite as a hardnosed coach (*Semi-Tough*) or tight-lipped law enforcer (*Happy Days, The Super, Benson*).

Peters, Bernadette: As young and beautiful Linda Galloway, she flirted with the Meathead in "Gloria Suspects Mike." Since then, she has only flirted with success—as Charlotte Drake in Lear's *All's Fair;* as a luckless hooker in Steve Martin's *Pennies from Heaven;* earning a Tony nomination for *Sunday in the Park with George;* and winning a Tony for her next hit, *Song and Dance.*

Rea, Peggy: A grieving relative in "The Saga of Cousin Oscar," a rich widow in "Barney the Golddigger," and seen in other *All in the Family* roles as well, Rea later turned up as Rose Burton on *The Waltons* and Lulu Hoggs (Boss's wife) on *The Dukes of Hazzard.*

Rodd, Marcia: Is Marilyn Sanders, who tries to convince Mike that he fathered her child in "Mike's Mysterious Son." She reappears in the episode "Maude," the pilot show for that series, as Maude's daughter Carol, a role later taken over by Adrienne Barbeau.

Wilson, Demond: He broke into the Bunker home in "Edith Writes a Song," then broke into the big time as Lamont Sanford on *Sanford and Son.* He later played Oscar Madison in TV's *The New Odd Couple.*

Episode Guide

Though episodes opened with essentially the same sequence throughout—Archie and Edith at the piano, singing "Those Were the Days," followed by views of the neighborhood and city—O'Connor and Stapleton redid it a few times over the years. Since the actors aged in the series, it made sense for them to look as old in the opening as they did in the episode itself.

With each reshooting, the two had the chance to approach details differently—so that over the years, we see Archie whining sometimes more than others about the welfare state, Edith's voice cracking in one shoot but not in others, and Edith's wardrobe improving from a dowdy dark olive dress to a geometrically patterned orange one to a drab beige-and-black number to one with an open collar, in the end, that was quite flattering. Perhaps most important to the actors, when the series began, was that their names followed the title. In the later seasons, the title followed their names.

As is true with many weekly series, *All in the Family* episodes were often not aired in the order in which they were made. The following list gives production order, along with initial air dates.

1970 – 1971 SEASON

Meet the Bunkers   0101   1-12-71

Because it's their anniversary, Edith has managed to drag Archie off to church. But, annoyed with the sermon, he takes Edith back home sooner than Mike and Gloria expected, surprising them in a sexual situation. The encounter sets the stage for the definitive Archie-versus-Mike debate.

Writing the President   0102   1-19-71

Furious that Mike has sent a derogatory letter to the president, Archie engages in more pomp and ceremony than it took to write the Magna Carta, painstakingly producing a laudatory one and fantasizing Nixon's grateful reaction.

Archie's Aching Back   0103   1-26-71

Though unhurt by a minor accident in his cab, Archie complains that Rhoda Greenspan plowed into it. Mike berates his anti-Semitism. Archie, sure he's no anti-Semite because he respects Jews for some things, engages the law firm of Rabinowitz, Rabinowitz, and Rabinowitz after he learns that George Jefferson opened his dry-cleaning business on the proceeds from an insurance settlement. His case evaporates when witnesses against him come forth—a station wagon full of nuns.

Judging Books by Covers   0104   2-9-71

Archie insists that Mike and Gloria's intellectual friend Roger has effeminate tastes and is therefore gay. He's unsettled to learn that Roger is straight, while his own chum—macho, arm-wrestling, top jock Steve—is a different sort of "man's man" than Archie assumed him to be.

Archie Gives Blood   0105   2-2-71

Mike plans to visit the blood bank and wants Archie to donate too. Archie refuses on the grounds that for all he knows his blood could go to a radical who got shot blowing up a building. Besides, Mike can't convince Archie that blood has only one color—red. Then Archie gives in, and runs into Lionel at the blood bank, where the tongue-in-cheek Lionel asserts that white blood in black people only confuses them. When Archie gets home, another debates ensues with Mike, this one about organ transplants.

Gloria Has a Belly Full   0106   2-16-71

In a rage that Gloria is pregnant though Michael can't support her, Archie shames Mike into getting an apartment—then changes his tune, becoming the sweetest possible dad, when Gloria suffers a miscarriage.

Now That You Know the Way, Let's Be Strangers   0107   2-23-71

Mike and Gloria invite two hippie friends to spend the night at 704 Hauser, but Archie yells foul when told the couple isn't married. The Stivics berate Archie—until the hippies prove so obnoxious about wanting to do things their way that they wear out their welcome with all concerned.

Lionel Moves into the Neighborhood   0108   3-2-71

Archie marshals every means at his disposal to keep an unknown black family from moving onto his block, including offering Lionel money to dissuade them. Lionel declines, since the family in question is his.

Edith Has Jury Duty   0109   3-9-71

Edith's jury duty goes into extra innings when she holds out against the other eleven jurors, who want to convict a suspected murderer—later shown to be innocent. Throughout, Archie reacts by growling that Edith's absence has inconvenienced him.

Archie Is Worried About His Job   0110   3-16-71

Archie's company has announced a 20 percent cutback in personnel. Archie stays up all night waiting for a phone call about whether he's on the list, while police officer Dave waits up with him to arrest a crank caller who is heading for Archie's in search of action. Mike, as long as he's up too, orders pizza.

Women's Lib   0111   3-23-71

Demanding that Mike deal with her as his absolute equal or not at all, Gloria embraces women's lib with a passion, whereas Mike will only go along if she first admits her inferiority. He excuses his disinterest by saying he's worried about his grades. In a rage, Gloria moves out. Archie temporarily loses a daughter and retains a freeloading son-in-law.

Success Story   0112   3-30-71

Mike and Archie tangle over pollution, dropouts, free clinics, and Archie's friend Eddie Frazier. Archie venerates Frazier's towering financial success. Mike questions Frazier's ethics, since he's a multimillionaire. When Eddie drops by, it becomes apparent that Eddie's son agrees with Mike.

The First and Last Supper   0113   4-6-71

Despite Archie's involvement in circulating a petition against blacks moving into the neighborhood, Edith accepts the dinner invitation extended to her and Archie by Lionel's parents. When Archie begs off with a story that Edith has hurt her ankle, the Jeffersons offer to come over to the Bunkers'. After Archie and Jefferson disagree on a variety of racial issues, Louise reveals that the man introduced as her husband George is really her brother-in-law, Henry. George, it turns out, categorically refuses to sup with a white family.

1971 – 1972 SEASON

Gloria Poses in the Nude   0201   9-25-71

When a famous artist friend offers to paint Gloria in the nude, the Stivics are thrilled and Archie scandalized. But Mike's open mind shuts down by stages as he dwells on the long, unchaperoned hours demanded by the arrangement.

The Saga of Cousin Oscar   0202   9-18-71

Cousin Oscar, unkind to Archie since childhood, costs him a fortune as a house guest—then costs even more by dying upstairs, with not a single relative willing to share funeral expenses. At first, Archie is prepared to bury him in a used casket or potter's field, but he softens and agrees to pay for a decent send-off.

Flashback—Mike Meets Archie   0203   10-16-71

Reminiscing as Gloria and Mike's first anniversary approaches, the family recalls the first time Mike met Archie. They couldn't have been more incompatible then, and they haven't improved much since.

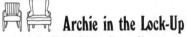 **Edith Writes a Song** 0204 10-9-71

Having composed a truly grating song about the importance of love, Edith wants to spend family money on setting it to music, with a view toward eventual publication. Archie, who'd prefer to buy a gun, seems justified when two men break into the house—but Edith wins them over with the sincerity of her good heart and bad song.

Archie in the Lock-Up 0205 10-2-71

Tipped off by Lionel's policeman cousin that trouble is imminent, Edith and Gloria beg Archie to go down and warn Mike and Lionel at the demonstration they've joined. There *is* real trouble: The cops haul Archie off to the slammer along with assorted deadbeats and space cadets.

Election Story 0206 10-30-71

Not surprisingly, Archie can't stand the candidate that Mike and Gloria have touted. Though he generally shuns local elections on the theory that they demean his vote, Archie decides he has to cancel out Mike's ballot. But he's turned away at the polls because he last voted so long ago that his registration has lapsed.

Edith's Accident 0207 11-6-71

Leaving a note on a car after she dents it with a can of cling peaches, Edith provokes Archie's wrath for her honesty but earns the esteem of her victim—a Catholic priest.

Mike's Problem 0208 11-20-71

Mike's impotent as the result of his fears that he might not pass final exams. He reluctantly confides in Archie, who suggests that he make a list of things to remember to do before falling asleep at night. Then, seeking expert advice, Archie asks Henry Jefferson how blacks got so good at sex.

The Blockbuster 0209 11-13-71

When the oil burner breaks down, Archie threatens to sell the house and move to California. He calls a real estate broker sight unseen—who turns out to be a black blockbuster.

The Insurance Is Canceled 0210 11-27-71

Archie loses his insurance for living in the wrong neighborhood. While at work, he has to choose which of three men to fire at work: Little Emanuel, a competent Puerto Rican; Black Elmo, a competent black; and Stretch Cunningham, an incompetent white.

Christmas Day at the Bunkers' 0211 12-18-71

Christmas at the Bunkers' finds Archie in the dumps. His tree looks like Charlie Brown's and he can only afford cheap gifts. Poor Archie has no money because he sent a shipment to London, England, instead of London, Ontario, and his company withheld his bonus as a fine.

The Man in the Street 0212 12-4-71

During lunch, CBS shoves a microphone at Archie, soliciting his opinion of Nixon's economic policy. His debut on the Cronkite news is 45 minutes away when the TV set goes on the blink. In vain, Archie goes wild to have the TV replaced or repaired in time, though he refuses Lionel's offer to watch the show from the Jefferson home. In desperation, Archie takes the family to Kelcy's, only the spot is preempted by an announcement from President Nixon.

Cousin Maude's Visit 0213 12-11-71

One by one, the Bunkers and Stivics succumb to flu, with Archie and Mike competing to have the highest temperature. Edith's cousin Maude arrives to nurse them back to health. Peppily pushy, she fusses over everyone but Archie, whose chair she sits in and refuses to relinquish. The two proceed to debate the relative merits of Franklin Roosevelt and Richard Nixon.

Edith's Problem 0214 1-8-72

Edith enters menopause giddily happy one moment, screaming *stifle* and *damn* the next. When Archie bends over backward to be understanding, Edith decides he's stopped loving her because he doesn't care enough to yell. Finally, he demands that if she's going to have a change of life, she'd better do it in thirty seconds. This cures her for about two more minutes.

The Elevator Story   0215   1-1-72

When Archie discovers that Edith forgot to mail his insurance payment, he dashes off from her birthday celebration at Pasquale's Italian restaurant to hand-deliver the envelope. Mere seconds into the insurance building's elevator, he and its other passengers—a disdainful, cultured black man, a neurotic secretary, a pregnant Puerto Rican woman, and her husband—get stuck between floors. To Archie's horror, the woman gives birth in the elevator. The infant's first blanket is Archie's copy of the *Daily News*.

Archie and the F.B.I.   0216   1-15-72

A government investigator arrives to grill Archie about his friend and co-worker Larry Grundy. Archie instantly assumes Grundy did something wrong, even after he hears that investigators are nosing around about A. Bunker, too. Archie and Larry destroy their friendship with cross-accusations, only to learn that the investigation was nothing more than a routine Air Force check related to a service contract at the plant.

Archie Sees a Mugging   0217   1-29-72

Forced to report a mugging that he wants no part of, Archie blames it on the Mafia as his excuse for not reporting it earlier—getting himself in the soup with the mob, the cops, and the maligned victim.

Mike's Mysterious Son   0218   1-22-72

A young woman leaves a little boy on the Bunkers' doorstep, identifying him as Mike's son. Mike denies it vehemently until he sees a picture of the woman. Yes, it's possible after all. Then the woman reappears to take her child back, saying he isn't Mike's. She left the boy in a weak moment when she felt that single mothers with children weren't welcome on the dating scene.

Archie and Edith Alone   0219   2-5-72

Mike and Gloria take off for eight days at a commune, leaving Archie and Edith to entertain each other. When Archie insults Edith's goodness one time too many, she gives him the cold shoulder until he comes crawling back to apologize.

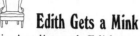 **Edith Gets a Mink**   0220   2-12-72

Cousin Amelia sends Edith a mink cape as a thank-you gift. Archie insists on returning it, but changes his tune when he knocks spaghetti onto it, has to have it cleaned by the Jeffersons, and makes a fast $300 in insurance when the Jeffersons ruin it. Edith, however, gives the money to Amelia.

Sammy's Visit   0221   2-19-72

Sammy Davis, Jr., having left a briefcase in Archie's cab in error, comes by Archie's house to retrieve it. Impressed and in awe, Archie extends himself to play the perfect host—inadvertently offending his famous guest with one racial goof after another.

Edith the Judge   0222   2-26-72

The laundromat owner and Archie are at each other's throats because Archie broke a machine by overloading it, and the machine wrecked Archie's clothes. They agree to submit the matter to Edith's arbitration, and Archie, expecting Edith to support him no matter what, is not overjoyed with her decision. She reveals that even though Archie weighed the laundry on his bathroom scale, he did overload the machine—because Edith had set the scale back five pounds to keep Archie from moping about gaining weight.

Archie Is Jealous   0223   3-4-72

Scandalized to learn that Gloria and Mike spent a weekend together before their marriage, Archie protests, whereupon Edith defends them by saying that she once spent a perfectly innocent weekend with a boy. Archie denounces her lack of judgment, particularly after she mentions that it wasn't entirely chaperoned.

Maude   0224   3-11-72

Maude invites cousin Edith and, reluctantly, Archie to the second wedding of Carol, her daughter by her second husband. Archie turns pale upon learning that Carol will marry a Jew, but he isn't the only one to hurl racial epithets once the groom reveals that he's bought a house without Carol's consent and expects her to quit her job to raise kids.

1972 – 1973 SEASON

Archie and the Editorial   0301   9-16-72

Provoked by a gun-control editorial, Archie goes on TV to represent the other side. His views have the effect of reinforcing everything the first editorial expressed, as does a subsequent experience at Kelcy's: A man who saw him on television asks to shake his hand, then robs him at gunpoint.

Archie's Fraud   0302   9-23-72

At the IRS office, Archie mouths off at a black guy in the waiting area, then learns the guy will be his tax examiner. At issue: the $680 that Archie made driving a cab. His solution: try to bribe the examiner with free cab rides.

Gloria and the Riddle   0303   10-7-72

Gloria poses a riddle with a women's lib twist. Mike and Archie bet a quarter on which of them will get the answer first. Neither wins, because Edith solves it before they do. *Because* it has a feminist answer, Mike feels enlightened and Archie rejects it out of hand.

The Threat   0304   9-30-72

The overly enthusiastic wife of Archie's Air Force buddy comes to spend the night as a house guest. When Archie inaccurately suggests that the woman made a pass at him, Edith asks her to leave. Archie takes entirely too long to feel guilty about what he's done.

Lionel Steps Out   0305   10-14-72

Archie's niece Linda has been staying with the Bunkers—and dating Lionel. Henry Jefferson and Archie Bunker, who both hit the ceiling, vie for the honor of being the biggest jerk about it. Archie is surprised to learn from Linda that her father (his brother) wouldn't mind at all.

The Bunkers and the Swingers   0306   10-28-72

Spotting a newspaper ad for couples who want to make friends with other couples, Edith merrily asks the twosome over. Archie hates the idea to begin with, then hates it considerably more when they reveal they're expecting a session of wife swapping.

 **Mike's Appendix** 0307   12-2-72

Mike needs an appendectomy and two doctors have been recommended to him, one of whom he knows to be female. Because she's a woman, Mike decides against her even though she charges less—then discovers after surgery that the other doctor is a woman too.

 **Edith Flips Her Wig** 0308   10-21-72

Edith, arrested for shoplifting, wonders if she suffers from the same kleptomania her aunt had. Archie goes to the store manager—whose wife is Jewish—and makes matters worse by insulting the Jewish race. Meanwhile, Edith seeks the advice of Father Majeski, who proves her innocence.

The Locket 0309   12-23-72

The antique locket Edith's grandmother gave her disappears. Archie twists the story to gouge his insurance company for enough money to buy a color TV, then hopes Edith will back him up even though the police have returned the stolen locket to her.

Mike Comes into Money 0310   11-4-72

When Mike inherits money from his Uncle Alex, he donates it to McGovern's campaign. Archie yells that the money should have gone to A. Bunker, not a candidate he loathes, so Mike secretly works a gas-station job at night to earn an equal amount for Archie.

Flashback—Mike and Gloria's Wedding, part one 0311   11-11-72

On the Stivics' second anniversary, the Stivics and Bunkers reminisce about Mike and Gloria's wedding, and Mike claims credit for having mellowed Archie from his earlier rabid bigotry. In the flashback, Mike could pass for a tall Charles Manson stand-in, and Gloria for Shirley Temple on the Good Ship Lollipop. Mike's Uncle Casimir insists on a Catholic service. Archie demands a Protestant church. Mike storms that if they're going to fight, he and Gloria can just live together.

 Flashback—Mike and Gloria's Wedding, part two 0312   11-18-72

Mike shaves off his beard and, becalmed after the issue of getting married in a Catholic or Protestant church, he and Gloria finally say "I do" in a civil ceremony in the Bunker living room. The judge performing the service is Polish.

Edith's Winning Ticket 0313 12-9-72

Edith holds a winning lottery ticket worth $500, which Archie can't wait to squander. Then Edith advises him that she bought the ticket for Louise Jefferson (though Louise hasn't paid for it yet). Archie tries to convince her that the money has no business leaving her hands or his home, but she gives it to Louise anyway.

Archie Is Branded 0314 2-24-73

A swastika is painted on the Bunkers' front door by someone who confused them for a neighbor. Archie hides it with a flag. A member of the Hebrew Defense Association arrives to offer protection and, when he leaves, is blown up in his car by the people from whom he meant to protect Archie.

Archie and the Bowling Team 0315 12-16-72

Archie, in heaven over the chance to get on the Cannonballers (the best bowling team in the district), discovers what it feels like to be on the receiving end of discrimination: he's blackballed. It's the last thing he expected to happen, since his competition is a black bowler who ties Archie's score in the tryouts. But the man is chosen over Archie because the team has been under fire for its racist composition.

Archie in the Hospital 0316 1-6-73

Back pains send Archie to the hospital, where the doctor can't discern the cause and Mike insists it's psychosomatic. Flat on his back in a hospital bed, Archie strikes up conversation and a friendship with Jean Duval, the patient on the other side of the curtain. When Archie walks around the curtain, he's shocked to discover that his charming new chum with the beautiful French accent is black. Archie's back on his feet again, thanks to "that old Black Magic."

Oh Say Can You See 0317 1-20-73

Archie, soured by his advancing signs of male menopause, only feels worse when he meets a high school chum who looks half his age and dates a very young woman. Archie's spirits instantly improve when he learns that his friend's "date" is a hooker.

Archie Goes Too Far   0318   1-27-73

Archie finds an old poem of Mike's, "To Vicki," in Mike's closet. Gloria rails that she thought he'd written it for her. Mike rants that his privacy has been violated. Gloria, Mike and Edith storm out, winding up at a pajama party to which Archie follows them, and almost apologizes.

Class Reunion   0319   2-10-73

Edith decides against going to her thirtieth anniversary class reunion because Archie won't join her. When she hears handsome Buck Evans will be there, she's ready to go alone, but Archie, hearing this, insists on accompanying her. Buck is fat, bald, and completely changed now—but to Edith, he's the same as ever.

The Hot Watch   0320   2-17-73

Archie feels lucky for a change. He's bought a $300 watch for $25. Mike suspects that it's stolen. When it breaks, Archie asks Lionel where people go to have watches repaired after they're broken in riots. Archie learns that his "registered Omega" is a cheap knock-off Omega, worth $8.00 at best.

Everybody Tells the Truth   0321   3-3-73

In this *Rashomon*-like tale, Mike and Archie have different versions of how they behaved when the refrigerator broke, and whether a white repairman's black assistant threatened Archie with a knife.

Archie Learns His Lesson   0322   3-10-73

Attending night classes to earn his high school diploma and maybe get a promotion to dispatcher at work, Archie swears Edith to secrecy lest Mike and Gloria discover he never finished high school. Overwhelmed by his studies, he tries to cheat, loses his crib notes when Edith pastes them on a board, passes anyhow—then loses the promotion when it goes to the boss's nephew.

Gloria the Victim   0323   3-17-73

Attacked by a would-be rapist on the way home, Gloria relates her story to a police detective who treats her to a hypothetical example of how victims are abused on the witness stand. Edith feels Gloria should nonetheless testify, but Archie and Mike instruct her to drop the charges.

The Battle of the Month 0324 3-24-73

It's Gloria's twenty-third birthday but %@$%*&#!!!, because it's also "that time of the month." Before hot tempers have run their course, Gloria calls Archie stupid, Mike calls Gloria stupid, and Gloria calls Edith a doormat, a zero, and a nothing. Then Edith comes through with advice that saves Mike and Gloria's marriage, earning from Gloria the accolade that she's really something—and from Archie, the observation that she's "something else."

1973 – 1974 SEASON

 ### Archie the Gambler 0401 10-13-73

When Gloria was three, Archie gambled heavily enough to lose a week's pay and his car. Edith stopped him by threatening to walk out. Now that Archie's at it again, Edith slaps him and demands he sign an apology.

Henry's Farewell 0402 10-20-73

Lionel's uncle—and Archie's sworn antagonist—is moving upstate. When Henry's brother George refuses to have an integrated party at his house, Archie is tricked into hosting the festivities at 704 Hauser, then George has to be conned into attending.

We're Having a Heat Wave 0403 9-15-73

It's hot going on scorching, with the mayor asking people to conserve energy by turning off their air conditioners, with Mike nagging Archie about Nixon's Watergate plumbers, and with a new family ready to move· into the Weedermeyer's house next door. When Henry Jefferson learns that the new family is Puerto Rican he, like Archie, is ready to sign a petition against it. Instead of moving next door, the Puerto Ricans buy a bigger house for the same money on the next block—and Irene and Frank Lorenzo become Archie's newest neighbors.

We're Still Having a Heat Wave 0404 9-22-73

Archie gets on Mike's and Gloria's cases for dressing skimpily to combat the hot spell, and he's reluctant to let Irene—a mere woman—fix his air conditioning. Archie manages to insult both Irene (for her views and interests) and Frank (for his vichyssoise), but Edith instructs him to behave, as these are friends she wants to keep.

Edith Finds an Old Man   0405   9-29-73

Edith brings home Justin Quigley, an old man in pajamas whom she found wandering the street. The man, a nursing-home runaway, makes Archie nervous, but Edith wants to help him, and so does the friend who wants him for a roommate—a septuagenarian female named Jo.

Archie and the Kiss   0406   10-6-73

A copy of Rodin's steamy statue, "The Kiss," enters the Bunker household as a gift from Irene to Gloria. Archie calls it a piece of filth. Mike says that even the Supreme Court wouldn't get into defining pornography. When Archie returns it to Frank Lorenzo, Gloria flies into a rage—which Archie attempts to subdue by buying her a hideous brown mermaid statuette with a flower and a carp on it. Archie believes it to be beautiful. The others make fun of his taste.

Archie and the Computer   0407   10-27-73

A computer foul-up—on a boxtop rebate for prunes—leaves Edith $47.75 ahead, but her efforts to correct the error only compound it. Archie doesn't want to stop "the goose that laid the golden prune." Then the Veterans Administration switches his name with that of a Mr. Binker, and lists him as dead. Archie quickly changes his tune about computer errors.

The Games Bunkers Play   0408   11-3-73

During an encounter-therapy board game with a few friends, revelations that Mike might be stuck-up, intolerant, and immature send him into a rage of stuck-up, intolerant immaturity.

Edith's Conversion   0409   11-10-73

Archie's kept in the dark when Gloria cooks Frank Lorenzo's horse-meat recipe for the family, and he has a fit when Irene and Theresa (her sister the nun) introduce Edith to Catholicism.

Archie in the Cellar   0410   11-17-73

The Stivics march off to a woodsy weekend seminar, Edith scoots to Scranton for a baptism, and Archie accidentally locks himself in the cellar, gets drunk on Polish vodka, and mistakes the black man from the oil company for God.

Black Is the Color of My True Love's Wig   0411   11-24-73

Mike is so enamored of Gloria in her dark wig that he can't wait to be alone with her. But he loses interest when she doffs the coif, and she loses respect for a husband who lusts after her when she looks like a different woman.

Second Honeymoon   0412   12-1-73

For their twenty-fifth anniversary, Edith surprises Archie with reservations at the Hotel Atlantic City. It's the same hotel, and the same room, they had on their honeymoon 25 years ago. Edith coos with delight to see the Atlantic Ocean still outside.

The Taxi Caper   0413   12-8-73

When Archie is mugged in his cab by the son of a city commissioner, he agrees to drop the charges in exchange for $100 from the lad's lawyer. The police, irritated that the kid has thwarted justice again, arrange to fine Archie out of his ill-earned profits.

Archie Is Cursed   0414   12-15-73

A men-vs.-women-in-sports argument between Archie and Irene leads to a pool game with money riding on the outcome. When Archie impugns Irene's femininity, Frank zings him with a Sicilian curse—and Irene hustles him for a fast ten dollars.

Edith's Christmas Story   0415   12-22-73

Edith puts up a cheery front despite having found a lump in her breast. Irene Lorenzo comforts her, having had a mastectomy years ago. Even more comforting is the doctor. When he tells Edith it's only a cyst, she jumps for joy and breaks her ankle.

Mike and Gloria Mix It Up   0416   1-5-74

Gloria vamps Mike when Archie and Edith go out for the evening. Mike, for all his noise about women's equality, is turned off by her assertiveness. He loutishly decides he would rather watch TV or play checkers.

Archie Feels Left Out   0417   1-12-74

Insisting that his fiftieth birthday is his forty-ninth, Archie boycotts the party—until 82-year-old Mr. Quigley persuades him that he's lucky to be alive with birthdays to look forward to.

Et Tu, Archie   0418   1-26-74

Joe Tucker, one of Archie's good friends, comes to town looking for a job. Afraid Joe wants *his* job, Archie bad-mouths him at the plant. Of course, Archie drew the wrong conclusion.

Gloria's Boyfriend   0419   2-2-74

A box boy from Ferguson's Market develops a crush on Gloria. She thinks it's sweet, but because the young man is retarded, Archie finds it dangerous, shoots off his mouth, and precipitates calamity.

Lionel's Engagement   0420   2-9-74

Louise Jefferson invites three out of four members of the Bunker household to Lionel's engagement party, while Archie more or less invites himself over George's vehement objections. At the party, both Archie and George are horrified to discover that the fiancée's mother is black and her father, white. (Neither Jennie nor her parents are played here by the team who took over the roles when *The Jeffersons* spun off. In this, Jennie: Lynne Moody; Mrs. Willis: Kim Hamilton; Mr. Willis: Charles Aidman.)

Archie Eats and Runs   0421   2-16-74

Archie eats mushrooms, then panics over reports that a batch of mushrooms on the market was recently found to be poisoned. He runs to the hospital for agonizing treatment, which turns out to be totally unnecessary.

Gloria Sings the Blues   0422   3-2-74

Afraid that she's fallen out of love with Mike, Gloria confides in Edith, who tells her it's a natural part of marriage. Revealing that she's had the same experience with Archie, Edith adds that the feeling will pass—and it does.

Mike's Graduation   0423   3-16-74

Four years of college are about to pay off for Mike, who will now be able to get a job and a home for himself and Gloria. Edith expects to miss them terribly. Archie starts counting the minutes. But the minutes turn into eons when Mike is offered a fellowship, and decides to stay with the Bunkers a little longer.

Pay the Twenty Dollars   0424   3-9-74

Archie gets a twenty for cabbing and gives it to George for dry cleaning. George calls it counterfeit, but Archie couldn't care less. It's up to the wives to make peace between the men without their knowing about it.

1 9 7 4 – 1 9 7 5 S E A S O N

Where's Archie?   0501   11-2-74

A big social occasion on Edith's calendar, her first Tupperware party, is wrecked by the news that Archie never arrived at the convention he was headed for in Buffalo.

Archie Is Missing!   0502   11-9-74

Going through Archie's personal effects for clues as to his whereabouts, Mike finds a photo linking Archie with Mildred Boom-Boom Turner. When Stretch Cunningham confirms that Boom-Boom is out of town, everybody assumes the worst. When Boom-Boom hears about it, she's incensed that anyone could believe her capable of liking Archie.

The Longest Kiss   0503   11-16-74

While everyone waits for Archie's triumphal return, Mike declares his affection for Royal Crown cola, Gloria grapples with her dread of lima beans, Irene stands on her head, George and Louise jitterbug, Edith jiggles in a hula hoop, and Mike and Gloria try to hold a kiss till Archie walks through the door.

The Bunkers and Inflation   0504   9-14-74

Archie's in for belt tightening when his union decides to go on strike.

Archie Underfoot   0505   9-21-74

Striking agrees with Archie more than it agrees with Edith, who has to cope with limited funds, Archie's bellyaching, and Archie in the way at home.

 **Edith the Job Hunter**   0506   9-28-74

Talk about humiliation! The Bunkers need money, and since Archie isn't earning it, Edith takes a job in the Jeffersons' dry-cleaning shop.

 **Archie's Raise**   0507   10-5-74

Good news for Archie. The strike is over, and the union has won him a 15 percent raise. Unfortunately, the increase still puts him behind the jump in the cost of living.

 Mike's Friend   0508   12-14-74

When Mike's brainy friend Stuart stops over, Mike obnoxiously excludes Gloria from the conversation. She wants to play charades; he instructs her to go check on the cookies. Gloria later tells Mike that she feels inadequate to fill his intellectual needs; he promises to send her to college after he graduates.

 Lionel the Live-In   0509   10-12-74

Lionel and George do a Mike and Archie—with the result that Lionel storms out of his own home to spend the night with the Bunkers. Edith plays the perfect hostess. Archie can't wait to send him back where he came from.

 Archie's Helping Hand   0510   10-19-74

Irene is looking for a job and Archie has no objection to her checking out his plant. In fact, he welcomes the chance to keep her and Edith apart. He doesn't consider that she'll get a job on the loading dock, and that his friends will never let him hear the end of it.

Gloria's Shock   0511   10-26-74

Mike ("Unilateral") Stivic strikes again, this time informing Edith and Archie that because the world is in such bad shape, he and Gloria plan not to have any children. They're surprised, as is Gloria, who wasn't consulted in the matter.

The Jeffersons Move Up   0512   1-11-75

In the episode that introduces the Jeffersons' new apartment and new neighbors, George takes his family to their East Side home in style—in a limo. He likes the place just dandy, but not the fact that Lionel's black mother-in-law and white father-in-law live upstairs.

Archie and the Miracle   0513   11-23-74

Archie finds religion when he narrowly misses being clobbered in an accident at work. Mike suggests that instead of thanking God, Archie might consider that God intended to flatten him, and that His aim was off.

George and Archie Make a Deal   0514   11-30-74

George needs Archie's signature on a petition in order to run for public office. Archie signs in exchange for discounts on his cleaning bill. But George rescinds the bargain rates when Archie's signature bounces. It seems Archie hasn't voted in so long, he's no longer registered.

Archie's Contract   0515   12-7-74

Claiming to have run an energy-conservation check on 704 Hauser, a salesman frightens Archie into signing a contract for aluminum siding. When Irene tells him the man was a phony, and George tells him how expensive it's likely to be, Archie wants to cancel the contract. The salesman won't budge. Then George brings a cop, Irene proves that the salesman's operating illegally, and Archie's off the hook. No, he doesn't thank his friends for saving his neck.

The Best of *All in the Family*   0516   12-21-74

Celebrating its first 100 episodes, *All in the Family* looks back on past episodes in this hour-long special narrated by Henry Fonda. Seventy-one clips from 41 past episodes cover moments ranging from Edith's shuffle to Gloria's transformation to the state of that uneasy union, Archie and Mike. Fonda calls the series "one of the most acclaimed and controversial...in television history."

Prisoner in the House 0517 1-4-75

Though Edith takes it in stride when she learns that their plumber's gentle assistant is on daytime work furlough from Sing Sing, Archie complains around the neighborhood and costs the man his job.

All's Fair 0518 1-18-75

Gloria resents Mike's having fallen asleep while she was discussing a problem. They reconcile through the techniques of "fair fighting." Gloria explains the methodology to Edith, who employs it in pestering Archie to let cousin Estelle visit. Estelle doesn't come. Edith ends up sleeping on the sofa. Archie recants.

Amelia's Divorce 0519 1-25-75

The Bunkers entertain Edith's cousin Amelia and Amelia's husband Russell, a plumber. Russell dotes on Amelia and showers her with expensive gifts. He also, much to Edith's surprise, cheats on Amelia. Amelia confides in Edith that she wishes she knew the secret of Edith and Archie's wedded bliss.

Everybody Does It 0520 2-8-75

Irene and Mike berate Archie for theft when he takes a box of nails home from the plant. In addition, he has pens he's kept, and tools that he's "borrowed." Mike acts superior until Archie catches him using a "signal" on a long-distance call to avoid paying charges.

Archie and the Quiz 0521 2-15-75

Edith, finding a life-expectancy quiz in a magazine, convinces Archie that his bad habits have him marked for almost immediate extinction. It takes a phony recomputation of the test to restore Archie's spirits and almost healthy glow.

Edith's Friend 0522 2-22-75

Attending an out-of-town family function without Archie, Edith renews her deep friendship with Cousin Roy. As captivated by him as ever, she's shocked to learn he was never a blood relation. Roy waxes romantic, and Edith pretends to get a phone call from Archie to discourage Roy from pursuing her.

No Smoking 0523 3-1-75

It's a battle of wills when Mike says he can give up eating for two days but Archie can't give up cigars for the same length of time. Taunting escalates and tempers grow uglier and uglier until they agree to weaken simultaneously, so that technically neither wins the bet.

Mike Makes His Move 0524 3-8-75

On the day of the Bunkers' mortgage-burning party, the Stivics are desperately seeking a place of their own, but Archie says they aren't trying hard enough. George Jefferson offers the solution of renting his house to the Stivics for a pittance, just to antagonize Archie. Mike refuses, but George keeps knocking the rent down—from $220 per month to $190 to $180 to $165, including carpet and drapes, with an option to renew on a month-to-month basis. Even though it means living next door to Archie, Mike accepts.

1975 – 1976 SEASON

Archie the Hero 0601 9-29-75

Archie comes home boasting about the woman whose life he saved in his cab, particularly since he gave the curvaceous beauty mouth-to-mouth resuscitation. He's anxious to spread the heroic tale until he learns that the woman was no lady but rather Beverly LaSalle, a transvestite.

Archie the Donor 0602 9-22-75

To get on his boss's good side and win a promotion, Archie signs up to support the man's cause, only to realize he's signed away his body to medical science.

Chain Letter 0603 10-20-75

When Archie refuses to answer a chain letter that Irene's been sending around, the toilet backs up, the oven door falls off, and Archie fears that Munson gave him hepatitis. He doesn't feel any better when the doctor who treats him is black.

Edith Breaks Out   0604   11-3-75

Picking on Edith for volunteering at the Sunshine Home, Archie claims they don't pay her because her work isn't worth a wage. He insists that she give up volunteering and she does—the Sunshine Home likes her so much they decide to pay her $2.00 an hour.

The Very Moving Day   0605   9-8-75

Gloria announces her pregnancy, and Mike goes from glad to mad, thinking they hadn't planned for this to happen, so Gloria must have plotted to bring it about by deliberately overlooking the necessary precautions.

Alone at Last?   0606   9-15-75

It's bitterly cold when the Stivics move into their new house, but Mike has forgotten to have the utilities turned on. Too proud to crawl back to Archie for a few more days' shelter, Mike determines that he and Gloria will somehow survive under their own roof.

The Little Atheist   0607   11-24-75

On Thanksgiving Day, the Bunkers and Stivics launch a brand-new debate. Archie expects his grandson to be raised a Christian. Mike and Gloria disagree. They're willing to let the boy make his own choice in his own time.

Mike's Pains   0608   10-6-75

The sex of the baby-to-be is predicted by the ring-on-a-string test (which Archie thinks is nonsense until the prediction tells him what he wants to hear). Mike has second thoughts about joining Gloria in the delivery room.

Mike Faces Life   0609   10-27-75

Archie is away at a convention, and Kressler's fires Gloria for being pregnant. When the Stivics can't get any satisfaction confronting the store management, they organize a picket line for preg-o power.

Grandpa Blues   0610   11-10-75

Archie has to get his blood pressure down to pass a company physical, but he goes home to a shouting match with Mike over what to name his grandson. Mike favors "Stanislaus," which Archie thoroughly despises. After Archie calms himself—surprise of surprises— he and Edith scamper upstairs to pitch whoopee *midday.*

 ## Gloria Suspects Mike   0611   11-17-75

Mike tutors a sexy female student to pick up extra cash, and Archie gets drunk with Mike to pry out how far they went. Mike reveals that he was tempted but didn't stray; Archie conks off to sleep before hearing the whole story.

 ## Archie's Civil Rights   0612   12-1-75

Archie, mugged at knifepoint, rescues himself by squirting tear gas at his assailant. The cops charge Archie with unlawful possession of a tear-gas weapon. In court, the judge saves Archie from a possible seven years in prison by discovering that the police officer obtained the evidence without a warrant.

 ## Archie the Babysitter   0613   1-12-76

Disapproving of the young babysitter the Stivics hired—and appalled when her boyfriend comes over to sit with her—Archie discharges her and has to watch Joey himself during a poker game in the Bunker living room.

 ## Gloria Is Nervous   0614   12-8-75

With the baby nine days overdue, Gloria and Mike are driving each other crazy, and Mike hyperventilates at Gloria's baby shower.

 ## New Year's Wedding   0615   1-5-76

Mike makes another decision without consulting Gloria. This time, he's invited friends of his to have their wedding ceremony in their living room.

 ## Birth of the Baby, part one   0616   12-15-75

Archie has to perform in a minstrel show or else be ditched by his lodge while—two weeks late—Gloria goes into labor in a restaurant, then gets trapped in a phone booth. Dr. Shapiro, on the other end of the phone, suggests putting the booth in an ambulance.

Birth of the Baby, part two   0617   12-22-75

The Bunkers get to the hospital ahead of the Stivics. Archie is still in blackface—shades of Ricky Ricardo in *I Love Lucy*'s birth of Little Ricky episode. Mike helps Gloria bring baby Joey into the world, but not before Archie bursts into the wrong room and terrifies a Mrs. Stipic.

Archie Finds a Friend   0618   1-26-76

Archie invests $1000 to make a million—in a remote-control doorbell ringer invented by Mr. Bernstein, the watch repairman. Edith opposes the deal and has her way in the worst possible way when Mr. Bernstein dies on the sofa.

Mike's Move   0619   2-2-76

Mike is up for a better job in Minnesota, so Archie rails about the dangers posed by its gopher holes. Then Mike's liberal views are put to the test when he loses the job to a fellow instructor who, in addition to being well qualified, is black.

Archie's Weighty Problem   0620   2-9-76

Archie chases Edith around the kitchen for beer when she pressures him to go on a diet and save his heart. Even though Edith, Mike, and Gloria diet too, he's ready for pig-out frenzy—until 92-year-old Mr. Quigley jogs by and sells him on the virtues of fitness.

Love by Appointment   0621   2-16-76

Gloria, too busy with Joey to be turned on by Mike, goes to Edith for answers, while Mike gets Archie's advice, which is surprisingly sympathetic.

Joey's Baptism   0622   2-23-76

When Archie can't talk Mike into baptizing Joey, he kidnaps the baby and takes him to a church, fails to bribe the Rev. Chong to perform the ceremony, and ultimately baptizes Joey himself.

Gloria and Mike's House Guest   0623   3-1-76

The Bunkers' furnace dies during the coldest weekend of the year. Edith and Gloria feel they should stay with the Stivics, but Archie and Mike can't bear looking at each other since the baptism incident. They don't have to worry. When they do get together, there's a neighborhood blackout.

Edith's Night Out   0624   3-8-76

When Archie refuses to take Edith out in her new red pantsuit, she goes where the action is on her own. At Kelcy's, Joe Foley scares her half to death by being friendly, then gets her to play the piano, where she becomes the life of the party. Archie shows up to realize he'd better slick up his act or she'll take the initiative and make her own fun with her many newfound friends.

1 9 7 6 – 1 9 7 7 S E A S O N

Archie's Secret Passion   0701   12-4-76

Archie panics because Edith has invited an old school friend to dinner—a woman with whom he once had a fling. He's relieved when Dolores doesn't provoke an ugly scene, but this is largely because their encounter was so brief that she's forgotten they'd ever been intimate. It's only because Edith asked her about it in the kitchen that Dolores is able to pretend to Archie that she remembered all along.

Archie's Brief Encounter, part one   0702   9-22-76

When a waitress named Denise makes a play for Archie, and his pals urge him to follow through, the basically faithful Archie trots home feeling romantic toward his wife. But Edith dashes off to bring false teeth to the Sunshine Home, leaving Archie alone and lonely enough to call on Denise in her apartment—where the two manage a lingering kiss.

The Unemployment Story, part one   0703   10-6-76

Mike, Gloria, and Edith are all set to celebrate when Mike wins professional honors. Archie would rather not talk about it. When Gloria berates him for his callousness, Edith clues her in: Archie is shaken because he lost his job.

The Unemployment Story, part two   0704   10-13-76

Archie is thrilled to be offered a job, even though it's as a janitor in a minority neighborhood. The man he beat out for the job, a college man, climbs out onto a ledge to commit suicide. Archie talks him back into the building—only to find himself out on the ledge, abandoned except by the people below, who urge him to jump.

Archie's Brief Encounter, part two   0705   9-22-76

Edith almost immediately discerns that Archie's been up to no good. She moves into the Sunshine Home permanently, and Archie is too surprised to know how to take it. (Run as the second half of a one-hour special with "Archie's Brief Encounter," part one.)

Archie's Brief Encounter, part three   0706   9-29-76

The brief encounter leads to the longest hours in Archie's life when Edith refuses to come home. Mike and Gloria scheme to bring Archie and Edith together with an invitation to see Joey. At first, they're both too hurt to reconcile. When at last they do, they sing about it on the porch.

Archie's Operation, part one   0707   10-20-76

Archie goes under the knife for gallbladder surgery. A black woman doctor gives him a shot in the backside, an intimate shave, and a transfusion of her blood—over Archie's consternation that his hemoglobin and her shemoglobin won't mix.

Archie's Operation, part two   0708   10-27-76

With his operation over and on the mend, Archie's feeling pretty good until he realizes how little of the cost is covered by medical insurance. He returns home to discover that Hank took his job—because he got a promotion. Even so, he'll be hurting financially from the hospital bills and the money he lost when he was out of work.

Mike and Gloria's Will   0709   11-20-76

Feeling mortal after he falls onto the subway tracks on Joey's first birthday, Mike names guardians for the baby. Archie and Edith don't appreciate his selecting Al and Trudy Bender over them. Gloria calms the crisis by suggesting that they not name anyone, and just promise not to die simultaneously.

Teresa Moves In 0710 11-13-76

With Mike and Gloria gone, the Bunkers take in a boarder to supplement their income—the same Puerto Rican admittance clerk who razzed Archie when he checked into the hospital. Soon Edith and Gloria are speaking Spanish, while Archie anticipates a rumble à la *West Side Story*.

Beverly Rides Again 0711 11-6-76

Archie is embarrassed that Beverly LaSalle, the transvestite nightclub entertainer whose life he once saved, has come to visit. Then it occurs to him that he can use Beverly to get even with a practical joker friend by setting them up on a date.

Mr. Edith Bunker 0712 11-27-76

Using her knowledge of CPR, Edith saves a man's life at the Sunshine Home. A local TV show comes to 704 Hauser to give her a citizenship award. Archie, hurt when the interviewer insults him for getting underfoot, storms off to Kelcy's to watch the broadcast from there.

Gloria's False Alarm 0713 12-18-76

Mike whines, simpers, and moans upon learning Gloria may be pregnant again. When he carps that the burden of birth control rests, by nature, on the woman, Gloria butts him over the coffee table and advises that it's his turn: he can have a vasectomy. She sends him off to the doctor, relents after he leaves, and finds out she's not pregnant just as he returns from having done the deed.

The Baby Contest 0714 12-11-76

Archie and Barney argue about who has the cutest grandchild. To settle the question, they enter theirs in a newspaper beautiful-baby contest. Both grandchildren are high in the running, but both are disqualified when it's discovered that their granddads stuffed the ballot boxes. Archie's miffed, but not as much as Mike and Gloria, who adamantly oppose the idea of beauty contests for babies.

The Draft Dodger 0715 12-25-76

Among the Bunkers' Christmas guests are a draft dodger back from Canada, and a friend of Archie's who lost his son in Vietnam. Archie is sure the man would be sickened to know he was eating with a draft dodger. But when the truth comes out, it seems he'd have been a lot happier had his son dodged the draft, and lived.

Archie's Chair   0716   1-15-77

Two institutions move on: Mike shaves his mustache; and Mike breaks Archie's armchair by sitting in it. Mike, Edith, and Gloria send the chair to Kressler's for repair; Kressler's misplaces it in a trash heap. Pop artist Lichtenrauch turns it into a symbolic work of art, but Archie won't relinquish the chair and the memories it holds, not even for $400.

The Boarder Patrol   0717   1-8-77

With the Bunkers away, Teresa's boyfriend wears her down and is just about to score when Archie and Edith return sooner than expected, having missed their bus out of town because Edith was in the restroom. Edith discovers what's going on, and exercises all her wits to keep Archie from finding out too. Not only is Archie fooled, but he can't help laughing over two young people who, left alone in a house, didn't dive at the chance to do something about it.

Mike Goes Skiing   0718   1-22-77

Mike stages an exaggerated display of exhaustion so that Gloria will let him take a ski weekend at Lake Placid with the guys. She agrees, despite his having picked the same weekend as Sheila Tishman's latest engagement party. Mike convinces Gloria to go to the party without him, which she does, fearing all the while that some snow bunny will throw herself at Mike. Actually, it's Gloria who, at the party, attracts a member of the opposite sex.

Stretch Cunningham, Goodbye   0719   1-29-77

Reluctantly, Archie agrees to deliver the eulogy at Stretch Cunningham's funeral, but he doesn't discover until the ceremony that the deceased was Jewish—and that all the years they were friends, Archie must have hurt Stretch terribly by deriding and ridiculing Jews to his face.

The Joys of Sex   0720   2-5-77

Wondering whether her sex life could stand improvement, Edith reads the book *How to Be Your Husband's Mistress*. Embarrassed when he finds out from

Mike, Archie forces himself to talk it over with Edith, telling her she makes him happy "in every way."

Mike the Pacifist 0721 2-12-77

Though a staunch opponent of violence, Mike is driven to bop a trouble-maker on the subway after the man—who has been arguing with his wife and working her over with a bouquet—threatens to kill her. For his troubles, Mike is accused by the woman of having murdered her husband. Archie is impressed by Mike's machismo, but Mike regrets the whole business, especially the fact that slugging the loudmouth felt pretty good.

Fire 0722 2-19-77

A fire breaks out upstairs and Edith frantically tries to save her photographs, her ceramic elephant, her Tupperware certificate of merit, Gloria's Brownie the Clownie dish, and every memento she can carry. Archie, hoping for an insurance windfall, takes pains to enhance the fire damage. When the insurance inspector determines that Archie's incompetence started the fire, Archie is lucky to come away with a few dollars.

Mike and Gloria Split 0723 2-26-77

Mike infuriates Gloria with a succession of patronizing comments about why she shouldn't mind being less educated than he is. A fight results, Mike lands in bed with Archie, and Mike finally gets the message that he's been behaving like a sap.

Archie the Liberal 0724 3-5-77

The Kings of Queens, Archie's lodge, had better admit minority members or court censure and worse will ensue. They figure to kill several birds with one stone by holding an absentee membership drive to bring in Solomon Jackson, a black Jew, assuring him he'll never have to attend a meeting.

Archie's Dog Day Afternoon 0725 3-12-77

After Barney and Archie argue over the messy habits of Barney's dog Rusty, Archie attempts a citizen's arrest. Barney makes a citizen's escape. Later, Archie unintentionally runs over Rusty with his cab. The dog survives with a broken leg. Archie pays the vet's bill, and Barney decides to get another dog to discourage Rusty from wandering off onto other people's lawns.

1 9 7 7 – 1 9 7 8   S E A S O N

Cousin Liz   0801   10-9-77

Edith's spinster cousin Liz has died and Archie looks forward to collecting something in the way of an inheritance. Veronica, Liz's roommate, confesses to Edith that they were more than roommates. Over Archie's pained objections, Edith gives Veronica Liz's silver tray as a keepsake.

Unequal Partners   0802   10-23-77

The Hefners invite the Bunkers for a fishing weekend, but Edith doesn't want to go because Mr. Hooper and Florence Talley, a couple from the Sunshine Home, will be getting married in the Bunkers' living room. Archie says he's going fishing anyhow. Edith says if he does, he can just keep going. To accommodate everyone, Archie rushes the couple through the ceremony—and Mr. Hooper locks himself in the closet until Barney agrees to take him and the new Mrs. Hooper along.

Archie Gets the Business, part one   0803   2-2-77

Kelsey has a heart attack and must give up his bar. Archie wants to buy it, but hasn't the ready cash. He raises the money by mortgaging his house—and forging Edith's signature on the mortgage. (First half of one-hour special.)

Archie Gets the Business, part two   0804   2-2-77

Edith is frightened for the future and angry at Archie when she discovers that he forged her signature to finance his purchase of Kelcy's. Then Mike, while not defending what Archie did, asks Edith to consider why he did it. Edith agrees to let Archie have his dream. (Second half of one-hour special.)

Edith's 50th Birthday, part one   0805   10-16-77

While everyone is over at the Stivic house preparing a surprise birthday party for Edith, a young man comes to the Bunker door. He identifies himself as a police detective looking for a rapist. She lets him in, only to discover he *is* the rapist. It looks as if she'll be unable to defend herself. Then she hits him in the face with a cake just out of the oven and runs to safety next door. (First half of one-hour special.)

Archie and the KKK, part one 0806 11-27-77

Archie sees some merit in joining a group of local super-patriots who are quite impressed by him. Then he learns that they are vigilantes who want to harass a local liberal. Their target just happens to be Mike Stivic.

Edith's 50th Birthday, part two 0807 10-16-77

Edith, escaping from the rapist, bursts into the Stivic home hysterical and unkempt. Because she's entered a surprise party for her birthday, everyone yells "Surprise!!!" and scares her half to death. Privately, she tells her family what happened. The men want her to let the matter drop, but Gloria convinces her to report the matter to the police. (Second half of one-hour special.)

Archie's Grand Opening 0808 10-30-77

Setting up for the grand opening of Archie's Place, Archie orders Harry around and talks down to Carlos. Harry quits. Carlos follows. Mike steps in to tend bar. Gloria waits tables. Archie's plant boss, Mr. Sanders, arrives and blasts Archie for calling in sick. Archie retaliates by quitting his job on the loading dock.

Archie and the KKK, part two 0809 12-4-77

When the KKK wants Archie to join them in burning a cross on Mike's lawn, he thinks fast and confesses that he has black blood in his veins (which is true, ever since his blood transfusion in "Archie's Operation"). He adds that if they go through with their plans, his black brothers might go on the warpath.

Archie's Bitter Pill 0810 11-6-77

With bar business pitiful, Archie careens toward financial ruin. Hank Pivnik slips him pills to boost his spirits. Archie gets high, wants to paint the porch at home at three in the morning, then gets hooked on pills. His family finally impresses upon him the seriousness of his situation, and he breaks down under the weight of his failures.

Archie's Road Back 0811 11-13-77

Out of the hospital after his O.D., Archie sees little point in returning to work. The piano has been repossessed, the phone disconnected, and the pinball machine is on its way back to Sicily. He vows to stay in bed until he dies. Since he won't get out, the family climbs in, and convinces him to coax Harry back to work as his partner.

Mike and Gloria Meet   0812   12-11-77

Flashback: The Bunkers go off for the weekend, leaving innocent Gloria at home with friend Debbie. Debbie invites her boyfriend over, and he brings a friend for Gloria: Mike. For Mike and Gloria, it's disinterest at first sight, until they discover mutual passions for ballroom dancing and Sir Walter Scott. Then Gloria has to worry about fighting Mike off.

Edith's Crisis of Faith, part one   0813   12-25-77

Mike and Beverly LaSalle (the transvestite) are jumped while taking a walk. Mike gets off easy compared to Beverly, who is beaten to death and dies on Christmas Eve. Edith, who was fond of Beverly, doubts she can continue to believe in God's love. (First half of one-hour special.)

Edith's Crisis of Faith, part two   0814   12-25-77

Christmas doesn't seem like Christmas to Edith, who is still in shock over Beverly's death. It hurts the family to see Edith so shaken—shaken to the point of shunning her faith on Christmas day. Then Mike tells Edith the only kind of Christianity he ever understood was the kind she always practiced, and she realizes that her faith is strong enough to give her comfort after all. (Second half of one-hour special.)

The Commercial   0815   1-8-78

At the laundromat, a grinning stranger hands Edith $50, rips up Archie's Disney World shirt, and pours ketchup on it. Next thing Edith knows, she is in a commercial, Archie is negotiating her fee down to a minimum wage, Mike is bewailing the ethics of commercials, and the commercial falls apart when Edith can't lie about the product in a whiteness test.

Aunt Iola's Visit   0816   1-22-78

Aging Aunt Iola visits the Bunkers. Edith, Mike, and Gloria find her adorable, but Archie considers her a nuisance and can't wait for her to leave. He panics when it looks like none of the other relatives will take her in, but she surprises him by having friends everywhere, including a gentleman friend she plans to stay with.

Super Bowl Sunday 0817 1-15-78

Archie plans to make big money by throwing a Super Bowl bash at his bar—and does—only to lose it when two hold-up men join the party, relieving him and his customers of their valuables and cash, and ordering them to drop their pants (to reduce their ability to give chase).

Love Comes to the Butcher 0818 2-5-78

Klemmer the butcher thinks that he and Edith are becoming an item when she shows him special attentions and invites him over for the evening. They sing songs together at the piano, and Klemmer, taking the words of the love songs to heart, declares his affection. Edith sets him straight while Archie, who has suspicions, decides to pay more attention to Edith himself.

Two's a Crowd 0819 2-12-78

Mike and Archie get locked in the storeroom of Archie Bunker's Place with nothing but hooch and each other. Archie justifies his prejudices by citing Noah's Ark: the elephant came with another elephant, not with a Polack. Archie lets slip that during the Depression, when he could only wear one shoe and one boot to school, the kids teased him with the nickname Shoebootie. He goes on to explain to Mike that a father who loves you can never do wrong. (With the exception of Mike's going-away episodes, this two-man show represents the last time Archie and Mike spend any appreciable time together.)

Stalemates 0820 2-19-78

Inspired by the example of two friends who have been in love forever but never married, Mike and Gloria go off to the Poconos for a weekend of marital rejuvenation. Awkward, uncomfortable, convinced they've lost more ground than they gained, Gloria laments the lack of spontaneity and contemplates divorce. Mike locks himself in the bathroom. They become spontaneous after Gloria breaks down the bathroom door.

The Brother 0821 2-26-78

Archie never talks about his brother, with whom he hasn't gotten along for ages. Then his brother shows up, reopens old wounds, gives Archie a mysterious letter with instructions not to read it until he's gone, and leaves. It turns out he may be gone for eternity. His brother faces a serious operation.

Mike's New Job 0822 3-5-78

Mike and Gloria walk into their living room to discover Archie attacking Edith on the sofa. But all Archie wants is a message that Edith is holding for Mike. It says he's gotten an associate professorship in California. Archie tries to talk the Stivics out of moving. Jefferson sells the house to the Bambinis, a family of midgets. The Stivics move in with the Bunkers for the remaining weeks before they move.

The Dinner Guest 0823 3-12-78

Though Edith has lavished love and time on a farewell dinner for Mike and Gloria, the two beg off to accept a posh invitation from Professor King, the head of Mike's department in California, who happens to be visiting New York. Archie shames them into staying, and the four have a horrible evening.

The Stivics Go West 0824 3-19-78

Mike has a new job on the West Coast so the Stivics are moving to California. In the midst of tears, goodbyes, and Mike's outpouring of gratitude, Archie puts up a brave front—asking only that Mike promise to take care of Gloria and Joseph.

1978 – 1979 SEASON

End in Sight 0901 10-1-78

When Archie and Harry have physicals preparatory to taking out partnership insurance, the doctor discovers a spot on Archie's liver. Afraid his days are numbered, Archie turns into a pussycat around the house. When he goes for more tests, he's ecstatic—the spot was only gas.

Reunion on Hauser Street 0902 10-8-78

Blanche is gone again and Archie decides it's time for Barney to find himself another woman. Archie thinks Barney and Boom-Boom Turner should get together, but Blanche reappears. Edith wants the Hefners to reconcile. Archie thinks Barney ought to dump Blanche.

Weekend in the Country 0903 10-29-78

Blanche has been jilted by the exterminator she ran away with, and the Hefners are reconciled. They invite the Bunkers to the woods for the weekend and embroil them in their bickering, with the net result that Archie, Edith, and Blanche wind up in the same bed.

Little Miss Bunker 0904 9-24-78

Edith's cousin Floyd tries to drop off his daughter Stephanie for two or three weeks. When Archie says no, Floyd abandons the child on the doorstep. When Stephanie overhears how little Archie wants her, she runs away. Archie tracks her down at the bus station, makes her feel appreciated, and takes her home.

Edith's Final Respects 0905 10-22-78

Edith goes without Archie to Aunt Rose's funeral. No one else attends. Rose, it seems, lost interest in Edith the day the Bunkers tied the knot. In this episode that is largely a monologue, Edith talks to the body in the coffin (the back of its head clearly visible on camera), sings "Getting to Know You," wishes Rose a nice trip, and watches the funeral director remove chairs from the room to accommodate the overflow in the next chamber.

What'll We Do with Stephanie? 0906 10-15-78

A letter arrives for Stephanie from her father. Steaming it open, Archie reads that her dad now works on a ship and doesn't intend to come for her. Archie wants Stephanie out but hasn't the heart to tell her. Since Edith won't tell her either, Archie lets Stephanie stay.

Archie's Other Wife 0907 11-5-78

Armed with his battery-operated gooser, Archie takes off for a VFW-type caucus out of town. In the course of water bags, shoes tied together, and Archie's toast to World War II—"the best war we ever had"—Pinky engineers the crowning practical joke of his career by arranging for Archie to wake up in bed with a young black stewardess.

Edith Versus the Bank 0908 11-19-78

Edith wants to surprise Archie with a new TV set for their 30th anniversary, but the department store won't give her credit and the First Friendly Bank denies her a loan. Bad enough the loan officer refuses, but he isn't even very good about disguising his contempt for a woman who is "just a housewife." Edith gets the money from Archie, by convincing him to pay her for the thirty years of housewife work she's done.

Return of the Waitress   0909   11-26-78

Boom-Boom has quit waitressing at Archie's Place, and Harry has hired a replacement—Denise—not knowing she and Archie once nearly had an affair. Archie prepares to take it, however awkwardly, in stride since Denise badly needs the job; but when Edith drops by, figures out who Denise is, and thanks Denise for her role in bringing Archie closer, Denise withdraws from the job.

A Night at the P.T.A.   0910   1-7-79

The P.T.A. is putting on a show for which Edith and Stephanie work themselves to a frazzle preparing a song-and-dance routine. The rehearsal scene echoes *42nd Street,* as do the moments of crisis (Edith gets sick and can't go on) and triumph (Stephanie goes out a youngster but comes back a star). Archie, who thought Stephanie would embarrass herself, admits that he's mighty proud.

Bogus Bills   0911   12-3-78

Bogus bills turn up in Archie's cashbox. Unfortunately, Edith took a few before he made the discovery. Now she's in jail for trying to buy his underwear with a counterfeit ten spot. Archie attempts to get to the bottom of things—at his bar, and down in the slammer.

Bunkers Go West   0912   12-10-78

Archie and Edith are happily expecting Mike and Gloria for the Christmas holidays. Then Gloria calls to say the trip is off because Mike's back went out. Edith merrily decides that if the Stivics can't come from California to visit the Bunkers, the Bunkers will go to California to see the Stivics.

The Appendectomy   0913   1-21-79

According to young Dr. Shapiro, Stephanie needs an immediate appendectomy, but Archie won't accept the diagnosis. To Archie, the only real Dr. Shapiro is this Dr. Shapiro's father. Besides, Archie remembers when

Junior, as a boy, used to "play doctor" with Gloria. Eventually, of course, Archie gives in, and shows Stephanie how much he really cares.

California, Here We Are, part one   0914   12-17-78

The Bunkers visit Mike and Gloria in Santa Barbara. The Stivics are glad to see them, but otherwise not glad about much. During a talk in the bathroom, Edith learns from Gloria that the Stivics are contemplating divorce.

California, Here We Are, part two   0915   12-17-78

Archie blames the Stivics' marital discord on Mike, and takes it for granted that Mike has been unfaithful. When he learns that Gloria, not Mike, has entered into a relationship, he takes the Meathead's side against his daughter.

A Girl Like Edith   0916   1-14-79

Klemmer—the man who used to have such a crush on Edith—is engaged to a woman named Judith. Edith invites them over for dinner. Judith, except for her hair and clipped Germanic diction, could pass for Edith's twin. While Klemmer pays more attention to Edith than to his fiancée, Archie attempts small talk on the whereabouts of Martin Bormann.

Stephanie and the Crime Wave   0917   1-28-79

Things are missing around the Bunker household and from Stephanie's classroom in school. Confronted, Stephanie confides that she took these things to keep as mementos of people she loves—fully expecting they'll be dumping her soon, just as people she loved did time after time in the past.

Stephanie's Conversion   0918   2-18-79

The Bunkers learn from the Reverend Chong, who learned from Stephanie, that Stephanie is Jewish because her mother was Jewish. Edith is hurt that Stephanie never mentioned it. Stephanie replies that her father warned her to keep quiet or risk Archie's wrath. Archie barely accepts the news and agonizes before agreeing to bring her up in her own faith—particularly since it means paying $100 for tuition for her religious instruction, and having to join the Temple Beth Shalom. Then, without any prodding whatsoever, Archie buys a Star of David pendant and affectionately presents it to Stephanie.

Barney the Gold Digger   0919   2-4-79

Blanche has run off on Barney again, this time with the furnace man. Barney threatens suicide. Archie fixes him up with Martha Berkhorn, a rich widow friend of Edith's. Martha is pretty but immense. Barney resents not being handed a young Elizabeth Taylor on a platter. Then the two hit it off and have to wonder what will happen if Blanche comes back.

Edith Gets Fired   0920   2-25-79

Edith is assigned to sit with Loretta Dillon at the Sunshine Home. Loretta is old, in pain, content with the life she has lived, and more than ready to die. She asks Edith to hold her hand and let her slip away, and *not* call for help. When Edith grants Loretta's last wish, the Sunshine Home fires Edith for gross negligence.

A Series Retrospective   [Unnumbered]   3-4-79

As *All in the Family* draws to the close of its last season, this 90-minute retrospective celebrates the series' 200th episode. Lear introduces clips from past episodes, and there are brief comments from the 100 couples (representing 48 states) who have been selected to attend the taping.

The Family Next Door   0921   3-18-79

The Jeffersons' house is vacant again, and Louise asks Edith to show it to prospective renters. Archie insists that Edith use the opportunity to preserve the "dignity" of the neighborhood, but she does not share his views.

The Return of Archie's Brother   0922   3-11-79

Archie's estranged younger brother Fred invites him to invest in a money-making scheme—a chain of Chinese eateries, the Fu Yoo Chinaterias. The rift between them seems to be healing until Archie meets Fred's new wife, a wide-eyed eighteen-year-old beauty.

The Return of Stephanie's Father   0923   3-25-79

Floyd Mills, Stephanie's father, returns to meet Archie and Edith in the lobby of a seedy hotel. Stephanie isn't invited. No wonder. Floyd doesn't want to take her back. He wants money to let the Bunkers keep her. When Archie realizes the life Stephanie is in for if he lets her go, he's all too happy to give Floyd a handout and what he hopes will be a final goodbye.

Too Good Edith   0924   4-8-79

Edith suffers from phlebitis, but despite doctor's orders to stay off her feet, she spends two days preparing corned beef and cabbage for the St. Patrick's Day party at Archie's bar. When, in great pain, she tries to tell Archie her problem, he's too busy to listen. Finally, she can't move her legs. Archie is broken-hearted when he learns the cause, and that his hard-headedness compounded her discomfort.

Legacy

"When you see contemporary shows on social issues, they harken back to the ground-breaking work of Norman Lear."
—Robert Batscha, president,
Museum of Broadcasting

In the years since *All in the Family* first caught hold of America's pulse, the term "Archie Bunkerism" has appeared in dictionaries; U.S. vice-presidential candidate Geraldine Ferraro noted that she represented Archie's congressional district "but Edith elected me"; *People* magazine dubbed *All in the Family* "the best TV show to put in a time capsule"; Larry Gelbart credited *All in the Family* with blazing the trail for *M*A*S*H*; and in an episode of *Taxi*—when Alex makes a phone call from a sleazy restroom and doesn't want to let on, he explains the background sound of the flushing toilet as a rerun of *All in the Family*.

In 1978, House Majority Whip John Brademas, then chairman of a House subcommittee responsible for overseeing the Smithsonian Institution, requested the Bunker chairs because "*All in the Family* programs reflect with accuracy, sensitivity and humor many important dimensions of American life. I think it would be most appropriate if two symbols of the series were to be preserved as part of the cultural legacy of our country." The chairs went on display in December of that year, and remain a permanent part of the "Nation of Nations" exhibit.

Since *All in the Family* began, Norman Lear has won honors ranging from the NAACP's 1972 Image Award and the Peabody Award to the first lifetime achievement American Comedy Award in 1987. His television and movie projects have included the made-for-TV movie *Heartsounds* and the "I Love Liberty" television extravaganza, which he produced and personally organized. He has been president of the Hollywood chapter of the American Civil Liberties Union, established Democrats for Change, and founded People for the American Way. Lear is seen here accepting the Central Synagogue Shofar Award from congregation president John H. Ball, for "upholding the highest traditions of Judaism in his affirmation of American values."

Involved in numerous development deals and projects since 1971, Carroll O'Connor is in the enviable position of being able to work or not work as he chooses. He retains an active interest in the theater, having written for it and having appeared on Broadway (*Brothers, Home Front*). On television, he has starred in such TV movies as *Brass, The Last Hurrah* (for which he also wrote the adaptation), and the TV play *Of Thee I Sing* (above, with Cloris Leachman).

Jean Stapleton, rated the country's top female star by *People* magazine in its 1979 readers' poll, gave up her Edith Bunker role when she felt she was starting to act like a dingbat. Since then, she has starred on Broadway in *Arsenic and Old Lace*, and regularly at her late husband William Putch's Totem Pole Playhouse in Pennsylvania; appeared on television in the special *You Can't Take It with You* and in such TV movies as *Angel Dusted*, *Aunt Mary*, and *Eleanor* [Roosevelt], *First Lady of the World*, for which she received an Emmy nomination; and turned down the Angela Lansbury role in *Murder, She Wrote*. She has been an active supporter of women's rights, and is Honorary Governor of the Pearl S. Buck Foundation. (Seen here as Eleanor Roosevelt, and with Grace C. K. Sum and Pearl Buck's daughter Janice C. Walsh).

Rob Reiner, who got tired of being called "Meathead"—by Archie, and by people who recognized him on the street—pursued his gifts as a writer and actor (*The Super, Free Country*, and a controversial satire of television programming, "The TV Show") and more recently, as a major director and sometimes writer of feature films (*This Is Spinal Tap, The Sure Thing, Stand by Me*, and *The Princess Bride*).

Once, when Sally Struthers was visiting Jerusalem, an Arab on a camel recognized her and shouted "Gloria!" In recent years, Struthers has been visible in TV movies (*The Great Houdinis, Intimate Strangers, Your Name Is Jonah*, and as Tiger Lily on the miniseries *Alice in Wonderland*), on Broadway in *Wally's Cafe* and the first female version of *The Odd Couple*, and starring in the TV series *9 to 5*. In the field of public service, she is deeply committed to the work of the Christian Children's Fund, the world's oldest and largest nonsectarian child welfare organization.

Rob Reiner, Sally Struthers, and Jean Stapleton on hand as Norman Lear presents the Bunker chairs to the Smithsonian Institution.

INDEX